Hope
Rediscovered

Among the many causes of anxiety in today's world are global concerns to do with social and economic inequality, the imperative of sustainable development, and the link between the damage we are causing the natural environment and climate change. These raise human – that is, moral and spiritual – questions about who we are, our destiny, how we can be helped to flourish, and what we hope for.

Hope Rediscovered is about being re-oriented in the face of such challenges. Bishop David Atkinson, who has an abiding interest in Christian ethics, pastoral theology and science, has put some key questions to the Gospel of John – a text which says much about human flourishing ('life in fullness'), and which draws heavily on Wisdom themes from the Hebrew Bible about understanding our human place in creation, and about practical living.

Like his followers, Jesus was beset with conflicts within 'the world'. The first-century Christian community, to which the Gospel was first addressed, discovered how to live hopefully in the way of Wisdom, energized by God's Spirit. The focus of this timely book is deep, practical wisdom for a troubled world.

Bishop David Atkinson undertook research in organic chemistry before being ordained into the Church of England and serving as Fellow and Chaplain of Corpus Christi, College, Oxford. He was a Canon Residentiary at Southwark Cathedral and Archdeacon of Lewisham, becoming Bishop of Thetford in 2001. He retired in 2009.

David Atkinson's *Hope Rediscovered* is a treasure-trove of wise insights and thoughtful reflection. It is a learned book, but never a dryly academic one; it is theologically sophisticated but communicated straightforwardly with vivid and often unexpected illustrations. Addressing our current ecological crises can be depressing and gloomy, but this book manages to be starkly realistic and yet genuinely hopeful. I greatly enjoyed it and was stimulated to think more deeply and act differently.

Dave Bookless, Director for Theology, Churches and Sustainable Communities, A Rocha International

David Atkinson's book is a necessary dose of encouragement for Christians. It portrays a faithful hope which is both biblically rooted and engaged with both some of the most important challenges facing us as people and as local and world communities.

Bernadette Meaden, Ekklesia Associate and researcher

The wise driver is not the one who knows why the road bends but the one who knows how to negotiate a winding road. Iin this book David Atkinson is such a driver as he applies the wisdom of God to finding hope for the world. In these pages he earths the wisdom of God in the humanity of Jesus as his life unfolds in the Gospel of John. If you're given to underlining get your pen ready to mark these pages as there are many original insights to treasure.

Bishop James Jones, former Anglican Bishop of Liverpool

A book that weaves its way helpfully between environmental reflection and the Gospel of John. David Atkinson will encourage you to read John in a new and hopeful way. Recommended reading for Christian environmentalists who want to go a bit deeper.

Dr Martin Hodson, Operations Director, The John Ray Initiative

The biblical wisdom issues in a radical call to social and personal change. At the heart of of the Christian message lies both hope and challenge.

Savitri Hensman, Christian writer and activist working in the voluntary sector

Dedication

For Graham and Julie with affection and gratitude.
And for Eden, Niamh and Jos, in love and hope.

Thanks

This book is dedicated first to Bishop Graham and Mrs Julie James with my warmest thanks for their many kindnesses shown to me when I worked with them in the Diocese of Norwich from 2001 – 2009; and secondly to my three youngest grandchildren – born since my earlier book *Renewing the Face of the Earth* was published – with gratitude for all they bring to our family.

It is also written with grateful memory of the late Professor Sam Berry, scientist and Christian leader.

I have in places drawn on my paper *Climate Change and the Gospel,* which I wrote for Operation Noah in 2012, and is published on their website.

I am enormously grateful to Archbishop Rowan Williams for permission to quote some lines from a sermon he preached in 2001, and for me to use these as a Foreword to this book. These words have been very inspirational to me since I heard them given from the pulpit of Southwark Cathedral.

I have been greatly helped by comments and suggestions on an early draft of some of this material from Dr David Attwood, Professor Timothy Gorringe, and Dr Brian Cuthbertson. I am very grateful to them all. My heartfelt thanks also to my wife Sue, who has read previous drafts as they have appeared, and whose generous, loving and compassionate service for others has kept reminding me that writing theology about life in this world is not the same as actually living it.

Charles

Grace & peace.

David

Hope Rediscovered

Biblical wisdom for an anxious world

David Atkinson

Ekklesia

First published in June 2018

Ekklesia
235 Shaftesbury Avenue
London
WC2H 8EP
www.ekklesia.co.uk

Production and design: Bob Carling (www.carling.org.uk)
Managing Editor: Simon Barrow

ISBN: 978-0-9932942-1-1

A Catalogue record for this book is available from the British Library.

Contents

Publisher's Preface

We live in troubled times. Environmental degradation, poverty, inequality and conflict are among the major challenges confronting our world. At both a personal and communal level, many are experiencing uncertainty and anxiety as part of the woundedness of our shared condition.

At times like this we need abiding wisdom more than ever. Anxiousness can readily lead us to embrace apparent 'solutions' that prove to be nothing of the sort. These include rigid ideologies and beliefs offering unassailable certainty, the dangerous lure of a 'strong leader', searching for quick technological fixes, or empty consumerism that finally fails to make despair go away.

In this book, David Atkinson confronts the big issues of our time and the frailties of our humanity. He does so with understanding, compassion and practical hope rooted in the Christian message. Taking the Gospel of John as the source of a wisdom that is both ancient and new, he explores what difference it makes to base one's life on the promises of God fleshed out in the person, work and destiny of Jesus of Nazareth.

This is an important book because it shows that the Bible can never belong to people who use it as a weapon to justify themselves by attacking or oppressing those they feel threatened by. It does so through a careful, patient reading of New Testament material that itself draws deeply on the Hebrew Scriptures.

What we discover is that the Jesus of John's Gospel invites us to join him and his companions on the costly path of reconciliation and transformation. We are offered a new sense of belonging through a community of hope, the rediscovery of wisdom, and God's gift of new life releasing us from the power of death.

It may come as a surprise to sceptics that the traditional Christian message as expounded here is anything but conservative in its implications. It is actually very radical; a much-misused word that rightly understood is about the capacity for change being nourished by deep roots.

In *Hope Rediscovered*, David Atkinson uncovers those roots with clarity and humility, showing how they can reframe our engagement with some distinctly contemporary dilemmas, and exemplifying why biblical (ancient–new) wisdom for an anxious world matters so much.

Simon Barrow, Director, Ekklesia

Foreword

At the heart of David Atkinson's book lies the Gospel of John and the important message it contains for our world.

Where Jesus is, there we shall be. That might serve to sum up the entire Gospel of John: it begins by marking out the place Jesus occupies, the place 'in the bosom of the Father' or 'next to the Father's heart', the place of that eternal harmonic energy that is for ever 'in relation to God', so profoundly and inescapably in relation that it is nothing but what God is; and then the story unfolds of how this life, lived in conversation with so many and so diverse persons, opens up that eternal place for human beings to inhabit. Following Jesus leads to this place, to his home: 'Rabbi, where are you living?' 'Come and see'.

All Christian calling is to follow Jesus. So all Christian calling is to find where he lives, where he is at home. And the Gospel of John shows unforgettably how he is at home simultaneously 'next to the Father's heart' and at the wedding feast, speaking in love and challenge to the woman of Samaria, arguing with the custodian of sacred words and places; on trial, on the cross, calling Mary Magdalene by name.

Next to the Father's heart; next to the heart of the reality in which he stands in his humanity. Our own journey to the heart of all things, the original love that grounds the universe, is by way of the realities in which we stand, the conversations into which we enter, seeking to bring to them that surrender to original love which burns in every act and word of Jesus's. As we learn to drop our defences before God's love, so we learn to drop our defences against the reality of God's world; and vice versa. The call is always to that double truthfulness in which Jesus lives, true to God, true to creation: the Word made flesh, the divine harmonic embodied in the world of conflict and suffering.

Rowan Williams

This Foreword is adapted from part of a sermon preached at Southwark Cathedral in April 2001.

Introduction

Grace and Truth

With the drawing of this Love, and the voice of this Calling
T.S. Eliot, 'Little Gidding', *Four Quartets*

My reasons for choosing John's Gospel as the basis for these reflections were very largely personal.

I was staying at Ghost Ranch – a Presbyterian retreat centre in the high desert of New Mexico. Our apartment was Casa del Sol – a small house some distance from the main centre – with views of the desert and mountains captured in paintings by Georgia O'Keeffe. There was a copy of *The Message* version of John's Gospel on a shelf, and I decided to read it from cover to cover. Afterwards I went outside, where there was a prayer labyrinth. As I slowly walked the labyrinth from the outside spiralling to the centre, thinking about what I had read, I felt myself drawn increasingly closely into what I can only describe as the love of God. It was a wholly unexpected experience of Someone coming close to me.

Years earlier, I had finished my doctoral research in organic chemistry, and was training for the Church of England ministry. My study room was on the second floor, its window overlooking the Clifton Downs in Bristol. I was due to take an exam on John's Gospel, so decided to shut my study door and read the whole Gospel through in one sitting. It took nearly three hours, and when I finished, I realized that something had happened to me. The only way to express it is to say that I had felt myself to have been addressed, perhaps even 'called'. A Word had been spoken, which in some way I had heard, and by which somehow I had been changed.

These two experiences seemed to bring me into touch with the Love and the Word of God. In some small and fairly uncertain measure, I think I had seen something of God's glory – as described in the Gospel: full of grace and truth. The drawing of that Love and the voice of that Calling remain with me today. I became excited by the promise held out by the words of Jesus recorded in John 10.10: 'I came that they may have life, and have it abundantly'; or, as another version has it, 'life in all its fullness'.

My academic study of John's Gospel was further inspired by some words from an early book by someone who later became a colleague, the priest/scientist Arthur Peacocke. In *Science and the Christian Experiment*[1] he wrote: 'Why *should* science work at all? That it does so points strongly to a principle of rationality, to an interpretation of the cosmos in terms of mind ... There is clearly a kinship between the mind of man and the cosmos, which is real, and which any account of the cosmos cannot ignore.' Peacocke pointed me to William Temple's *Nature, Man and God,* and from there to Temple's *Readings in St John's Gospel,* and so to a theological excitement with John's Gospel's use of *Logos,* God's Word, God's Wisdom.

A second, equally personal, set of concerns lies behind this book. In recent years I have worked on environmental studies, sustainability and climate change. Increasingly these issues and others have raised questions about the nature of the world we live in, and of human identity and values. Who are we as human beings in God's world? What is our destiny? What could 'life in all its fullness' mean in our current contexts of environmental degradation, economic uncertainty, anxiety, even despair? What does it mean for human beings to 'flourish'? Increasingly I have found debates and discussions pushing us back to questions that are ultimately moral and spiritual. People in many places, it seems, are searching for a fresh understanding of wisdom – wisdom by which to interpret our human condition, and wisdom to live by in all the frailties of contemporary life. It should be no surprise, then, that I started – as it were – to put these questions to the Gospel of John: what perspectives of spiritual wisdom might the Word of grace and truth bring to bear on such issues in our very different world?

What sort of human life and human living does the writer of John's Gospel have in mind when he writes of 'life in all its fullness'? The phrase comes right in the middle of the Gospel which begins with a testimony about Jesus Christ: 'we have seen his glory', and ends with the statement that the Gospel was written 'that you may come to believe that Jesus is the Messiah, the Son of God, and that through believing you may have life in his name.' Fullness of life, we may infer, is – for John's Gospel – to do with the life of Jesus Christ, a life that displays God's glory, and a life that can be shared with those who 'believe in him'.

My purpose in this book is to offer a series of reflections drawing on major themes in John's Gospel, asking as we go what these tell us both about Jesus Christ, and about the 'fullness of life' that he said he

---

[1] Arthur Peacocke, *Science and the Christian Experiment,* Oxford, 1971 p. 133f. cf. also William Temple, *Nature, Man and God,* Macmillan, 1934; William Temple, *Readings in John's Gospel,* Macmillan 1939–40.

came to bring. It explores what these themes might mean for Christian discipleship today. It does not by any means cover everything in the Gospel. It is most certainly not a 'commentary' in the usual sense. The first part of John's Gospel introduces the disciples – and us the readers – to Jesus, in his closeness to God as a Son to the Father, and in his thoroughly authentic humanity, through his teaching, his signs of healing, his way of living. The second part of John's Gospel moves from the Last Supper to the arrest, suffering, death and resurrection of Jesus, and his creation of a new community of believers to share the life of his Spirit, and to live hopefully in the world.

We begin with the question 'Where shall Wisdom be found?' in the context of our contemporary uncertainties. Then we explore God's Wisdom embedded in Nature, understood as 'God's creation' (chapters 2 and 3). Where the Hebrew Bible talks about 'Wisdom', John's Gospel uses the symbol of 'the Word' (chapter 4). God's Wisdom and God's Word are embodied in the rich authentic humanity of Jesus, God's Son (chapters 5 – 6). The fullness of life of which Jesus speaks (chapter 7) often comes into conflict with a world which does not recognize and honour God (chapter 8, 9 and 10), but that fullness of life is the gift and promise of God for the new community of Christ's people (chapter 11). Drawn together by the risen Jesus and empowered by God's Spirit, Christ's people are called afresh in each generation to bear witness in the world. That witness of mission, a discipleship of restraint, a life of repentance, hope and worship, is life in the light of the resurrection of Jesus and empowered by his Spirit (chapter 12). All this lies behind Jesus' words to his disciples, 'I am come that they might have life in all its fullness'.

Chapter One

Where Shall Wisdom be Found?

- There is much to cause anxiety in our world
- The words of hope in the Gospel of John were written into a context of anxiety
- Despite our very different world, John's Gospel offers spiritual wisdom
- Three major concerns today are the poverty gap, sustainability and environmental degradation
- These issues of equity, economy and ecology raise many questions that at root are spiritual
- Many people today are searching for spiritual wisdom
- The Gospel of John, which draws on Hebrew Wisdom teaching, will be our guide

---

How are we going to cope?

The poster outside the church said: 'Do not let your hearts be troubled, and do not let them be afraid.' Inside the church things were rather different. I was at a conference about coastal erosion in Norfolk, and the likely loss to the sea – over the next decades – of some houses, a fine church, and maybe even a village. It has happened before. The coastal Suffolk village of Dunwich had been the capital of the kingdom of East Angles and a major port. In the thirteenth century a storm surge had eroded the coast and much of the village was lost to the sea. Over the centuries many surviving buildings, including churches, have been lost – the latest being the tower of All Saints in 1922. Some people at the Norfolk conference wanted the government to provide more coastal defences for their village. Others said that building new defences here would make erosion much worse further along the coast. One lady said, with a sigh, 'Well, at least it won't happen in my lifetime!' That is probably true, though it will happen in someone's lifetime. And the sigh was probably more a sigh of denial than anything else. It said:

'This is too big for me to handle. I wish it would all go away. What is going to happen? I do not want to think about it, because if I do, I really don't know how I am going to cope.'

It was anxieties of this sort to which the quotation on the poster outside the church was addressed. The words are from John's Gospel, and recall Jesus speaking immediately after the Last Supper. Judas the betrayer has left in the night. Jesus is preparing his disciples for his imminent 'departure', which meant his death. It seems like an ending to their time of walking with him, learning from him, hoping in him. Their world was changing. They were not sure how they were going to cope. It is at this point the Gospel records Jesus' words:

> *Do not let your hearts be troubled. Believe in God, believe also in me ... I am the way, and the truth, and the life.* (John 14:1,6)

and a bit later:

> *Peace I leave with you. My peace I give to you ... Do not let your hearts be troubled, and do not let them be afraid.* (John 14:27)

The author is not only recalling the words of Jesus at this particular point in Jesus' ministry, he is selecting his material in the Gospel with a very particular purpose in mind. At first sight, these words could seem like an individual pietistic retreat from the world into the spiritual comfort of the thought of heaven. But digging deeper into the Gospel, we find a grittier, more this-worldly, politically aware, corporate understanding of life in God's world, and a faith that helps people to cope in life's ordinarinesses. We find the author addressing the need to reassure and strengthen the faith of the disturbed, oppressed and divided small Christian community for whom he was writing. The world they knew was changing fast. Some were losing their grip on their identity as Christians. They were facing persecution and antagonism from outside their community. They were not sure how their faith would cope with what was happening around them. These words of Jesus were also for them. The Gospel author is helping them rediscover hope.

The community of the Beloved Disciple

We can perhaps imagine this Christian community in the last decade of the first century, somewhere in the Jewish Dispersion (maybe Ephesus, maybe Alexandria, maybe somewhere else).[2] It is a community that has been nurtured on the traditions about Jesus, passed

---

2   I have received considerable help from Ruth Edwards, *Discovering John*, SPCK, 2003, Richard Bauckham, *The Testimony of the Beloved Disciple*, Baker, 2007, David Rensberger, *Overcoming the World*, SPCK, 1998, Wes Howard-Brook, *Becoming Children of God*, Orbis Books, 1994; as well as from many standard commentaries.

on through teaching, preaching, gossip, reminiscence, often orally, perhaps sometimes written down. It is a community drawn together around the Beloved Disciple, referred to in the Gospel: someone who had been with Jesus, though never one of the Twelve. It is a community that has internal tensions, but most markedly one that has come into conflict with Pharisees and other Judean leaders. It is in dispute with its local synagogue precisely over its faith in Jesus. It is struggling with some half-believers like Nicodemus. It includes people who get it wrong, and try again, like Simon Peter. It is socially mixed, with some rich people, some poor. It is in touch with Greeks and Samaritans as well as with Jews. Part of the intention of the Gospel writer, he tells us, is 'that you may believe that Jesus is the Messiah' (John 20:31) – that is, in Jesus, God is acting to bring healing and renewal to a broken and struggling world, and to restore it towards God's purposes in creation. But the Gospel writer has a second task also. He wants to give courage and purpose to the Christian community in its God-given task of living out the life of Jesus in its contemporary world of tension, persecution, oppression and opposition, and so sharing in Jesus' ministry of healing a broken creation. They are not to let their hearts be troubled, nor should they be afraid.

Our so different world ...

In very many ways the community around the Beloved Disciple could not even have begun to recognize our contemporary culture at all. Ours is a culture of printing and science. It has been changed by Newton and Darwin, Marx and Freud. Our world includes the fairly recent growth of neo-liberal capitalism with its assumption of limitless economic growth. Our world is seeing environmental degradation, the loss of species and of biodiversity, and the exponential growth of the human population – at the rate equivalent to a city the size of Birmingham every five days. We are aware, through television and the internet, of the rapid spread of globalization. There are powerful global corporations larger than some national governments. We are having to think new thoughts about genetic modification, nuclear weapons, drone warfare, and artificial intelligence. We see the growing impact of the immense revolution in information technology and modern means of communication, not least social media. We see the expansion of areas of extreme poverty, and the growth of the gap between the richest and the poorest people – and between the richest and poorest parts of the world. In recent years, we have witnessed the growth of fundamentalisms of many sorts, sometimes with use of terror, and the diminishment of respect for and trust in social authorities of different kinds.

We are constantly confronted with how our faith impinges on the huge questions that seem to be put to us. What are we to make of the political turmoil of the Middle East, not to mention the political up-heavals in Europe and in the USA? Christians are being persecuted for their faith as never before in Syria and Iraq. Western nations are becoming increasingly secularized in the sense that faith in God is no longer taken for granted, but is simply 'one human possibility among others'.[3]

Sometimes it is more homely and domestic issues that are the causes of our uncertainty. Where will I live? Will I be able to afford a home? How long will we need to use a food bank? How can I pay for my child's uniform? Who is going to look after our elderly mother? More generally our pace of life, with the speed of modern transport, rapid communication and constant quest for more, lies behind many of our fears. The imperative to succeed and the way many in our cul-ture define themselves by what they do, or what they achieve, and our measurement of well-being largely in financial terms – with the as-sociated tolls of air pollution, traffic accidents and modern diseases – as well as social mobility and the separation of people from their families and roots – all this and so much more, contributes to our con-temporary anxieties and our fears. And the burgeoning consumer cul-ture is spurred on by an advertising industry whose primary purpose is to make us discontented and continually wanting something else. Our world is very different indeed from the culture for which John was writing his Gospel.

... and yet the same

Despite all the differences, in many significant ways the community around the Beloved Disciple towards the end of the first century was very similar to any Christian community today. It was made up of be-lievers dependent on God for their life and well-being, human beings who believed themselves to be made in the image of their Creator. They were followers of Jesus of Nazareth, inspired by his life, redeemed by his death and resurrection, trying to hold on to hope in his lordship and coming reign. They were energized, taught and guided by God's life-giving Spirit. They were nourished by God's Word and regular in corporate worship, and were committed to the mission of working for God's kingdom of 'justice and peace and joy in the Holy Spirit' (Romans

---

3   Charles Taylor *A Secular Age*, Harvard: Bleknap Press, 2007, p.3.

14:17). That was the community which the Gospel writer was seeking to encourage and strengthen – to help them live without anxiety and fear in the face of all the uncertainties confronting their faith; to help them to cope.

Three major issues for us today

Our society is changing fast. The story of our modern culture is of phenomenal human achievement, and at the same time a picture of human sin, selfishness, failure and cruelty. At one end of the Mediterranean we can see a billionaire Chief Executive relaxing on his third luxury yacht, while on the same day at the other end of the Mediterranean – not far from where the community of the Beloved Disciple used to gather – we can see scores of Syrian and Somali refugees, fleeing war zones, hunger and poverty, drowning when their inflatable boats are capsized by a storm.

This tragic story vividly illustrates three major and growing issues that are increasingly pressing their importance on all human beings. These will be a special focus of this book: (i) inequality: the growing gap between the richest and the poorest; (ii) sustainability: how are growing numbers of people going to live together on this planet; and (iii) the impact of climate change. These all seriously affect our ability not only to flourish as human beings, but even to cope at all. It is issues such as these that we wish to put to the author of John's Gospel with the question: Why should not our hearts be troubled? Why shouldn't we be afraid? How are people to flourish in this world? Are there grounds for hope?

(i) The first issue is the growing gap between the richest and the poorest. While there is good news that in many parts of the world extreme poverty is diminishing, the bad news is that there are still vast numbers of people living in poverty, and the gap between the richest and the poorest is growing very fast.[4] The structures of inequality are destroying social well-being, and in some places social stability. It is not possible for any of us to flourish, and hard for many to cope, if

---

4   As Dr Irene Guiju, Head of Research at Oxfam has noted:
    • Forbes rich list for 2013 said 85 of the world's richest people own as much as 3.5 billion of the poorest.
    • In 2105, the world's richest 1% had the same wealth as the remaining 99% added together.
    • In the UK, in 2015, 1% of people owned 23% of the wealth.
    To give one example from the developing world: in Zambia in 2010, 74% of the population was still living below the $1.25 poverty line. Although economic growth is up, inequality is growing rapidly, leading to much more extreme poverty. In January 2018, a factsheet from Oxfam Australia highlight a 'broken economic system' that is concentrating ever more wealth into the hands of the rich and powerful, while many ordinary people are not able to scrape by. In a report published to coincide with the gathering of some of the world's richest people at the 2018 World Economic Forum in Davos, Oxfam said billionaires had been created at a record rate of one every two days over the previous 12 months, at a time when the bottom 50% of the world's population had seen no increase in wealth. 82% of the global wealth generated in 2017, they said, went to the wealthiest 1%.

9

those unlucky enough to be born poor are denied opportunity, and have their potential smothered.

In Pope Francis's magnificent Encyclical *Laudato Si* (2015) *'On Care for our Common Home'*, he commented on, among many other things, global inequality. He said 'we have to realize that a true ecological approach always becomes a social approach: it must integrate questions of justice in debates on the environment so as to hear *both the cry of the earth and the cry of the poor.'*

The Archbishop of Canterbury, Justin Welby, also spoke about inequality in a speech in the House of Lords on 5 July 2016, in relation to the divisions in British society following the Referendum about membership of the European Union. In it, he said: 'The biggest thing it seems to me that we must challenge, my Lords, if we are to be effective in this creation of a new vision for Britain – a vision that enables hope and reconciliation to begin to flower – is to tackle the issues of inequality. It is inequality that thins out the crust of our society. It is inequality that raises the levels of anger and bitterness.' He spoke of the tools available to tackle inequality – education, health, mental health, housing – and then continued '... But my Lords, if those tools are to be used effectively, they are no use held in some kind of vacuum of values. We need a deep renewal of our values in this country. We need a renewal of a commitment to the common good. We need a renewal of solidarity. We need a sense of generosity, of hospitality, of gratuity, of the overflowing of the riches and the flourishing that we possess.' Does the Gospel of John have any spiritual wisdom to offer about justice and equality? That is one of the questions we will explore in this book.

(ii) The second major issue is sustainability. The issue of sustainability[5] has only reached prominence in recent decades. The reality has at last dawned on us that we are actually destroying the life systems on which all life depends. The myth of unlimited plenty, the expanding consumerist culture, the failure to recognize our depletion of vital earth resources, our reckless burning of fossil fuels, coupled with our assumption of the goal of unlimited economic growth – all this has

---

5   The link between the environmental agenda and the development agenda was made clear in the now classic definition of 'Sustainable Development' given in *Our Common Future*, the 1987 Report of the Brundtland Commission on Environment and Development, set up by the United Nations: 'Sustainable Development is development that meets the needs of the present without compromising the ability of future generations to meet their own needs.' This focuses on needs, and makes assumptions about the availability of social structures and natural and technological resources to meet those needs. The Brundtland definition has been criticized for its 'creative ambiguity', and the assumption that it is possible both to work for sustainable development while protecting resources for the present and the future, and also to work for the alleviation of poverty in the present, while not exceeding the environmental limits which nature imposes. There is widespread political belief that simply choosing the right technologies and reshaping the world's economic institutions will enable the world to continue aiming for economic growth while honouring planetary boundaries. However, there must be serious doubt about the feasibility of indefinite growth within the planet's ecological limits, not to mention human sin and selfishness, and the persistent failure of political institutions to reshape damaging economic structures.

brought to the clearest focus and to highest priority what the Anglican Marks of Mission called the obligation on us 'to safeguard the integrity of creation and sustain and renew the life of the earth'.

In his recent major study, *The Age of Sustainable Development*,[6] Jeffrey Sachs argues that sustainable development is the greatest, most complicated challenge humanity has ever faced. The world is uncertain, complex and confusing, faced with powerful vested interests, and with long lead times in building infrastructure. The problems are multi-generational. We have little time left to face up to the challenge of moving economies and societies on to sustainable development. If we do not make this change peacefully, equitably and urgently, Sachs argues, it will be forced on us by ecological disruptions in coming decades.

Underneath all this are huge numbers of questions, economic and ethical, ecological and social, about who we are as human beings, what our relationship is to the rest of the created order and other living beings and, in particular, how we relate to each other. Does the Gospel of John have any spiritual wisdom to offer us as we struggle with food, security, economic priorities, the consumer culture and the inclusion of people on the edges?

(iii) The third major issue is how we are to respond to environmental degradation, especially climate change. The opening ceremony of the 2012 London Olympics showed England's green and pleasant land transformed by the smoking chimneys of the industrial revolution. There is so much to be grateful to God for in science and technology. But one of the things the early industrialists did not know is that by burning fossil fuels, by deforestation, by some industrial agriculture, we are putting a blanket around the earth, which is changing the climate. My grandparents did not know this, nor did my father and mother. But we do.

The UN Intergovernmental Panel on Climate Change (IPCC) published its Fifth Assessment Report in 2013 and concluded that it is now unequivocal that the climate is changing and it is extremely likely that human influence has been the dominant cause in the last few decades. With no change to the rate of emission of greenhouse gases into the atmosphere, the earth is on course for a further rise in average temperature of somewhere between 1.5 degrees C and a catastrophic 4 degrees C.[7] And that will create an even more unstable climate. The

6   Jeffrey D. Sachs, *The Age of Sustainable Development*, Columbia University Press, 2015.
7   Many commentators have said – 5 years ago – that even 2 degrees is 'beyond dangerous' (e.g. Kevin Anderson and Alice Bows, 'Beyond "dangerous" climate change: emissions scenarios for a new world', *Philosophical Transactions of the Royal*

people most affected will not be in the UK or USA, but in Sub-Saharan Africa and Southeast Asia – people who have done the least to cause the damage, and are the least equipped to adapt.

Since then, reports about loss of all summer sea ice in the Arctic predict not only sea-level rise, but also the likely release of methane (an even more potent greenhouse gas than carbon dioxide) from the ocean floor.[8] Meanwhile, governments who signed up to the global Paris agreement to curb carbon emissions are still digging for coal and fracking for gas, apparently unaware of, or stupidly disregarding, the implications of what they have signed up to. 'After all,' comments George Monbiot, 'it's only the future of life on Earth that is at stake.'[9]

Alongside climate change, we are witnessing significant loss of bio-diversity, which affects the well-being of many creatures as well as the food chain, and increasing numbers of species becoming extinct. There have been mass extinctions several times over the course of evolution; this time it is being caused by us. What sort of world will our grand-children grow up into?

In summary, these three major issues put questions to us about **equity**, about the **economy**, and about our **environment**.

How might the spiritual wisdom of writings such as the Gospel of John help us to respond to some of these issues? Our question about how we are to cope has widened into a range of broader questions about our human identity and destiny. Questions such as:

- What is God asking of us now in relation to care for God's earth and the well-being of all God's creatures?

- What are our responsibilities to the parts of the world that are poorer, have done little to cause the damage to our environment and are the least able to adapt?

- How do we let future generations speak to us of their needs? (It is our carbon emissions that will still be around in their climate.)

- What sort of trust should we place in technology; are we secretly hoping that a technical fix will be the answer to all our fears?

Society, vol. 369, 13 January 2011), and that the IPCC is being too conservative in its estimates. We may be on course, such commentators say, unless we change direction, for 5 degrees C rise or more by the end of this century. This may not sound much, but when you think that the temperature difference between ice ages and the warm period in between is only about 6–7 degrees, we are talking about roughly half an ice age change in a matter of decades. The earth has never had to adapt so quickly before.

8   Peter Wadhams, *A Farewell to Ice,* Allen Lane, 2016.
9   George Monbiot, 'No fracking, drilling or digging: it's the only way to save life on Earth', *The Guardian,* 28 September 2016.

- Why do we keep fostering the illusion that growth in Gross Domestic Product (GDP) is the most important thing?
- Why do we maintain our dependence on fossil fuels, when we know that burning fossil fuels – which currently energise the industrial world and underpin our GDP – results in a major cause of damage to the planet? Why do we (why does the Government) try to hold two contrary views together: cutting carbon emissions on the one hand, and maximising fossil fuel extraction on the other?
- What are we to do about the unfair trade rules that frequently put finance above the welfare of human beings or above the wider environment of God's earth?
- Why do we seem so ready to downplay, deny or displace the urgency of environmental concerns such as climate change?10
- What does all this say to us about priorities for the Church in furthering the mission of God?
- What does it say about our individual discipleship, lifestyles and priorities?
- How do we handle our fears, vulnerabilities and anxieties about the future? How, indeed, are we going to cope?

These are all, at base, moral and spiritual questions. We will come back to them in different ways as we pursue our reflections on the spiritual wisdom of John's Gospel.

Who are we? And what is our destiny?

Some of the moral and spiritual questions that need to be addressed about equity, the economy and the environment are essentially questions about who we are as human beings and how we relate to God, to others and to the rest of God's creatures. In his book, *Destination of the Species: the riddle of human existence*,[11] Michael Meacher offers his attempt after 'years of musing', he says, to address the questions about humanity: 'Who are we? What is our destiny?' He says that a 'systematic review of all the scientific evidence strongly suggests that the Dawkins and neo-Darwinian view that the universe is driven by pitiless, directionless chance is seriously wrong and misleading.' One of the huge puzzles about human life is that we are here at all. Meacher's book takes us from the origin of the universe to the evolution of the human species, indeed to the evolution of human spirituality, and ends

10 cf. George Marshall, *Don't Even Think About It: Why our brains are wired to ignore climate change*, Bloomsbury, 2013.
11 Michael Meacher, *Destination of the Species: The riddle of human existence*, O Books, 2010.

up asking who we are now and where, as a species, we are going. He concludes:

> *The current political and economic governance structures place too much emphasis on competitiveness, aggrandizement, greed and self-interest for humans to achieve their real destiny of living, creatively and cooperatively, within the minutely balanced systems of the cosmos.*

Meacher argues that although we are increasingly able to understand the 'rules' that govern these systems, we are apparently not willing to abide by them:

> *Our destiny is still defined in terms of our power, our technological mastery over the whole natural world, our capacity to conquer and colonise the cosmos. We neglect the emergent property of our spirituality, the single most important attribute of human uniqueness, and our capability now in a globalized world to universalize human welfare we subordinate to our primitive drive to dominate. The challenge now for humans is not to transform the world, but to transform themselves.*[12]

If we transpose that into the language of the Gospel, I think Meacher is saying that human sin, greed and selfishness get in the way of living 'life in all its fullness' in accordance with God's purposes for the world. So if, as Christians believe, we are spiritual beings, and live and have our being in God, what does this imply for what Meacher calls 'human welfare'? What – in Christian understanding – does human flourishing mean? What is our human place within God's wider creation? And how are we to live, and cope?

The quest for spiritual values

There is a growing realization that the key issues are not primarily economic or political, but *spiritual*. They are about our vision, our values: about who we are and what is our destiny.

Some years ago, the great Greek Orthodox Christian leader, His All Holiness Ecumenical Patriarch Bartholomew, wrote:

> *The crisis we face is ... not primarily ecological but religious; it has less to do with the environment and more to do with spiritual consciousness. It is a crisis concerning the way we imagine the world.*[13]

Towards the end of his Encyclical, *Laudato Si: On Care for Our Common Home*, the Pope writes 'Christian spirituality proposes an alternative understanding of the quality of life, and encourages a prophetic and contemplative lifestyle, one capable of deep enjoyment free of the

---

12   Meacher, op. cit. p.224.
13   Foreword to Margaret Barker, *Creation,* T & T Clark, 2012.

obsession with consumption'.[14] The Pope also referred to 'the ethical and spiritual roots of environmental problems' (9), and drew attention to the way we see ourselves: 'We have come to see ourselves as [Sister Earth's] lords and masters, entitled to plunder her at will' (2).

Pope Francis is but one voice among many urging human beings to find a different way of living in the world. He offers a view of life which is not obsessed with consumption, but which is open to the Spirit of God active within the ordinariness of the world, a life which is not constrained by human abilities and frailties, but which is freed and guided by the Wisdom of God.

One of the interesting and increasingly frequent features of many contemporary debates is the extent to which people from all perspectives are seeking help from traditions of morality, spirituality or religious wisdom. Understanding well-being only in terms of growth in GDP simply will not do.

People are grasping for something more, something about human fulfilment and meaning which current economic theories simply do not touch. As long ago as 1973, E. F. Schumacher wrote *Small is Beautiful*, which he subtitled *A study of economics as if people mattered*.[15] And two years later Bishop John's Taylor's classic *Enough is Enough*[16] called for Christian people to see that discipleship requires rich Christians to fight against excess – of consumption, of waste, of pollution: 'we are being made to expect too much. We are taking too much. We are scrapping too much. We are paying, and compelling others to pay far too high a price.'

A poignant recent contribution comes from Fiona Reynolds, now Master of Emmanuel College, Cambridge, but formerly Director General of the National Trust. She writes: 'We seem to have forgotten that the human spirit is not satisfied by material progress alone. It is time for us to reconnect with nature.' We live in an era, she acknowledges, 'where fewer of us are driven by religious imperatives, but we are not lacking in spirituality.'[17]

The 2014 publication from the British Academy, *Prospering Wisely*, which explores the contribution of the humanities and the social sciences to our understanding of the meaning of 'prosperity', refers to 'the quest for a better, deeper, more valuable life'. It speaks about 'improving people's well-being', and 'the elements that make for a good

---

14   Pope Francis, *Laudato Si*, para. 222.
15   E. F. Schumacher, *Small is Beautiful*, Penguin, 1973. Compare also Jonathon Porritt, *Capitalism as if the World Matters*, Earthscan, 2005.
16   J. V. Taylor, *Enough is Enough*, SCM, 1975.
17   Fiona Reynolds, *The Fight for Beauty*, One World, 2016, p.311.

life and a healthy society'. It quotes Archbishop Justin Welby: 'A flourishing economy is necessary but not sufficient. A healthy society flourishes and distributes economic resources effectively but also has a
deep spiritual base which gives it its virtue.'[18]

At one point the BA paper says, 'Religious belief is one of the issues
where a perspective from the humanities is indispensable for policy
makers,' but rightly goes on to add this key sentence: 'Prosperity by
itself is not enough: it must be married with wisdom.'

The challenge being posed is for a change of heart and mind, away
from the sins of over-consumption, and towards justice, generosity
and care for the common good. We need a spiritual wisdom for today.

Where shall Wisdom be found?

People from many different perspectives and world-views are turning
back to spiritual writings in search of a wisdom that can illuminate the
questions we have been exploring.

One of the life-giving contributions that Christian faith can make to
these debates is an encouragement to return to what was called God's
Wisdom.

Divine Wisdom is the preoccupation of one particular genre of
writings in the Hebrew Bible: Proverbs, Job, Ecclesiastes, some parts
of some psalms and of some prophetic writings – and in some of the
books of the Apocrypha such as Sirach and the Wisdom of Solomon.
At its heart is the question raised in the Book of Job, 'Where shall wisdom be found?' (Job 28:12). In the Hebrew Bible, 'Wisdom' is closely
linked with God's creation of the world, and the order and rationality
we find there. It is also concerned with the relationships that human
beings have with each other, with their environment and especially
with God.[19] This second aspect is what Eric Heaton called 'the ability
to cope',[20] and which Derek Kidner more colourfully described as 'godliness in working clothes.'[21]

Hebrew Wisdom literature, then, says something about God, about
how the whole created order holds together within God's providence,

---

18 Archbishop Justin Welby, quoted in 'Living Better: Our culture and identity' (http://www.britac.ac.uk/prosperingwisely/
    living_better/our_culture_and_identity.htm).
19 Walter Brueggemann (*Theology of the Old Testament*, Fortress Press, 1997, p.680) wrote: 'Wisdom theology is theology
    reflecting on creation, its requirements, orders and gifts. The data for such theology is lived experience – whose regularity
    and coherence has an unaccommodating ethical dimension.' cf. Sharon Ringe, Wisdom's Friends, Westminster, 1999, p.29:
    'Wisdom names a bridge between Creator and creation ... Wisdom literature seeks to discern and describe the order
    inherent in the structures of society that give shape to human life: God's ways are known in the order of the world itself.'
20 Eric Heaton, *The Hebrew Kingdoms*, OUP, 1968, p.165: 'Wisdom is the ability to cope.'
21 Derek Kidner, Tyndale Old Testament Commentaries: *Proverbs*, Tyndale Press, 1964. cf. also Paul Fiddes (*Seeing the World
    and Knowing God*, OUP, 2013). Fiddes remarks that Aristotle distinguished between two aspects of wisdom: the intellectual
    wisdom of discerning what is ultimately real, lasting, universal and true (*sophia*); and the practical wisdom of moral
    decision making (*phronesis*). He suggests that the Hebrew understanding integrates both of these aspects. 'Wisdom' has
    something to do with a search for meaning (intellectual wisdom) and is also concerned with how to live well (practical
    wisdom).

about our human interdependence with the rest of the natural world and also our human vocation under God responsibly to care for God's earth. Wisdom moves from philosophical categories of meaning, to the very practical questions of day-to-day morality and (in Christian terms) discipleship. It is something about learning to understand God's world and how everything holds together, as well as learning how to live in God's world and dealing with the choices that face us each day. Wisdom asks: Who are we? How should we live? What makes for human flourishing? How are we to cope? And that brings us back to our reflections on John's Gospel.

Why the Gospel of John?

John's Gospel, more than the other three Gospels, I think, draws on Wisdom themes. It assumes a Wisdom perspective on creation. It makes use of both the intellectual aspects of Wisdom in its exploration of the Word, truth, life, light, Spirit and also draws on the earthy symbols of bread, water, gate, way, health and vine, which are all found in the more practical aspects of Hebrew Wisdom literature, and which John's Gospel uses to illustrate the fullness of life as it is seen in Jesus. The Gospel emerged out of the experiences of the Beloved Disciple, and the community around him. We must not try to read the Gospel as biography, nor as chronological history. It is a *gospel* narrative and its material has been very carefully and deliberately selected, under the inspiration of God's Spirit, to do several things. First, to introduce the readers to Jesus as God's Messiah. In fact, some commentators see the Gospel rather like a statement for the defence in a law court, in which Jesus is vindicated in his conflict with 'the world' (that is humanity living without reference to God).

My purpose in this book is very selective, and concentrates mostly on a second purpose for which I believe the Gospel was written: to strengthen the Christian community's faith in Jesus at a time of struggle and uncertainty. The writer uses symbolism a great deal; the text can often be understood at different levels of meaning; often it leaves us with mystery – or with wondrous great streams of thought which seem to expand the more we ponder them. By means of the symbols, the pictures, the motifs, the encounters, the theological themes interwoven through the Gospel narrative about Jesus' life and ministry in Galilee and Jerusalem, the author is introducing the risen Jesus, alive now in the power of God's Spirit, to his readers at the end of the first century – as well as to us, his readers at the start of the twenty-first century, with our questions about equity, economy and environment, and what it means for humanity to flourish.

In all this, the Gospel writer draws on Wisdom. Wisdom helps the readers understand what is going on in the world, and their place within God's creation. Wisdom also helps them live, and cope, and keep going hopefully as disciples of Jesus in his healing mission when the going is hard. It tells us who we are, and what is our destiny. It shows us how to cope. It points us to the spiritual meanings of human flourishing. In a vivid phrase, the theologian Hans Küng once wrote[22]:

> *'God's kingdom is creation healed.' Part of Christian discipleship and mission is to share in that healing.*

And it is Jesus in John's Gospel who not only says, 'do not be afraid', but also:'I came that they might have life in all its fullness' (John 10.10).

---

22 Hans Küng, *On Being a Christian*, Collins, 1977, p.231.

Part I

God's Wisdom Embedded in Creation

In Part I, we give an extended discussion of two of the primary assumptions of John's Gospel – that God is Creator of all, and that God's Wisdom, embedded in Creation, holds all things together. This will initially take us away from John's Gospel and back to the Hebrew Bible and its Wisdom writings. It will be our way in to a theology of nature, a way of understanding our human relationship to the rest of the created order, and give us a basis for a Christian perspective on ecology, and on some of the environmental issues that face us. It will help us understand who we are in relation to God's creation, and our human responsibilities under God in care for God's earth. All this will be background to our fuller exploration of the major themes of John's Gospel in the rest of the book.

And I have felt
A presence that disturbs me with the joy
Of elevated thoughts; a sense sublime
Of something far more deeply interfused,
Whose dwelling is the light of setting suns,
And the round ocean and the living air,
And the blue sky, and in the mind of man,
A motion and a spirit, that impels
All thinking things...

William Wordsworth,
Lines written a few miles above Tintern Abbey

Chapter Two

Creation as God's Delight and Gift

- What do we mean by 'Nature'?
- Christians see Nature as 'God's creation' which comes to us as gift.
- The Hebrew Scriptures speak about God's Wisdom embedded in all creation.
- Wisdom is God's delight, and we also delight in God's world.
- However, some aspects of Nature – and of Wisdom – are darker. Creation is in jeopardy.
- We have to acknowledge human sin and selfishness.
- Yet God's creation was made 'fit for purpose', and we humans are part of it, yet with a role of care for all God's earth.
- We need to live with all God's other creatures, care about biodiversity, and live within God-given boundaries.

One of our key questions is what relationship we human beings have with the rest of Nature. What is our Christian understanding of our role in God's earth?

In the beginning ... (John 1:1)

The opening words of the Gospel of John, '*In the beginning was the Word*', take us immediately back to the opening words of the Hebrew Bible: '*In the beginning, God*'. At this point we step back from our focus on John's Gospel, in order to discuss two of the major assumptions which underlie much of what John has written: God as Creator, and Nature as God's Creation in which God's Wisdom is embedded, holding all things together. The wonderful poem at the start of our Bibles, Genesis chapter 1, is a reflection on Nature as God's creation. In much of the Hebrew literature, Wisdom offers us a way to understand God's gift of creation, and our human place within it. It gives pointers to how we are to live and care for the rest of God's creation if we are to flourish, and how to cope when things are hard. But, first, what is meant by 'Nature'?

What do we mean by 'Nature'?

The word 'Nature' for many people first of all evokes awesome wonder. A visit to the Grand Canyon can be breath-taking, and even awaken worship. There is a painted notice on the railings at the edge of the Grand Canyon that reads: 'Bless the Lord, O my soul. O Lord my God, you are very great' (Psalm 104:1).

But, of course, there is also in Nature that which is awesomely destructive and damaging. Tsunamis and hurricanes, floods in India and Bangladesh, volcanic eruptions, droughts in East Africa and parts of Australia, ice-storms in America's mid-West, firestorms in the canyons above Los Angeles fuelled by the fierce Santa Ana winds. People speak of the 'power of Mother Nature'. Long ago the prophet Nahum said of God: 'His way is in whirlwind and storm' (Nahum 1:3). And we cannot forget Tennyson's famous line about 'nature red in tooth and claw'. There is that about Nature which seems cruel and heartless, and rightly puts serious questions to people of faith.

Whether through beauty or destructiveness, this way of seeing Nature is a common feature of our culture: Nature is simply there, apart from any human influence, and Nature moves us human beings emotionally, to wonder or to horror.

But there are other ways of 'seeing Nature'. In *Man and the Natural World*,[23] Keith Thomas illustrates many changes in social attitudes in England from AD 1500 to 1800, which affected how Nature is 'seen', from exploitation to stewardship. 'In the seventeenth century it became increasingly common to maintain that nature existed for God's glory and that he cared as much for the welfare of plants and animals as for man.'[24] The end of the nineteenth and early twentieth century, inspired by people like John Muir, the Scots-born naturalist, saw the growth of movements to preserve 'wilderness', and – initially in America – to develop major national parks such as Yosemite Valley, though it has to be acknowledged that sometimes the 'wilderness', as in Yellowstone, was an imposed, rather artificial, 'Nature' created at the cost of the livelihoods of indigenous people.

---

23 Keith Thomas, *Man and the Natural World*, Allen Lane, 1983; Penguin 1984.
24 Ibid., p.166.

Christians see Nature as 'God's creation' which comes to us as gift

Later in the twentieth century, as Alister McGrath indicates, there have been other different ways of 'seeing' Nature: a mindless force, causing humanity inconvenience and demanding to be tamed; an open-air gymnasium offering leisure and sports facilities; a wild kingdom, encouraging pursuits such as scuba diving, hiking and hunting; a supply depot, producing minerals, water and food for human wants and needs.

McGrath's primary point is that the definition of 'Nature' is actually a social construction[25] and involves seeing the world in a certain way'.[26] We do not simply see Nature, we see Nature 'as' something. Christians see Nature as 'God's creation'. This is the significance of Pope Francis' call to humanity to return to seeing Nature as gift: the gift of 'a Father who creates and who alone owns the world'.

On Ash Wednesday 2012, the Christian charity Operation Noah issued a paper called *Climate Change and the Purposes of God*,[27] which included the words: 'All we have, life and the means of life, comes to us as gift.'[28]

Human life in God's world is response to gift. In other words, we humans are not autonomous beings – we are dependent for all things on God the Giver. To recognize this should restrain our constant tendencies to anthropocentrism – that is to say, our tendencies to assume that everything is there for us, and that we are the centre of everything. There is a proper place for human responsibility under God, but there is a wrong sort of anthropocentrism that needs to be restrained. By recovering our sense of our dependence on God, and indeed our mutual interdependence within creation, we are not talking of the sort of 'deep ecology' in which everything becomes 'Nature'. That can lead to a form of pantheism. We are rather saying that, with all other creatures, we depend on God for our life: our oxygen, food, water and energy. But also that as human beings we are called into relationship with and responsibility to God for the care of the creation, all of which depends on God. The earth is the Lord's.[29]

---

25 Alister McGrath, *A Scientific Theology, Vol. 1: Nature,* Bloomsbury, 2001, p.109.
26 *Ibid.*, p.113.
27 www.operationnoah.org.
28 cf. Psalm 104:27–30: 'these all look to you to give them their food in due season; when you give to them, they gather it up; when you open your hand, they are filled with good things. When you hide your face they are dismayed; when you take away their breath, they die and return to their dust. When you send forth your Spirit, they are created; and you renew the face of the ground.'
29 To quote the Psalms again: 'the Earth is the Lord's and all that is in it' (24:1); 'the Lord has compassion on all that he has made' (145:9). All things look to God for their life and livelihood: 'O Lord, how manifold are your works! In Wisdom you have made them all' (104:24).

Wisdom: God's delight

Two major themes of the early chapters of the Book of Proverbs are that the world is ordered and held in being by God's Wisdom, and that God delights in all that God has made.

About 2500 years ago a wise person wrote:

> *The Lord by wisdom founded the earth; by understanding he established the heavens;*
> *by his knowledge the deeps broke open, and the clouds drop down the dew.*
> *My child, do not let these escape from your sight;*
> *keep sound wisdom and prudence,*
> *and they will be life for your soul.* (Proverbs 3:19f.)

and another said:

> *... if you find wisdom, you will find a future, and your hope will not be cut off.* (Proverbs 24:14)

The Wisdom of the Book of Proverbs is wonderfully free from religion.[30] No tabernacle or temple, no priests or scribes, no sacrifices or rituals. Instead a farrago of pithy sayings about relationships and money, wine and work, sex and death, animals, gossip, justice, royalty, language and lethargy. In other words, as we saw Derek Kidner describe it: 'godliness in working clothes'. But behind the moral wisdom of the sayings of Proverbs lies a view of the world in which God's Wisdom is embedded. Wisdom is God's agent in creation. She is there with him in the beginning. She is God's 'delight'. Here is Lady Wisdom speaking:

> *The Lord created me at the beginning of his work ... When he established the heavens, I was there, when he drew a circle on the face of the deep, when he made firm the skies above, when he established the fountains of the deep, when he assigned to the sea its limit, so that the waters might not transgress his command, when he marked out the foundations of the earth, then I was beside him, like a master worker; and I was daily his delight, rejoicing before him always, rejoicing in his inhabited world and delighting in the human race.* (Proverbs 8:22, 27–31)

Wisdom's world is one of discovery and excitement. Everything is to be explored. Wisdom's path is one of delighted, playful discovery, a sense of wonder and enjoyment. Are there echoes of the Lord God walking in the Garden in the cool of the evening, just to enjoy the flowers and the breeze? Or of the morning stars singing together and all the heavenly beings shouting for joy (Job 38:7)?

The poet who wrote Psalm 104 speaks of God's wisdom and joy in

---

30 cf. David Atkinson, *The Message of Proverbs*, IVP, 1996.

all the creatures and ends with a dominant note of joy: *'May the Lord rejoice in his works'* (v.31). God's Wisdom is embedded in creation, and is a source of God's delight.

Our delight in God's gift

The high point for me of Haydn's *Creation* is the magnificent chorus, quoting Psalm 19: 'The heavens are telling the glory of God'. The psalmist is speaking out of his commitment of faith in God the Creator, of God's revelation in the universe, and of the psalmist's own experience of God in his life. The psalm goes on not only to speak of the wonder of God's handiwork, but about God's ordering of things, of the moral law of God within a person's conscience, and of the promise of God putting things right. To the psalmist, the universe has precisely the properties he would expect if there is at its foundation a loving Creator God, whose beauty is seen in the starry heavens, whose rationality is seen in the ordering of creation, whose goodness is known in moral awareness and in the experience of grace and forgiveness.

But it is not obvious to everyone. In one of the saddest sentences I have read, Richard Dawkins writes from within his own commitment of faith in an atheistic, rationalistic materialism: 'The universe we observe has precisely the properties we should expect if there is, at bottom, no design, no purpose, no evil and no good, nothing but blind pitiless indifference.'[31] Yet even Richard Dawkins (rightly) argues that science itself, properly understood, leads to a sense of wonder and delight. He is unhappy with John Keats' implication that Newton's physics ('natural philosophy') had 'destroyed all the poetry of the rainbow'. Keats writes:

> *Philosophy will clip an Angel's wings,*
> *Conquer all mysteries by rule and line,*
> *Empty the haunted air, and gnomed mine –*
> *Unweave a rainbow ...* [32]

Rather than unweaving the rainbow, Dawkins argues instead that science can lead us to the point where 'a Keats and a Newton listening to each other might hear the galaxies sing'.[33] And Dawkins calls his fine major book on evolution *'The Greatest Show on Earth'*. It is the nearest he allows himself to come to the sense of wonder and worship we find in the poetry of the closing chapters of the Book of Job, or indeed of the psalmist: 'the heavens are telling the glory of God.'

---

31 Richard Dawkins, *River Out of Eden*, Orion, 1996, p.155.
32 John Keats, *Lamia*.
33 Richard Dawkins, *Unweaving the Rainbow*, Penguin, 2006, p.313.

I am reminded of that wonderful piece from the seventeenth-century poet Thomas Traherne:

> You never enjoy the world aright, till the Sea itself floweth in your veins, till you are clothed with the heavens, and crowned with the stars: and perceive yourself to be the sole heir of the whole world, and more than so, because men are in it who are every one sole heirs as well as you. Till you can sing and rejoice and delight in God, as misers do in gold, and Kings in sceptres, you never enjoy the world.[34]

Part of our human responsibility in the care of God's creation, in response to God's gift, is to safeguard the possibilities of delight and joy in God for ourselves and for others and for future generations. As Gerard Manley Hopkins has it, 'the world is charged with the grandeur of God'. But it needs us to look in the right direction. How we see 'Nature' depends on the way we are looking:

> Earth's crammed with heaven,
> And every common bush afire with God:
> But only he who sees, takes off his shoes,
> The rest will sit around it, and pluck blackberries.[35]

The psalmist who speaks of God's joy goes on to speak of his own: 'I rejoice in the Lord' (Psalm 104:34).

This suggests that a dominant note in a theology of Nature should be that of humble and joyous gratitude: joy in what God has made; joy in God's gift. For all that we have, life and the means of life, comes to us as gift: gift of God's goodness, generosity and love, for as John's Gospel later puts it: 'God so loved the world' (John 3:16). In God's Wisdom, heaven and earth come together. Or, in a phrase from James Jones,[36] this is the 'earthing' of heaven.

Wisdom: the wild order of things; creation in jeopardy
We have been trying to understand 'Nature' as God's creation, God's gift and the source of delight to God and wonder and worship to us. But sometimes Nature fills us rather with anxiety and fear, and seems to be a place of inexplicable suffering. In the Wisdom writings, there is another perspective on Nature, darker and more perplexing. Professor Frances Young's unpublished poem *Sophie's Call* refers to God's Wisdom as 'the wild order of things'.[37] Here is just a small part of a long poem:

34 *Centuries of Meditation* (1960 edition Clarendon Press), 'The First Century' section 29.
35 Elizabeth Barrett Browning, *Aurora Leigh*, Oxford Paperbacks, 1998.
36 James Jones, *Jesus and the Earth*, SPCK, 2003, p.60.
37 Quoted with the author's permission in David Atkinson, *The Message of Job*, IVP, 1991.

The wild beauty I see at the heart of things;
Conceived in the mind of the unknown Ancient of Days
She is the elemental principle,
The underlying pattern beneath the chaos ...

I am Sophie, the wild order of things ...

Often the underlying pattern in the world is hidden to us, and we see only what appears as chaos, or at least without meaning. God's way is sometimes 'in the whirlwind and the storm.' Although the enigmatic Wisdom book Ecclesiastes ends up, despite everything, with a word of hope, the writer spends most of his time looking down at the frustration of it all. There is not much about God in this book, though God as Creator gets a mention in the very last chapter: "Remember your Creator in the days of your youth' (Ecclesiastes 12:1). Why? Because you are getting old and will die, just as this whole creation is dying. The majority of Qoheleth's book is a depiction of waste and frustration. The author does not engage with the cruelty and apparent wastefulness of the evolutionary process. But he gets close. Vanity of vanities, all is vanity. What comes around goes around. Everything gets recycled in some way. What is the point of it all?

And yet there are a couple of glimpses of hope. The author can just see beyond the frustrations of the present to something deeper, something more profound, even more real. God is in heaven, he says, and you are upon earth (5:2). Yet 'he has put eternity into man's minds' (3:11). That is why the young man is to remember his Creator, and why, eventually, Qoheleth ends in the way he does: 'The end of the matter: all has been heard. Fear God and keep his commandments: for that is the whole duty of everyone. For God will bring every deed into judgement.' In other words, even though everything looks futile and vanity, and as though nothing has meaning under the sun, and that nothing ultimately matters at all, the end is this, which we can receive as good news: everything matters – God judges every deed – so fear God and keep his commandments.

We must not deny the harsher side to Nature. We have said that sometimes Nature overwhelms us with horror as well as with worship. To use one of Walter Brueggemann's phrases, we can often speak of 'creation in jeopardy'.[38] There is within God's creation that which is

---

38   In his *Theology of the Old Testament*, Walter Brueggemann writes of creation as Yahweh's partner. He acknowledges as we have done the role of Wisdom, and creation's capacity to enhance worship, as well as the blessing and fruitfulness of God's creation. But then he rightly speaks of another Old Testament theme, which he calls 'creation in jeopardy.' The ancient threat of chaos is still very present, and some psalms and prophets refer to it. The modern theologian Karl Barth speaks of an 'alien factor': an opposition and resistance to God's world-dominion. Is this the Serpent in Genesis 3; is it the Satan in the opening of Job? Is it 'the rule of this world' in John's Gospel? Brueggemann quotes Terence Fretheim's work [see note 16] and especially his treatment of the plagues in Egypt at the time of the Exodus. Fretheim's reading of Exodus 1–15 leads him to suggest that Pharaoh's policies stand for 'a deep disruption of creation', which somehow the God of Providence has allowed.

broken, seemingly cruel, without obvious purpose. God's Providence has somehow allowed a 'deep disruption of creation'. There is a 'wild order' to things. God's world is not yet perfected.

Sin and Selfishness

One aspect to the brokenness of the world is human sin and selfishness.

There are times when human sin and selfishness – or downright evil – have repercussions on a global scale. In our day we can name human activities that have brought huge destruction on people and planet – the holocaust and the gulags to give two examples; ecological devastation, deforestation and human-induced climate change to name others. So a number of the so-called 'natural' horrors have a human cause. And many aspects of our current economic thinking may well contribute significantly to environmental degradation. For example, much current economic thinking fails to take seriously the depletion of resources on which all life depends – indeed, economists tend to regard the capacity of the earth to support life as an 'externality' (that is, an economic factor for which no one is held responsible). Economists tend not to worry about the loss of biodiversity or the extinction of species, nor the persistent damaging commitment to burning fossil fuels as a primary source of energy.

In 1997, the Greek Orthodox leader, Patriarch Bartholomew, said in a speech in Santa Barbara, California, referring to people who seem not to care:

> *If human beings treated one another's personal property the way they treat their environment, we would view that behaviour as anti-social. We would impose the judicial measures necessary to restore wrongly appropriated personal possessions. It is therefore appropriate, for us to seek ethical, legal recourse where possible, in matters of ecological crimes.*

> *It follows that, to commit a crime against the natural world, is a sin. For humans to cause species to become extinct and to destroy the biological diversity of God's creation ... for humans to degrade the integrity of Earth by causing changes in its climate, by stripping the Earth of its natural forests, or destroying its wetlands... for humans to injure other humans with disease ... for humans to contaminate the Earth's waters, its land, its air, and its life, with poisonous substances ... these are sins.*

As long ago as the sixth century BC, the prophet Isaiah referred to environmental damage as an example of human sin, and the breaking of what he calls the 'everlasting covenant':

> *The earth dries up and withers, the world languishes and withers; the heavens languish together with the earth. The earth lies polluted under its inhabitants; for they have transgressed laws, violated the statutes, broken the everlasting covenant.* (Isaiah 24:4f.)

Isaiah's younger contemporary, Hosea, wrote this:

> *There is no faithfulness or loyalty, and no knowledge of God in the land. Swearing, lying, and murder, and stealing and adultery break out; bloodshed follows bloodshed. Therefore the land mourns, and all who live in it languish; together with the wild animals and the birds of the air, even the fish of the sea are perishing.* (Hosea 4:1–3)

There are destructive forces in Creation[39] – good, but not yet made perfect – as well as destructive forces in 'the world' of people. John's Gospel speaks starkly of the judgement of God: '*And this is the judgement, that the light has come into the world, and people loved darkness rather than light because their deeds were evil*' (John 3:19).

There is an ambiguity in our understanding of God's creation: God's delight in his world, which was made for perfection, but is not yet there; a world which has been spoiled and is under God's judgement.

God's creation is good: fit for purpose, but not yet perfect

The creation narrative of Genesis 1 shows the wonderful pattern of God's world, six days leading to a seventh – all creation leading towards worship – and humanity in God's image as the last of a long line of creatures made for God's enjoyment. It is very clear that other species matter to God: they are not simply there for their usefulness to us. Had God not first made all the other creatures, we humans would not be here. This is the world of which God again and again said, 'This is good!' God's creation reflects God's goodness: it is good – that means, 'fit for purpose'. 'Good' does not mean 'already perfect'. Genesis 1 also makes clear that we humans are part of the rest of Nature or, as we would say, part of the whole evolved creation, and therefore dependent on God for life, and for well-being, and interdependent with all the rest of creation. Our theology, our discipleship, our ethics, our mission, must therefore – as we have said – be one of proper dependence, and interdependence, of createdness, not of an assumed autonomy.

Further, we are made, male and female, to be 'the image of God'. The language of 'image' is of royal service: humanity charged with

---

39   There is, of course, another large and important discussion, beyond the scope of this book, concerning how the suffering of animals, in what seems to us wasteful and cruel ways, fits into the providence of God. Two good books are Christopher Southgate, *The Groaning of Creation: God, Evolution and the Problem of Evil*, Westminster , 2008; and Elizabeth A. Johnson, *Ask The Beasts: Darwin and the God of Love*, Bloomsbury, 2014; cf. also Terence E. Fretheim, *Creation Untamed: the Bible, God and Natural Disasters*, Baker, 2010.

particular responsibility under God for the cultivation, care and protection of all God's creation. It is sometimes said that because human beings are the cause of the damage to the natural environment, it is human beings who can solve it. While we have a responsibility under God for creation care, the preservation or restoration of creation cannot simply be a human task if the creation is continuously created and upheld and sustained by God, and will ultimately be redeemed. Creation, or to use Gunton's, phrase, 'God's project' of which we are one part, is in the process of being healed and restored and made perfect.

The pattern of Genesis 1 is also the pattern of the Temple,[40] and the whole cosmos can be understood as God's temple, or what Calvin called the 'theatre of God's glory'.[41] Humanity, God's image-bearer, can then be seen as God's 'priest'[42] – part of the created order, and yet with a responsibility under God to represent God in relation to an interdependent creation, and to enable creation to sing God's praise.

God's Garden: life within limits

The calling as God's image-bearers to be creation's stewards and priests needs to be set in strong contrast with the roles we human beings have frequently actually adopted in relation to the earth. Peter Jacques, for example, writes 'the current trajectory of human consumption of the Earth's ecosystems is both unsustainable because it cannot continue without causing deep social crisis from systemic exhaustion, and because it is already creating social crisis through deeply unjust distribution of wealth and wellbeing'... 'humanity must end this death march if we want a livable planet' ... 'Human activities, especially since the Industrial Revolution and accelerating after World War II, have altered basic operating conditions for life on Earth, by altering the chemistry of soils, atmosphere and fresh and marine water systems, extinguishing species, and disrupting whole landscapes, all in a very short time.'[43]

Sallie McFague says of her recent book[44] that a central thread is 'the gnawing question of how to live well on planet earth in the twenty-first century'. She puts it this way: 'We are facing an economic and environmental meltdown of more serious proportions than any generation of human beings before us. It is no exaggeration to speak in apocalyptic language, at the most elemental levels of basic physical needs, of the prospects for people and the planet.'

---

40 cf. Margaret Barker, *Temple Theology*, SPCK, 2004.
41 J. Calvin, *Institutes*, I.6.2.
42 Although Richard Bauckham (*Living with Other Creatures*, Paternoster, 2012, p.151) cautions against the use of this term because of its hierarchical connotations, I think it is still useful in the context not of hierarchy but of service.
43 Peter Jacques, *Sustainability*, Routledge, 2015, pp.1,5,30.
44 Sallie McFague, *Blessed are the Consumers: Climate Change and the Practice of Restraint*, Fortress Press, 2013, p.35,2.

The ambiguity of our human life and predicament on earth is powerfully illustrated in the much earlier Genesis text that we know as Genesis chapters 2 and 3. These chapters are predominantly a story of intimacy between Adam and God, but also a story of how things went desperately wrong. Adam is placed within a Garden. Probably written about the time of King Solomon, Genesis 2 may reflect the importance played in Jerusalem by 'the king's garden.'[45] Maybe the writer wanted to emphasise the importance of the royal service required to care for the garden on behalf of the King. Humanity is earthed within the rest of the created order, and yet alone among the creatures is addressed by God and charged with the responsibility of royal service ('to guard and to keep' the Garden). The human is enabled to live in relationship, is given the capacity for moral choice, experiences shame, guilt and alienation, and knows that he will die. However, Adam does not die – or at least not physically then. He is clothed by God's provision, and driven out of the garden for his own protection. But then we find that there are cherubim with flaming swords guarding the way back to the tree of life.

The Garden environment is a sign of God's abundant generosity. 'Every tree that is pleasant to the sight and good for food' (Genesis 2:9). The 'tree of life' symbolises the life of God – the presence of God bringing life to the midst of the garden.[46] And yet there is one restraint placed on humanity: 'You may freely eat of every tree of the Garden, but of the tree of the knowledge of good and evil you shall not eat' (Genesis 2:17). The serpent gives the reason in chapter 3: 'God knows that when you eat of it ... you will be like God' (Genesis 3:5) – and the serpent goes on to tempt the human to do just that. The restraint God places on life in the Garden seems to be this: 'You are to grow in the knowledge of God on the basis of obedience to God's ways.' In other words, life in God's Garden is both the enjoyment of God's abundant generosity, and is also restrained by the need to live within God-given limits. Humanity flourishes within a God-given boundary.

So in Genesis 2, the picture of humanity is ambiguous. Through God's gift, humanity is set in a place of delight, of responsibility and royal service. Through human choice and human sin – seeking to 'be like God' – damage is done to the life of God's Garden and the relationships within it. In a world in which creation is fragile and sometimes broken, humanity is protected by God, but is now separated from the

---

45 cf. the later references in 2 Kings 25:4 and Jeremiah 39:4; 52:7; quoted in William T. Brown, *The Seven Pillars of Creation*, OUP, 2012.

46 The symbolism of the tree appears again in the design of the tabernacle and the temple for the people of covenant faith – the seven-branched candlestick is the tree of life – God's presence in the midst of God's temple.

tree of life. Access to God's presence is no longer obvious. It will take 'a second Adam to the fight' to restore the authority to live as children of God. In 'God's project'[47] humanity has a particular responsibility under God in bringing creation to its perfection. Adam, the original 'child of God', is made out of the dust of the ground – which we now know to be the dust of dying stars; 'you are dust and to dust you shall return.' As Anne Primavesi[48] underlines, if we see ourselves as of the earth, rather than think the earth exists for us, our whole perspective is radically changed. Adam, made of the dust of the earth, is given responsibility for the earth.

We have already referred to our dependence on God's gift for life and livelihood. We must now add to that our human interdependence with all other creatures. We are 'of the earth', alongside all other creatures in which God delights.

Nature, God and our human responsibilities

We can now offer some preliminary reflections on our human responsibilities for how we live in God's world today. We need (i) to live within God-given limits in dependence on God, and we need (ii) to live with other animals, in interdependence as fellow-creatures with them.

(i) Living within planetary limits

The language of 'living within limits' is very pertinent to the environmental crisis we face. A publication from the Club of Rome as long ago at 1972, called 'Limits to Growth', challenged the assumption of unlimited consumption, and warned of the devastation ahead if the world continued to consume the planet's resources at the same unrestricted rate. Though the paper was criticized for some of its details, more recent research in Stockholm has also spoken of 'planetary boundaries'. In 2009, Professor Johan Rockstrom published a paper in *Nature* concerning what he called 'a safe operating space for humanity'. Oxfam built on this in their 2012 paper, 'A Safe and Just Space for humanity',[49] in which they argue that humanity flourishes within social boundaries on the one hand, and planetary boundaries on the other. Social boundaries include such things as sufficiency of food, water, health, income, education, gender equality, social equity and jobs. By 'planetary boundaries' they mean living within the limits imposed by climate change, freshwater use, the nitrogen and phosphorus cycles, ocean acidification, pollution, ozone depletion, loss of biodiversity and some

---

47   To borrow a phrase from Colin Gunton, *Christ and Creation,* Paternoster, 1992; cf. The Triune Creator, Eerdmans, 1998.
48   Anne Primavesi, *Exploring Earthiness,* Cascade, 2013.
49   See also Kate Raworth, *Doughnut Economics* (Random House, 2017)

changes in land use. On some of these markers, they argue, humanity is already living beyond the carrying capacity of the planet. If everyone wanted to live as many of us in the developed world now do live, there is simply not enough planet to go round. Human flourishing – living well – is multi-dimensional, and is getting harder to achieve for increasing numbers of people trapped by poverty and injustice.

(ii) Living with other creatures

The vision of creation in the Wisdom writings is a theocentric one in which the animals have their place. They are sometimes used for food, sometimes for sacrifice. They are always there for God's purposes and often for God's delight long before humanity was thought of (Genesis 1; Job 38:1ff.). God even seems to enjoy the sport of the frightening monsters such as Leviathan (Psalm 104:26) and Behemoth (Job 40:15). The other creatures besides human beings have their own identity and place before God. They all – just by being themselves – 'praise the name of the Lord' (Psalm 148).

Whereas sometimes animals need to be tamed, there is much in the Hebrew Bible and in the Synoptic Gospels about the compassionate treatment of animals, God's provision of food for them, and God's care for each of them.[50] The messianic hope of Isaiah's peaceable kingdom, when the wolf lives with the lamb and the leopard lies down with the kid (Isaiah 11:6–9), seems also to be depicted in Jesus' time of friendly presence 'with the wild beasts' in the wilderness (Mark 1:13), and looks forward also to the 'new heaven and new earth' with the vision of wolves and lambs feeding together, and the lion eating straw like the ox (Isaiah 65:25).

In the light of this perspective, we need to heed Richard Bauckham's words: 'All too often in the history of Christian thought and in the history of western thought, humans have been elevated above the natural world as though we did not really belong to it. We have tried to relate to other creatures as demi-gods rather than as fellow-creatures, and the results have been in many cases catastrophic. But this is not a biblical view. Humans are *distinctive* among other creatures, but the creation narratives also make quite clear our *kinship* with other creatures ... Had we paid sufficient attention to this, we could not have come to regard the earth and its creatures as dispensable, as though we did not really belong to it. Once we recover our sense of our kinship to all other creatures, we cannot be indifferent to the fate of other creatures

---

50 My thanks to Richard Bauckham for *Living with Other Creatures,* Paternoster 2012, especially ch. 4: 'Jesus and Animals'.

on earth.'[51]

Richard Bauckham points to the Book of Job, to which we have earlier referred, as illustration of God's delight in biodiversity, and that the whole of creation lives to glorify God. There is a sacredness to God's creation (which is by no means the same as pantheism), and as Bauckham says, 'if we gave more attention to the creatures as our fellow-worshippers, we would not be so prone to instrumentalise them, to regard them as having value only if we can make use of them for our own needs and desires.'[52]

Part of our concern for the well-being of our environment is for the growing loss of biodiversity, and the probable extinction of growing numbers of species – current extinction rates are about 1000 times higher than 'natural' rates and what some now label the Sixth Great Extinction is, this time, largely caused by us. There is considerable debate within the conservation movement as to what the right responses should be. As Dave Bookless writes: 'At the heart of the crisis within biodiversity conservation is a simple question which divides the global conservation movement. What gives nature its value? Is conservation's raison d'etre purely instrumental, preserving habitats and species because of the 'ecosystem services' they provide for human thriving, or can we speak of intrinsic or inherent values within species and ecosystems and, if so, on what are these values based?'[53]

For a Christian, those values are rooted in the delight and gifts of God's good creation: the values of God's Wisdom that enable us to live wisely in God's world. These are themes to which we return in our discussion in Part II of the way John's Gospel depicts the Wisdom of God embodied in Jesus.

51 *Ibid.*, p.223.
52 Bauckham, *Living with Other Creatures*, p.222.
53 Dave Bookless, 'Let Everything that has Breath Praise the Lord: the Bible and biodiversity', Cambridge Papers vol. 23. No3, Sept. 2014.

Chapter Three

God's Wisdom Holds
Everything Together

- **The Bible presents a life-giving triangle of relationships rooted in God's promise and God's faithfulness: God–Humanity–Earth.**

- **Wisdom is seen as the Mediator, holding everything together.**

- **At times, particularly with the growth of modern science in the seventeenth century, 'God' has been eclipsed, and the triangle of relationships fractured.**

- **Wrong views about human beings 'having dominion' have made things worse.**

- **However, the Bible holds out the hope of creation being healed through the life, death and resurrection of Jesus Christ. Through him, life-giving relationships can be restored.**

John's Gospel, much more than many other New Testament writings, draws heavily on the Hebrew concept of Wisdom. As we shall elaborate much more fully in Part 2, Jesus – God's Word made flesh – is presented as the Mediator between God, Humanity and the Earth – a life-giving 'triangle' of relationships which we first encounter in the Hebrew Bible.

A triangle of relationships: God–Humanity–Earth
We are first introduced to a triangle of relationships, described as a 'covenant', based on God's promise and faithfulness, which links God and God's people with their promised home: God–Israel–the Land.[54]

---

54 cf. W. Brueggemann, *The Land: Place as Gift, Promise and Challenge in Biblical Faith,* 2nd ed., Fortress Press, 2002. For the people of Israel, 'the land' reflected in significant ways their relationship with God. As Brueggemann shows, land was first a promise made by God to Abraham; the journey to the land of promise is the story of Exodus; land was received as God's gift, and there were laws to ensure the proper use of God's land. Misuse of God's land – and treating it as a commodity rather than 'an arena for human interaction that respects both neighbour and the land' contributed to the judgement of exile, when the people of Israel found themselves landless, homeless and without hope. Brueggemann moves on to New

That triangle, told in the story of God's people, then became a symbol of a much larger and more basic 'cosmic covenant'[55] between God–Humanity–Earth. Such a covenant, also rooted in the promise and faithfulness of God, is implied in the first chapter of the Bible when, after the emergence of all other creatures, humanity is created to be 'the image of God'. It is explicit in the story of Noah and the rainbow: 'God said, "This is the sign of the covenant that I make between me and you and *every living creature* that is with you"' (Genesis 9:12). The earth is then seen as 'God's promise and gift to humanity'[56] – a place in which to live well, to relate, to grow, to flourish, and where all creation is therefore to be respected as God's gift and not be treated as a 'commodity'. It is in this sense that Pope Francis' encyclical refers to the earth as 'our common home'.

Wisdom as Mediator

Lady Wisdom has her role as a Mediator within this triangle of relationships. Sometimes described as 'the Word', sometimes as God's Spirit, She is the deep meaning behind the relationships of God's creation, and She is the one who holds everything together – the strength and stay of all things. Various Wisdom texts show this. The wonderful passage in the Book of Job chapter 28, after the pain of Job's losses and the unhelpful responses of his various friends, acts as a sort of 'chorus' in the tragedy. It gives us space to breathe and think before the dialogues continue and eventually God speaks in the whirlwind. Rather unexpectedly, Job 28 is about mining ore from the mountain. It is through digging in the dark that silver and gold, iron and copper and precious jewels can be found. But – the chapter continues – although human beings can find and benefit from these resources of the earth, we cannot in the same way dig for Wisdom! *'Where shall Wisdom be found? And where is the place of understanding? ... It cannot be bought for gold, and silver cannot be weighed out as its price ... It is hidden from the eyes of all living ... God understands the way to it, and he knows its place.'* Wisdom is personified, immanent in all creation. She is the order given to the world, the most precious thing of all. Yet human beings – even though they can achieve the hardest of things, and unearth the richest jewels, cannot determine where Lady Wisdom is to be found. Wisdom is 'established' by God at the heart of creation. She is there

---

Testament categories of crucifixion and resurrection to refer to the move from landlessness to the rediscovery of 'home'.

55   cf. Robert Murray, *The Cosmic Covenant*, Sheed & Ward, 1992. cf. also John Goldingay's comments on Isaiah 24:1–13 in *New International Biblical Commentary*, Isaiah, Paternoster, 2001, p.138: '[In Genesis 9:8–17], that covenant is purely a commitment on God's part to be faithful to the world ... Israel's covenant relationship is then an application of the general covenant relationship to Israel in particular. It is designed to benefit the world as Israel becomes a covenant for the people.'

56   Brueggemann, op. cit.

in the world, even though her meaning, implanted by God, remains a mystery until God discloses it.[57]

Other Wisdom writings open up some of the mystery. We have quoted from Proverbs chapter 8, which describes Wisdom as God's agent in creation, God's Delight. A few chapters earlier, we find this:

> *Happy are those who find wisdom and those who get understanding, for her income is better than silver, and her revenue better than gold. She is more precious than jewels, and nothing you can desire can compare with her. Long life is in her right hand; in her left hand are riches and honour. Her ways are ways of pleasantness, and all her paths are peace. She is a tree of life to those who lay hold of her; those who hold her fast are called happy.* (Proverbs 3:13–18)

Later texts are more specific about the way Wisdom 'holds everything together.'

> *Wisdom is a kindly spirit ... Because the spirit of the Lord has filled the world, and **that which holds all things together** knows what is said ...* (Wisdom 1:6–7)

Later, in Wisdom 7:22–28, we find this remarkable paragraph:

> *There is in her a spirit that is intelligent, holy, unique, manifold, subtle, mobile, clear, unpolluted, distinct, invulnerable, loving the good, keen, irresistible, beneficent, humane, steadfast, sure, free from anxiety, all-powerful, overseeing all, and penetrating through all spirits that are intelligent, pure and altogether subtle. For wisdom is more mobile than any motion; because of her pureness she pervades and penetrates all things. For she is a breath of the power of God, and a pure emanation of the glory of the Almighty; therefore nothing defiled gains entrance into her. For **she is a reflection of eternal light, a spotless mirror of the working of God, and an image of his goodness. Although she is but one, she can do all things, and while remaining in herself, she renews all things**; in every generation she passes into holy souls and makes them friends of God, and prophets; for God loves nothing so much as the person who lives with wisdom.*

And yet another Wisdom writer, while celebrating the splendour of God's creativity in the sun, moon, stars and rainbow, and in Nature, continues:

> *In it are strange and marvellous creatures, all kinds of living things, and huge sea-monsters. Because of him each of his messengers succeeds, **and by his word all things hold together**. We could say more but could never say enough; let the final word be: 'He is the all.'* (Sirach 43:25–27)

Among the many attributes of Lady Wisdom, one is that it is She in whom all things hold together. This is a theme to which, as we shall

---

57   cf. G. von Rad, *Wisdom in Israel*, SCM, 1972, p.144ff.

see later, New Testament writers refer when speaking of Jesus Christ.

The break-up of the triangle of relationships: humanity as 'masters' of Nature

The sad truth is that in our culture the covenanted triangle of relationships, God–Humanity–Earth, has been fractured, and that fracture has contributed to the difficult issues and anxieties with which we are now trying to cope – of which loss of sustainability, population growth, environmental degradation and climate change are among the most serious. We have lost the sense that 'the earth is the Lord's', and that we humans are part of Nature, 'of the earth', and so dependent on God and other creatures for our well-being. We have also lost our sense of a God-given responsibility to care for God's creation on God's behalf.

The cosmic covenant (God–Humanity–Earth) features in the writings of theologians such as Irenaeus, Augustine and Francis of Assisi. But it has been lost. Sir Francis Bacon, barrister and parliamentarian, was a philosopher often credited with opening up the thinking that led to modern science.[58] There is, of course, a very great deal of science and technology which has enormously benefited humanity and for which we can thank God. Indeed, science itself works because of the correspondence between our minds and the ordered rationality of the universe that science explores – a rationality to which the Scriptures gave the name Wisdom. Francis Bacon extolled the virtues of scientific conquest, but used the language of forcing Nature to yield her secrets for the benefit of humanity as the highest human calling – often using words that today we regard as strongly sexist and patriarchal. It is largely to Bacon that we owe the development of a mechanical model of the universe, which came to such prominence in the work of Newton. However, it is sometimes forgotten that Bacon – a person of faith in God – linked the quest for knowledge with the virtues of wisdom, courage, justice and moderation,[59] and described science as 'the finding out of the true nature of all things whereby God might have the more glory in the workmanship of them, and men the more fruit in the use of them'.[60] He even said that 'man is but the servant and interpreter of nature'.[61] Bacon developed a wholly new understanding of humanity's place in the natural world. Free from religious control, human will becomes the measure of nature. The hugely positive benefits

---

58 Louis Dupré puts the main damage to what he calls the 'orthodox synthesis' earlier, at the end of the medieval period, when, he argues, the triangle of relationships between God, humanity and the earth begins to come apart (*Passage to Modernity*, Yale, 1993).

59 J. Weinberger's *Introduction to Francis Bacon, The Great Instauration and New Atlantis*, Harlan Davidson, 1980 edition, p.xxix.

60 Francis Bacon, op. cit., p.57.

61 Ibid. p.31.

of science – which Pope Francis's encyclical rightly acknowledged – emerge alongside a loss of the sense of God's immanence in creation. God was dispatched to some deistic transcendent distance, where he could not interfere. A similar unsatisfactory understanding of our human relationship to nature is found in Descartes, where he speaks of the new science as a 'practical philosophy' which can put to good use 'the fruits of the earth and all its commodities', and 'thereby make ourselves, as it were, masters and possessors of nature'.[62]

It is this shift in thought during 'The Great Instauration' (as Francis Bacon called the flowering of new knowledge in the 1620s) that lies behind much of our contemporary crisis of not knowing who we are in relation either to God or to Nature. It lies behind Michael Meacher's questions: 'Who are we?', and 'What is our destiny?' It greatly affects our response to the question of how we are to flourish. It also lies behind the development of what Naomi Klein[63] calls 'extractivism' – a dominance-based relationship in which we humans place ourselves above the earth's ecosystems and believe we can – indeed must – control and exploit the earth as if it were an inanimate machine simply there for our benefit alone.

The covenanted triangle of relationships, rooted in God's promise and God's faithfulness, lies behind both our emphasis on our dependence on God, and also – one of the key features of contemporary ecological science – our interdependence with all God's creatures.

The eclipse of God
The fracture in the triangle of relationships shifted God to a separate, distant relationship with the creation. This challenged our human dependence on God as one of God's creatures, and led rather to an assertion of our human autonomy, independent of God's will and God's ways.

Michael Northcott, in his book *A Political Theology of Climate Change*,[64] talks about the 'separations', or 'pulling apart' that started with Francis Bacon's mechanistic model of nature. God is separated from the world: matter becomes separated from mind and spirit; nature from culture; science from ethics; facts from values. Carolyn Merchant writes of *The Death of Nature*.[65] Philip Sherrard called his book, *The Rape of Man and Nature*.[66] Bill McKibben wrote of *The End*

---

62 Rene Descartes, *Discourse on Method* (1637), Penguin Books, 1968, p.78; cf. also Charles Webster's discussion in *The Great Instauration*, Duckworth, 1975.
63 Naomi Klein, *This Changes Everything: Capitalism vs. The Climate*, Allen Lane, 2014.
64 Michael Northcott, *A Political Theology of Climate Change*, SPCK, 2014.
65 Carolyn Merchant, *The Death of Nature*, Harper and Row, 1980.
66 Philip Sherrard, *The Rape of Man and Nature*, Golgonooza, 1987.

of Nature,[67] and Alister McGrath has called for *The Re-enchantment of Nature*.[68] Climate change, in James Lovelock's colourful metaphor, is 'Gaia's revenge'.[69] It is of interest, incidentally, that in the New Testament, the concepts of throwing apart, dividing, separating, setting at variance, are covered by the word *diabolos*, that is 'demonic'. The ministry of Jesus, by contrast, is predominantly healing, gathering up fragments, restoring, and putting back together.

What is at issue here, to repeat, is the fracture of that triangle of relationships between God, humanity and the earth, and so the loss of the Christian understanding of humanity serving under God in the care of the world. To pick up a phrase from John Donne – Francis Bacon's contemporary – in his sad reflection on what the new science of his day had produced, "'Tis all in pieces, all coherence gone.'[70] The human damage caused to the environment is one illustration of the disintegration that results from displacing God from the relationships of God with humanity and the earth. To use a phrase that Thomas Torrance borrowed from Martin Buber, this is 'the eclipse of God'.[71]

But don't Christians talk about 'having dominion'?

The fracture in the triangle God–Humanity–Earth also challenged our human relationship with all God's other creatures, and opened the way to seeing ourselves as 'masters and possessors of nature'.

We have noted that at times many people – though not all – took the Genesis language of 'dominion' and 'subdue' (Genesis 1:28) to mean 'exploit as much as you like, without regard for the welfare of other creatures'. Sadly this has too often been true of Christians. Lynn White's famous charge against Christianity, that it is the most anthropocentric of all religions,[72] and so the cause of our environmental crisis, is partly true but only to the extent that Christians have colluded with that aspect of the enlightenment approach to nature which replaced awe and humility with exploitation and management. The perspective of the closing chapters of the Book of Job, by contrast, is to move us from the wildness of creation to the wisdom of the Creator – to hear behind the

---

67 Bill McKibben, *The End of Nature,* Bloomsbury, 1989/2003; cf. also McKibben, *Eaarth,* St Martin's Griffin, 2011.
68 Alister McGrath, *The Re-enchantment of Nature,* Hodder, 2002. Many environmentalists are 'enchanted' with nature, and are at a loss to understand why this view seems not to be shared by Christians.
69 James Lovelock, *The Revenge of Gaia,* Allen Lane, 2006.
70 'And new philosophy calls all in doubt, / The element of fire is quite put out, / The sun is lost, and th'earth, and no man's wit, / Can well direct him where to look for it. / And freely men confess that this world's spent, / When in the planets and the firmament / They seek so many new; they see that this / Is crumbled out again to his atomies. / 'Tis all in pieces, all coherence gone, / All just supply, and all relation; / Prince, subject, father, son, are things forgot', John Donne, *An Anatomy of the World,* The First Anniversary.
71 T. F. Torrance, *God and Rationality,* OUP, 1971.
72 Lynn White Jr., 'The Historical Roots of Our Ecological Crisis', a paper given at the 1966 meeting of the American Association for the Advancement of Science; *Science,* **155**, 1967, p.1203–1207.

singing of the morning stars or the tumults of the waves or the roar of the hungry young lion – to hear behind these the voice of God in the whirlwind. The New Testament invites us to do the same, even if in a different key: to see beyond the birds of the air, the Heavenly Father who feeds them; beyond the lilies of the field, the God who clothes them with glory (Matthew 6:25ff.).

Many environmentalists are cautious of – indeed, opposed to – the Christian Church because they assume that exploitation and extractivism is what Christians believe. In fact, however, as Richard Bauckham makes clear,[73] until the rise of modern science, most Christians did *not* believe that this Genesis verse meant that human beings should have total control over the whole world, but rather that as beings 'made in God's image' we have a responsibility under God to care for God's creation.[74] It was the growth of modern science and technology in the seventeenth century – though often pioneered by Christian people (many of the first members of the Royal Society were Puritan Christians), and having brought much blessing to the world – that led at the same time to the 'disenchantment' of Nature and the (wrong) belief that science was about forcing Nature to yield her secrets to our human dominion.

Creation healed?

The question is: can that coherence be restored. Can Lady Wisdom once again be seen to 'hold all things together'?

From Wisdom's perspective, we need to affirm both a picture of creation as God's delight, and also a picture of creation in jeopardy, infected by human sin, selfishness and stupidity. We recognize the chaos of much of the world, and the anxieties this creates about our ability to cope. But it is only when this is acknowledged that we can look beyond chaos to the vision of creation healed. There are indeed pointers in the Hebrew Bible to God's compassion and desire to restore creation. There is language of 'a new heaven and a new earth', a vision of prosperity, security, fruitfulness, blessing and peaceableness throughout creation.[75] But it is in the New Testament picture of Jesus Christ, embodying the Wisdom of God, that we find grounds for substantial hope that God has remained faithful to his covenant promise, and that the whole of creation – not just human beings – is part of his 'project' to bring all things to their perfection in a healed creation.

---

73   Richard Bauckham, *Bible and Ecology*, DLT, 2012.
74   In the Genesis text, 'dominion' is best thought of as 'ruling' with the sort of care and compassion that God shows – humanity is as it were 'in royal service' – taking care of God's creation on God's behalf. 'Subdue' is probably best thought of in terms of cultivation and agriculture.
75   For example: Isaiah 55:12f.; 65:17f.

John's Gospel on creation

The Gospel of John does not say very much directly about creation as such, but the theme is implicit throughout the Gospel, and is foundational for its message. The first verse, 'In the beginning ...' (John 1:1), recalls God's work of creation in Genesis 1. At the end of the Gospel we read of Jesus 'creating'.[76] It appears that the author is very deliberately underlining the fact that the God whose creation is referred to in John 1:1 is the Jesus who is still active in creation.

One aspect of John's Gospel worth mentioning here is that the author does refer to other animals, if not very prominently. The metaphor of lamb is used of Jesus, the Lamb of God, and of the sheep for whom he is the Good Shepherd, and indeed the lambs and sheep that the apostle Peter is called to feed. There is reference back in history to Jacob's flocks of sheep, and to the sheep with the cattle and doves near the tables of the moneychangers in the Temple. Sacrificial lambs are implicit in the references to the Day of Preparation for the Passover. The Holy Spirit is depicted as a dove, there is a quotation about a donkey in relation to Jesus' entry into Jerusalem, a cock crows in the High Priest's courtyard. Then there are the fish: two of them with five barley loaves in the young boy's packed lunch, and a rather larger number in the fishing net on the Sea of Galilee, when the risen Jesus was cooking a fish breakfast on the beach.

What John's Gospel does say quite a lot about, however, is the 'new creation'. There are signs of new creation happening all through the Gospel. The dialogue with Nicodemus in chapter 3 refers to new birth. After the healing of the paralyzed man on the Sabbath in John 5, Jesus says 'My Father is still working and I also am working.' In other words, through his healing and re-ordering Jesus is continuing God's creative work. In chapter 1, Jesus speaks of the ladder between heaven and earth. He transforms insipid water into an abundance of wine (John 2). He cleanses the Temple, which is another sign of a renewed and healed creation. He uses the dust of the earth as an agent of healing. He reforms the meaning of Sabbath and provides bread from heaven from the bread of earth. He teaches about water and light and harvest. In a remarkable passage in John chapter 6, Jesus calms a storm on the lake, and says to the terrified disciples in their boat: 'I AM: do not be afraid.' Using the divine name 'I AM', which we will notice much more in a later chapter, Jesus demonstrates his power over the created elements, and at the same time gives his anxious disciples grounds for hope. Do not

---

76 The LXX (Septuagint) of Genesis 1:1 speaks of God 'creating' using the word *epoiesen* – the Greek word used in John 20:30: 'Now Jesus did (*epoisen*) many other signs ...' and in John 21:25: 'many other things that Jesus did (*epoisen*) ...'

be afraid. I AM. You can cope.

Throughout the Gospel there is an eye to a future new creation of the new community, born from the resurrection and energized by God's Spirit, ready to take forward 'the work of God'. It is at the resurrection that Jesus' role as the 'second Adam', charged with care of God's creation, comes most clearly into focus, as Jesus is described – all unknowingly – by Mary Magdalene as 'the Gardener'. Many commentators have understood this to refer back to the story of the Garden of Eden. Tom Wright's summary at the close of his comment on Jesus' resurrection[77] puts it well:

> Mary's intuitive guess, that he must be the gardener, was wrong at one level and right, deeply right, at another. This is the new creation. Jesus is the beginning of it. Remember Pilate: 'Here's the man!' Here he is: the new Adam, the gardener, charged with bringing the chaos of God's creation into new order, into flower, into fruitfulness. He has come to uproot the thorns and thistles and replace them with blossoms and harvests.

Jesus Christ is God's image-bearer, the new Adam, creation's priest.

Living hopefully

The fracture in our human relationship with the rest of God's creation has sometimes led in a different direction. Not to our human mastery, but to our despair. 'Nature', it is said, is too big to handle, too frighteningly powerful. Nothing we can do can make any difference. So we are tempted to give way to a fatalism: 'Let us eat and drink, for tomorrow we die' (cf. 1 Corinthians 15:32). It is that sort of despair that lies behind some of the anxieties and fears of our world. Whether coastal erosion in Norfolk, or the poverty gap, sustainability or climate change: the issues seem too big, and we are afraid.

Christian theology and Christian discipleship and mission now take place in a world from which God has been largely 'eclipsed'.[78] Richard Dawkins is not alone in his reference to seeing the world in terms of 'pitiless indifference'. Two decades before he was writing, Jacques Monod concluded his study of the place of humanity in the universe by saying:

> The ancient covenant is in pieces: man at last knows that he is alone in the unfeeling immensity of the universe, out of which he emerged only by chance. Neither his destiny nor his duties have been written down. The kingdom above or the darkness below: it is for him to choose.[79]

77   Tom Wright, *John for Everyone*, SPCK, 2004, p.146, on John 20:11–18.
78   In *A Secular Age* (Belknap Press, Harvard University, 2007), Charles Taylor demonstrates that the processes of secularization move from the loss of belief in God in the public sphere and the consequent privatization of religion, through the falling off of religious belief and practice among believers, to a society where belief in God is no longer unchallenged but has given way to belief being simply one option among many others.
79   Jacques Monod, *Chance and Necessity,* Collins, 1970.

By contrast, the gospel sounds a strong trumpet call of hope. Christian faith absolutely does not believe that 'the ancient covenant' is in pieces, but rather lives in the hope of a restoration of the covenant between God and the whole of creation; a repair of the disjunction between God, humanity and earth; a reconciliation of body with spirit, nature with culture, science with ethics. Then humanity, united as a community of Christ's people by the Spirit with the life of the risen Christ, can discover again our human place with responsibility as God's image-bearers, creation's priests, endowed with a status in God's creation, not to be 'lords and masters' but rather corporately as servants and stewards.

The Christian gospel is about restoration and renewal and resurrection. And it is rooted in an understanding of the world as gift of God's creative love, dependent on God's promise and faithfulness, held in being by God's Wisdom, energized by God's Spirit, and lived out in the witness of the community of Christ's people.

Repentance

We are being called, in working out our part in today's mission, to recover our place in God's creation, and recognize God's compassion for all that is made. Our first step needs to be one of repentance for where we have gone wrong. Our human relationship to both God and the earth are underlined in the Operation Noah Declaration, *Climate Change and the Purposes of God*.[80] First, 'The beauty and harmony of God's creation is for all cultures a source of human wellbeing, spiritual nourishment and joy.' But, secondly, it also sounds this call to repentance: 'Continuing to pollute the atmosphere when we know the dangers, goes against what we know of God's ways and God's will. We are failing to love not only the earth, but also our neighbours and ourselves, who are made in God's image. God grieves over the destruction of creation, and so should we. Repentance means finding creative, constructive and immediate ways of addressing the danger ... For our generation, reducing our dependence on fossil fuels has become essential to Christian discipleship.'

We need both repentance for sin and selfishness and all that damages God's earth, and also to be part of God's project for the healing of creation, working towards the coming of God's kingdom 'on earth as it is in heaven'. That way, we, as creation's priests, can give a voice for the whole creation to sing the Creator's praise.

---

80 Operation Noah, Ash Wednesday Declaration 2012, Climate Change and the Purposes of God; available at www. operationnoah.org.

Part II

God's Wisdom Embodied in Jesus

In Part II we explore how John's Gospel shows us God's Wisdom embodied in Jesus Christ – the authentic human being who demonstrates in his life and ministry what walking in the way of Wisdom entails. Jesus lives out the practical wisdom of living in God's ways in God's world, showing us 'life in all its fullness'. He displays God's glory in God's abundant generosity, deep compassion, anger at the forces of evil, and self-giving love and service.

The glory of God is a human being fully alive
from Irenaeus (2nd Century AD)

Chapter Four

God's Two Hands: Wisdom and Word

- The Wisdom of God embedded in creation is embodied in Jesus of Nazareth.

- The 'Wisdom' of the Hebrew Bible is the same as 'the Word' in John's Gospel.

- The surprise is that God's Word (Wisdom) becomes incarnate: the Creator becomes a creature.

- In God's Word/Wisdom all things hold together, and through them the coherence of our relationships with God and other creatures can be restored.

- Incarnation means restraint: living within the limits of the material world.

- Incarnation also means sacrifice: God's self-giving for the sake of others.

- The life of creation is God's Spirit, leading all things to their destiny in God's purpose.

- The language of 'the Word' soon becomes the much more personal language of the Son and the Father. God the Holy Trinity (Creator/Word/Spirit) is about loving relationships – a pattern for our relationships within God's creation.

- John's Gospel speaks about 'believing into' Jesus, and so becoming children of God.

The Wisdom of God, who holds all things together in God's creation, is embodied in a person – Jesus Christ, God's Son. That is what the first paragraph of John's Gospel tells us. In chapter 5 we will explore the very human life of Jesus of Nazareth, his healings, teachings, encounters with people, believing that he is the one who shows us what authentic humanity should be, the one in whom humanity flourishes.

Before we get there, however, we need to explore some of the themes of the Prologue to the Gospel, in which the writer picks up some of the metaphors that describe God's Wisdom. Like the single beam of light scattered by a glitter ball into a thousand moving sparkles, God's Wisdom seems to burst onto the page of the Prologue of John's Gospel with so many flashes of brilliance that we cannot catch up with them: Word, life, light, truth, glory, grace, fullness.

> *In the beginning was the **Word**;*
> *The Word was with God;*
> *The Word was God: He was in the beginning with God;*
> *All things came into being through him;*
> *What has come into being with him was **life**;*
> *The life was the **light** of all people;*
> *The light shines in the darkness, and the darkness did not overcome it;*
> ***The true light which enlightens everyone was coming into the world;***
> *He was in the world, and the world came into being through him, yet the world did not know him;*
> *To all who received him, who believed in his name, he gave power to become children of God;*
> ***The Word became flesh** and lived among us;*
> *We have seen his **glory**: the glory as of a Father's only Son, full of **grace** and **truth**;*
> *From his **fullness** have we all received grace;*
> ***Grace and truth** came through Jesus Christ;*
> *No one has ever seen God; it is God the only Son, who **is close to the Father's heart**, who has made him known.*

These scattered sparkles are all aspects of Wisdom – and indeed the Hebrew Wisdom writings use all these metaphors in different places. The most important reason for seeing many of the themes of John's Gospel in terms of Wisdom is that when John uses the rather masculine concept 'Word', he is referring to what the Hebrew Bible meant by Lady Wisdom.[81] Sometimes the metaphors get muddled up. For example, one of the greatest theologians of the early church, Irenaeus, Bishop of Lyons in the second century, tried to make sense of things by saying

> *God creates with two hands: the Son and the Spirit, the Word and the Wisdom.*

In this chapter we will try to unpack the significance of some of these Wisdom themes. The Prologue moves us from the rather abstract concept of 'Word' to the very personal language of 'God's only Son, close to the Father's heart'. God's Word (=Wisdom) becomes 'flesh' in Jesus of Nazareth, the Son of God.

---

81 Proverbs 1.20 etc., and cf. John Ashton, *Understanding the Fourth Gospel*, OUP, 1991, p.527.

God's Wisdom is God's Word

In the beginning was the Word. (John 1:1)

What was in the Gospel writer's mind that led him to use the concept of 'Word'? There are a number of strands of thought coming together in the Gospel's Prologue, like the wires in a many-corded flex. The author of the Gospel winds the wires together, and produces a new thing – a many-coloured flex that is not quite like anything that anyone has ever seen before.

The first 'wire' is the Torah – that is the fatherly instruction from God which we often call God's Law. This is how many of the Jewish rabbis understood Wisdom.

The second is the link between God's Wisdom and God's Word in some parts of the Hebrew Bible, especially Proverbs as well as the apocryphal Books of Wisdom and Sirach.

Thirdly, sometimes writers speak of Wisdom, sometimes of the Spirit, as though they were almost interchangeable. In Genesis 1, God creates by both commanding Word: 'Let there be' and by God's animating Spirit: 'the Spirit of God swept over the face of the waters.'

A fourth strand may well come from the Stoic world into which John's Gospel was written. To the Stoics, 'Logos' (Word) meant something like 'rational principle' and the creative energy by which the cosmos is held together.[82]

All these wires are wound together in a new multi-coloured flex. John's Gospel does not correspond exactly with any of them, but it makes its own creative use of them all. The Hebrew emphasis on Word as action and the Stoic emphasis on Logos as Reason come together. Wisdom, which is the same as the Word, holds all things together. The Beloved Disciple as the author of John's Gospel is trying to say something about rational principle, but also about moral virtue, divine instruction and command, practical living, knowledge for the sake of goodness, source of wonder and praise. Wisdom is not only a doctrine to be believed, but also a way of life to be lived. There is intellectual wisdom and there is practical wisdom.

So in a couple of sentences, the writer of the Prologue to John's Gospel cleverly brings together God (Creator, Word and Wisdom, and Spirit), with the creation ('all things'). Creation derives both from the rational ordering of God's mind, as well as being a practical expression

---

82 The Jewish writer, Philo of Alexandria, tried to merge Stoic understandings of Logos with the Hebrew understandings of Word, Wisdom and Law. He thinks of Logos as an agent of creation, a thought in the mind of God. But 'logos' is also used of the rational mind of human beings by which we can come to know God.

of God's loving will. And we human beings can both discern God's rationality and order in the created cosmos, and also discover how to live, and cope, in the light of God's will and God's ways. Or, to put it another way: science and values belong together.

Word and Wisdom incarnate

Completely original thoughts are very rare. Alfred North Whitehead once characterized the whole European philosophical tradition as 'a series of footnotes to Plato'. Banksy became famous for creative graffiti appearing on public walls at night when no one was looking. On one of these he quoted a saying from Diogenes: 'One original thought is worth a thousand mindless quotings.'

But there is a uniquely bold and utterly new thought in the Prologue of John's Gospel: it comes in John 1:14.

> *The Word was made flesh and dwelt among us ... and we have seen his glory.*
> (John 1:14, ESV, Anglicised)

No one had ever thought of the Word or Wisdom of God as being part of the material world. Many of the philosophers believed in a major divide between 'spirit' and 'matter'. This verse in John's Gospel shockingly brings together matter and spirit, earth and heaven. The 'becoming flesh' – the incarnation – of Jesus of Nazareth is something utterly new in the material world of God's creation. Our 'flex', so to speak, is both 'live' and 'earthed'. The thought that God's Wisdom – embedded throughout God's creation and holding all things together – could become embodied in a person was a shatteringly new idea. The theological word for this is 'incarnation.'

To try to get some handle on how to think about this, we can draw on the thinking of the scientist/philosopher Michael Polanyi.[83] His scientific reflections on the nature of the world indicated that reality can be thought of as 'multi-levelled', each level with its own mode of interpretation, from physics and chemistry at the bottom, then higher levels of biology, psychology, sociology, ethics and theology. Each 'level' depends on, but is not reducible to, lower levels. Within that model (and it is only a model), we can think of the incarnation of Jesus Christ, God's Word and Wisdom, becoming flesh right down to the level of our genes. In a vivid metaphor Thomas Torrance,[84] describes the incarnation as 'the intersecting vertical coordinate' that gives all the other levels of reality their coherence and meaning.

---

83   e.g. Michael Polanyi, *Personal Knowledge*, Routledge, 1958; *Knowing and Being*, Routledge, 1969.
84   T. F. Torrance, *Space, Time and Incarnation*, OUP, 1969.

Coherence restored

I referred earlier to the triangle of relationships between God, the earth and humanity that was so decisively affected by the new thinking, in the seventeenth century, of Francis Bacon and others. Although that thinking became hugely important in the development of modern science, it also led to the deistic detachment of God from the earth. As a culture, we suffered what T. F. Torrance called 'the eclipse of God'. However, in the incarnation of the Word in the birth of Jesus Christ, God himself becomes immersed in the earth as a human being. In the incarnation of God's Word and Wisdom in Jesus, that triangle of relationships between God, humanity and the earth is restored. Oliver O'Donovan wrote of:

> ... the message of the incarnation, by which we learn how, through a unique presence of God to his creation, the whole created order is taken up into the fate of this particular representative man at this particular moment of history, on whose one fate turns the redemption of all.[85]

The incarnation of divine Wisdom brings repair for our cultural splits between body and spirit, nature and culture, science and ethics. We referred earlier to John Donne's sadness at what the 'new philosophy' of his times was producing, and which he had described it in terms of 'all coherence gone'. By contrast the incarnation points to 'coherence restored': God, humanity and Earth reconnected.

Wisdom as Mediator

Wisdom is She in whom all things hold together. When Wisdom is embodied in Jesus Christ, we can discover that coherence in a broken world can be restored, and God and humanity brought into life-giving relationship again.

In this sense, Wisdom is God's Mediator. There is a powerful image used in the first chapter of John's Gospel, that of Jacob's ladder, mediating between heaven and earth, with God's angels going up and down on it. This symbolized for Jacob that the God of heaven was present with him on earth. The place where Jacob is sleeping with his head on a stone in the desert is discovered to be the 'house of God' (Bethel) and the 'gate of heaven' (Genesis 28:10f.). In the Gospel author's use of the image, the 'Son of Man' himself becomes the ladder (John 1:51).

The image of Wisdom the Mediator is what is in mind when the majestic Christological hymn in Colossians 1:15–20 refers to Jesus Christ.

85   O.M.T. O'Donovan, *Resurrection and Moral Order*, IVP, 1986, p.15.

*He is the image of the invisible God, the firstborn of all creation; for in him
all things in heaven and on earth were created, things visible and invisible …
all things have been created through him and for him. He himself is before all
things, and in him all things hold together … in him all the fullness of God was
pleased to dwell, and through him God was pleased to reconcile to himself all
things, whether on earth or in heaven, by making peace through the blood of his
cross.*

In 1961, Joseph Sittler spoke from this text in his address to the World
Council of Churches. He was talking about Christian unity. It is the vision of the Cosmic Christ in whom 'all things hold together' which provides Sittler with what he calls a 'life-affirming Christology of nature'.
The triad of 'God, humanity and nature' is the basis, he says, for our
calling to unity with one another and with all creation.

The writer to the Ephesians expresses a similar thought:

*Blessed be the God and Father of our Lord Jesus Christ … With all wisdom and
insight he has made known to us the mystery of his will … to gather up all things
in him, things in heaven and things on earth.* (Ephesians 1:3–10)

The Letter to the Hebrews says much the same: '… in these last days
[God] has spoken to us by a Son, whom he appointed heir of all things,
through whom he also created the worlds (Hebrews 1:2).

Holding together

The phrase 'hold together' points us to mutual interdependence. Our
human life and flourishing is inextricably bound up not only with our
relationship with God, but also with our interdependent relationships
with all God's creation, and the well-being of the planet on which we
depend for food, oxygen, sustenance, health, energy and so on. This is
why the Fifth Mark of Mission for the Anglican Consultative Council is:
'To safeguard the integrity of creation, and sustain and renew the life
of the earth.'[86]

I think we urgently need to recover a sense that 'the earth is the
Lord's', and our calling to live within God's will and God's way of
Wisdom. It is Wisdom's way that leads us back to coherence. We need
to recover a sense of mutual interdependence within creation – which
for us, as we shall see further in a later chapter, requires justice, generosity and restraint.

---

86 (i) To proclaim the Good News of the Kingdom; (ii) To teach, baptise and nurture new believers; (iii) To respond to human
need by loving service; (iv) To seek to transform unjust structures of society, to challenge violence of every kind and to
pursue peace and reconciliation; (v) To strive to safeguard the integrity of creation and sustain and renew the life of the
earth ('Bonds of Affection', 1984, ACC-6, p.49; 'Mission in a Broken World', 1990, ACC-8, p.101). See more at: http://www.
anglicancommunion.org/ministry/mission/fivemarks.cfm#sthash.TgAt0Gzm.dpuf

Incarnation as Wisdom's restraint

The Word was made flesh and dwelt among us. (John 1:14, ESV, Anglicised)

The incarnation of God's Word/Wisdom made flesh clearly gives a vital importance to the material world. The world of rocks and stones, or cockroaches and giraffes, of you and me, is all 'ennobled' by the presence in our material world of God's own self – God's Wisdom and Word.

More than that: God has – as some theologians put it – 'pulled back' to make space for the creation. God's loving action in creation is a form of self-denial so that others may live. So the incarnation is, in a sense, Wisdom's restraint. The incarnation means that God limits God's own being to the constraints of this physical earth, within the limits of a material universe, subject to the laws of thermodynamics and entropy, in which people need food and energy, health and security, and are interdependent with all other creatures upon God's love and God's gift. When God's Wisdom and God's Word became flesh, they became part of a world in which the life-giving energy from the Holy Spirit is channelled to us in part by the sun, through the carbon cycle, in an atmosphere which sustains sufficient oxygen, at a habitable temperature for food security, clean water and a habitable earth. Incarnation means living within limits, within planetary boundaries. Now God has become a creature among all other creatures. This puts a value on all creatures, and not just on humanity.

Incarnation, then, is a sort of 'kenosis': the theological word used to describe God's self-emptying – God's making space for others, God's restraint. For life to flourish, we need to take more seriously the limits to physical life on this planet, and learn to restrain ourselves to live within those limits. As Sallie McFague put it, 'Kenosis … works at all levels by restraint, pulling back, sharing, reciprocity, interrelationship, giving space to others, sacrifice.'[87]

Incarnation entails self-giving sacrifice

Incarnation therefore means that in Jesus God constrains God's own being by the needs of a broken world. As we shall discuss much more fully later, Jesus' way is that of self-giving love, service and sacrifice; a love constrained by the need for healing, restoration, sustenance and hope in a world that has in many ways got lost. So the language of

---

87 Sallie McFague, *Blessed Are the Consumers: Climate change and the practice of restraint*, Fortress, 2013, p.36.

incarnation takes us to words like humility, service, self-giving, sacrifice, restraint, living within limits, love.

We can perhaps discern this restraint of the Wisdom of God in the constraints of the evolutionary process: life is laid down so that life can be renewed – what in theological terms we may describe as a form of sacrifice. Sacrifice is at the heart of the whole biological process as organic life develops. Some new life cannot come into being without death. The food chain is at the same time destructive of life and also life-giving. There is a principle of vicarious suffering whereby new life is achieved only by sacrifice. The natural rhythms of death and new life in the plant kingdom, and the death of the antelope as food for the lion, in their different ways show the paradox of sacrifice in the natural world. Life laid down is the source of new life.

But the natural biological processes point towards richer meanings at a higher level in the human world, namely the meaning of self-giving love. The Suffering Servant of Isaiah 53, who for Christians has become understood as pointing towards Jesus Christ as God's Messiah, exemplifies a sacrificial suffering through to something higher, fuller, more whole.

Sacrifice can be understood in terms of costly self-giving and the bringing about of life through the agency of death, and as such is characteristic of both the being and the work of God. The God who is revealed in Christ is continually sacrificing himself, as much by giving himself in the activity of creation as in the work of redemption through his Son. He is the author of life through self-giving. God so loved that he *gave*. Wisdom is seen in the self-giving of God in the life and death of Jesus Christ, in his humble self-giving service for others, and his personal demonstration that no one has greater love than to lay down one's life for one's friends (John 15:13).

This is such an important insight for the situation in which we now find ourselves. Our science is showing us that all life depends on 'self-giving' and death, and yet our culture is predominantly marked by individual self-interest, self-gratification, self-sufficiency and the assumption that we can live independently not only of one another, but of the rest of creation on which in fact all our life depends. If our earth and humanity is to survive, we human beings – especially those of us who live in the richer parts of the world – are going to have to learn again about restraint, self-giving and self-denial.

Wisdom and the Spirit

'In him was life' (John 1:4). After introducing us to the Word (the Wisdom) of God, John's Gospel immediately brings in another major theme in his writing: life. Life in the Bible is often linked to the Holy Spirit, 'the Lord and Giver of Life'. Here is God and 'in him we live and move and have our being' (Acts 17:28).

As we said earlier, Word and Spirit belong together within God's creative love. *The Wisdom of Solomon* describes God's Spirit as the animating life of God's Wisdom. 'The spirit of the Lord has filled the world, and that which holds all things together knows what is said' (Wisdom 1:7).

It is the Spirit that gives life (John 6:63), and Wisdom is identified as Spirit: 'Wisdom is a kindly spirit... the spirit of the Lord has filled the world, and that which holds all things together knows what is said' (Wisdom 1:6–7).[88] The second-century theologian Irenaeus even speaks of Wisdom as 'the feminine face of God'.

John's Gospel has much to say about the Spirit – mostly in the second half of the Gospel where the focus is on the Spirit energizing the life of a Christian community of disciples, and we shall discuss more fully later how the Spirit of God's Wisdom is at work in that community of Christ's people.

All we need at this point, however, is to underline the point that the healing work of God's Spirit is not only applied to the disciples, but includes all of God's creation. God's Spirit gives life to all creation, and renews 'the face of the ground' (Psalm 104:30).

We may be given a clue to the ongoing creative work of the Holy Spirit in Genesis 2:2. Some commentators suggest that when God 'rested' from work, God was preparing the way for future blessing and eventually for the perfection of all creation. James D. Hunter[89] put it well: 'The spirit that God breathed into his creation was life itself, not only in its manifest beauty and delight but also in its potentialities. The goodness of his creation, then, was anything but inert. It was dynamic, vibrant, and full of latent promise.'

Abraham Kuyper offers this translation of Genesis 2.2: 'God rested from all his work which he had created to make it perfect.' He comments: 'Thus to lead the creature to its destiny, to cause it to develop

---

88 cf. 'She is a breath of the power of God and a pure emanation of the glory of the Almighty ... she is a reflection of eternal light, a spotless mirror of the working of God and an image of his goodness' (Wisdom 7:25–27).
89 James Davison Hunter, *To Change the World,* Oxford, 2010, p.3.

according to its nature, to make it perfect, is the proper work of the Holy Spirit.'[90] The Holy Spirit, the Giver of Life, leads the whole creation to its destiny. It is God's Spirit that animates humanity. 'The Spirit of God has made me' says Job (33:4), 'and the breath of the Almighty gives me life.'[91]

The Word becomes the Son: God the Holy Trinity

The language of the Prologue changes markedly after we have read of the incarnation of the Word. The early verses seem a bit abstract. They are about 'the Word'. But after verse 14, 'The Word became flesh and lived among us, and we have seen his glory, the glory as of a father's only son', we do not read any more about 'the Word'. Instead the writer talks about 'the Father's Son'. We move from speaking of Jesus in the theological and intellectual language of the Word, to the practical, earthy, material, ordinary language of personal relationships, Father and Son. 'No one has ever seen God. It is God the only Son, who is close to the Father's heart, who has made him known' (John 1:18).

Thereafter the Gospel's primary theme is the relationship of Jesus with the Father, which gradually develops as we approach the Passion and death and resurrection of Jesus, into the theme of the disciples' relationship with Jesus in the Spirit, and therefore the disciples' own relationship with God in the community of Christ's people. The Gospel is deeply personal and relational. The fullness of life of which it speaks is essentially about the life that the Father gives through the Son in the power of the Spirit. It is the life of 'the children of God', the community drawn together by the risen Christ.

The Prologue to John's Gospel is therefore bringing us in touch with what theologians of the early Church called 'God the Holy Trinity'.

Celia Deane-Drummond gives a wonderfully concise summary:

The joint action of Word and Wisdom in creation is expressed in the incarnation of the Son. In the person of Jesus, the Son becomes Wisdom incarnate and Word incarnate. This is a unique interpenetration of the Godhead with the material world. Whereas in the act of creation Word and Wisdom serve together to shape the creative process, in the incarnation of the Son both Word and Wisdom become part of the fabric of creation itself. It is through the Holy Spirit that the Son becomes incarnate as Jesus Christ in history. This is a fundamental affirmation of creation by God, namely that God enters fully into the material world in the history of Jesus of Nazareth. The significance of Christ for creation is this ultimate act of love and humility.'[92]

---

90 Abraham Kuyper, *The Work of the Holy Spirit*, Eerdmans, 1900, 1975. p.21.
91 The animating Spirit of Life is also the giver of gifts and talents. 'The Lord spoke to Moses: See, I have called by name Bezalel ... I have filled him with divine spirit, with ability, intelligence, and knowledge in every kind of craft, to devise artistic designs, to work in gold, silver, and bronze, in cutting stones for setting, and in carving wood, in every kind of craft' (Exodus 31:2–5). Artistic, scientific and technological creativity are depicted in this paragraph as gifts of the divine spirit.
92 Celia Deane-Drummond, *Creation Through Wisdom*, T & T Clark, p.140.

God the Father is the source of all things in God's creative love; God the Son, the Word and the Wisdom, is the one in whom we and all creation are held together; and God the Giver of Life, the Spirit, is the energy of God's will and purpose, who leads all creation towards its perfection. 'From him and through him and to him are all things.'[93]

God the Holy Trinity thus speaks both of God's transcendent majesty over all things but also – and this is perhaps what Francis Bacon lost – of God's immanent presence in the world, God's power and compassion in the ordinariness of living in this world. If we can follow Wisdom's way to find again the coherence of the integrated triad, God–Humanity–Earth, then we might rediscover who we are, and who we are to be. We might rediscover our role in relation to God's earth, our interdependence with all other creatures and our human responsibility under God to care for them. We might learn what it is to live well. We might discover what our Gospel calls 'life in all its fullness'.

Trinity and Ecology

An understanding of God the Holy Trinity may be able to help us deepen our understanding of ecology.[94] By looking at the relationships between God the Father, the Son and the Spirit, we can learn something of God's relationships with the whole of creation. In other words, if we understand God as 'persons in relationships of love and communion', then God's whole creation can be thought of as God's loving relationship with the world of creatures. The heart and source of everything in the universe is personal love. The whole universe springs out of God's love. So we human beings need to see ourselves as belonging within a 'web' of life that depends on God's love, every creature in its own way depending on God's presence and gift of life. We recall how the Genesis texts about creation keep saying 'Let there be …'. God gives human beings the freedom to be themselves. God also gives all creatures – indeed the whole physical universe – the freedom to be what they are.

The community of those who 'believe into' Jesus

The personal relationships of love and communion shared between God the Father and the Son give birth to a new community of disciples who are invited to share in that love and communion. The Prologue to John's Gospel calls them 'children of God'.

> To all who received him, who believed in his name, he gave power to become children of God. (John 1:12)

---

93 Romans 11:36.
94 This section draws on Denis Edwards, *Jesus the Wisdom of God: an ecological theology,* Wipf and Stock, 1995.

The 'children of God' are described as those who 'believe in the name of Jesus.' The Beloved Disciple has some interesting things to say about believing. A few times he uses the usual phrase 'believe that' – in other words, 'give assent to'. We find this in Martha's reply to Jesus at the grave of Lazarus: 'Yes, Lord, I *believe that* you are the Christ.' But mostly the author uses *eis*, which means 'into', with the sense *'believing into'* Jesus, that is receiving the life of God through Christ by faith (1:12; 3:36); giving wholehearted commitment to Jesus as the One whom God the Father has sent (6:29). To believe *into* Jesus is to have eternal life (3:16; 11:25–26); is to 'incorporate' him by 'eating' the Bread of Life and so finding spiritual hunger satisfied and thirst quenched (6:35; 7:38); is to be made one with Jesus and the Father (17:20–21). 'Believe *into* God, believe also into me' (John 14:1).

It seems that the community of the Beloved Disciple had to deal with some groups of believers who did not fully either accept Jesus as God's Messiah, or 'believe into' him. For example, there were some followers of John the Baptist (3:22–36) and the Gospel emphasizes John the Baptist's insistence that they look away from him and believe rather in Jesus.

However, there was also a group of people in Jerusalem who apparently believed in Jesus just because of the signs he was doing, but Jesus 'would not entrust himself to them' (2:23–24). Maybe Nicodemus was one of this group. The Gospel gives us some short paragraphs about him.

Nicodemus

Nicodemus is one of the key representative figures in the Gospel[95] – someone who stands for a group of others in their relationship to Jesus. Nicodemus is a rich man who has influence, a Pharisee, a leader of the Judeans. At one point he tries to defend Jesus' rights in law before some of his hostile colleagues (7:50–51). And, very late in the day, he emerges with another rich benefactor (Joseph of Arimathea), who is described as a 'secret disciple' to provide some myrrh and aloes for Jesus' burial (19:39). But he is best remembered as probably a sort of half-believer – part of the group of those to whom Jesus did not trust himself (2:24). He came by night to try to find out what Jesus was really about. Quite probably the community of the Beloved Disciple for which the Gospel was first written included half-believers like this – and part of the author's purpose is to strengthen their faith so that they might 'believe that Jesus is the Christ', and so have life in his name.

95 David Rensberger, *Overcoming the World*, SPCK.

Nicodemus does not seem to know quite where he stands. He needs, says Jesus, to be born anew – that is born 'from above' with new life from God. 'Water and Spirit' probably refers to the water of baptism (since this section of the Gospel is so closely followed by a paragraph about baptism [3:22ff.]). In other words, Nicodemus, the respected religious leader, referred to by Jesus as 'a teacher of Israel' – and those in the community for whom he stands – needs not only to 'know' (3:2) about Jesus and his ministry, but to act, to decide, to respond to the blowing wind of God's Spirit, to make a commitment. They must believe *into* the Son of Man, and so have eternal life. They become 'children of God' with a new intimacy of relationship with God the Father. To be a member of the community of Christ's people means a new allegiance altogether.

New Life
The Gospel writer's comment on all this is very stark. The new life on offer is gift of God's love. God so loved the world that he gave his only Son, so that everyone who believes into him may not perish but have eternal life (3:16). However, the choices facing the community of Christ's people are clear: to those who do not believe into Jesus, we find the language of condemnation, judgement, loving the darkness, evil deeds; to those who do believe into Jesus, there is the language of salvation for the world, coming to the light, so that it may be clearly seen that their deeds have been done in God (3:17–21). The writer is using strong words to make a vital point: we are talking here about matters of life and death. For a Christian community under persecution, such as the one from which and for which the Beloved Disciple was writing, half-belief of the self-righteous Nicodemus sort is not an option. Choices have to be made, allegiances clarified. Judgement becomes a matter of which roads are travelled. But the offer of life is available: 'To all who received him, who believed in his name, he gave power to become children of God' (John 1:12).

Who are we? And what is our destiny? How are we to live, and to cope? The Gospel of John says that the coming of Jesus Christ, God's Word and Wisdom, into the world creates something new. As the Gospel develops we find Jesus bringing into being a community of men and women who share Christ's life and are called to bear witness to his glory. This is not a human achievement ('not of blood or of the will of the flesh'), but is gift of God's love. It is in this community of Christ's people that those who 'receive him and believe in his name' discover who they are: children of God. They discover that their destiny is 'to be where Jesus is' (cf. John 17:24). And they can experience something of the 'life in all its fullness' (cf. John 1:16; 10:10), which God offers through Christ in the Spirit, a life seen – in all its joy, and in all its struggle and suffering – in the authentic humanity of Jesus of Nazareth, in whom God's Wisdom is embodied, and through whom God's glory is seen.

Today, therefore, we need to understand ourselves from two perspectives at the same time. First, to repeat once more, we are interconnected and interdependent with all other creatures. And second, we are self-conscious beings called to relationship with and responsibility under the God the Holy Trinity.[96] God the Holy Trinity is our primary 'environment'; it is in God that we live and move and have our being.[97] It is – to use one of Jürgen Moltmann's lovely phrases – within the 'wide open space of God's joy'[98] that we have the freedom to live.

---

96   cf. Edwards, op. cit., p.143–144.
97   quoted in Acts 17:28.
98   Jürgen Moltmann, *The Living God and the Fullness of Life*, WCC Publications, 2016, ch.5.

Chapter Five

'Here is the Man!'

- John's Gospel introduces us to Jesus, the Son of God. Jesus is described as being 'close to the Father's heart', and his relationship with God the Father is a dominating theme of the Gospel.

- The Gospel also shows us Jesus the 'Son of Man'; he is 'the Man', the authentic human being, in whom human life is lived to the full.

- The outworking of the fullness of life is seen in Jesus' earthly ministry: with people at the margins of society; through his healings; in his celebrating creation by re-shaping the Sabbath; by providing food; walking in the light of truth; providing security and a sense of belonging; educating; serving; responding to rejection with love.

- The goal of Christian discipleship is to 'be where Jesus is' – and we look at what that might mean in today's world in relation to our aspirations for sustainable development.

'Here is the Man!' (John 19:5); In him was life (John 1:4)

1. The 'earthing' of heaven

Once, when I was speaking in a church about Christian responses to climate change, the minister asked: 'What has all this to do with Jesus?' I think the questioner was afraid that I had been lured by the false gods of environmentalism, and was not really preaching the gospel of Jesus Christ. I also suspect that he had been brought up with the sort of faith that makes a strict divide between the material world and the spiritual world, between flesh and spirit, between science and values – so my approach appeared to him a denial of the Spirit and a pandering to the flesh. What mattered was the salvation of souls.

Bishop James Jones tackled this question head-on in his book *Jesus and the Earth*.[99] Taking special notice of the many 'Son of Man' sayings

99 James Jones, *Jesus and the Earth*, SPCK, 2003.

in the Synoptic Gospels, and recalling that 'Son of Man' in Hebrew is 'Son of Adam', James Jones explored the Son of Man's authority on earth; he discussed the 'earthiness' of Jesus, who came eating and drinking – which led Jones to a discussion of food security and the question of sustainability; he celebrated the 'coming of the Son of Man' and the 'earthing' of heaven (which opened up issues about God's creation and the care of non-human as well as human beings – and about hope in God). Jones explored Jesus' own engagement with the earth, through parables in his teaching, in the Garden of Gethsemane and in the Garden of Resurrection, where Jesus is depicted as the new Adam, the Gardener of the new Eden. Jesus is the Saviour, Jones argued, not only of human beings, but also of the whole cosmos.

All this, I believe, is wonderfully true. This chapter will take some of these themes further. And yet the New Testament has something even deeper to say about Jesus Christ. James Jones does briefly refer to this, but he does not elaborate a theme that we have indicated is prominent in the Prologue of St John's Gospel and also in some of the New Testament Epistles. This is the theme of Wisdom.

In this chapter, we venture beyond the Prologue into the rest of the Gospel, and we will find many echoes of Wisdom writings there too, not least that God's Wisdom brings heaven and earth together. The Bible neither takes us to pantheism, in which nature is identified with God, nor to the deism that has such a lofty view of God's transcendence that God is lifted out of any concern with ordinary material things. Nor does it offer the sort of super-spirituality that detaches us from the earth and our earthiness. 'This world' and the 'world above' are both aspects of God's earth here and now. In God's mediating Wisdom, heaven and earth come together. The Word is made flesh. As James Jones put it, this is the 'earthing' of heaven in Jesus. So my reply to the minister who asked, 'What is this to do with Jesus?' is that the life and death and resurrection of Jesus concern more than the salvation of our souls: they are concerned with the healing of the whole of creation.

2. Here is the Man!

In each of three of the corners of Trafalgar Square in the centre of London there is a huge, impressive statue. One is of a King of England, two are of army Generals. They all look imperial and important. They speak of power. But the fourth plinth has no permanent statue. In recent years, different sculptors have been asked to provide a short-term statue to go on the empty fourth plinth. In 1999 Mark Wallinger made a sculpture of a small, life-sized, unimpressive, ordinary human be-ing, cut out of plain marble, wearing only a loincloth, and a crown of thorns. The contrast with the imperial symbols on other plinths was remarkable. Mark Wallinger called it 'Ecce Homo', which is Latin for 'Look: the Man'. 'Here is the Man'.

This was the description which Pontius Pilate gave to Jesus in John's Gospel, referring then to Jesus' humiliation, dressed up by mocking soldiers in crown of thorns and purple robe: 'Here is the Man!' (19:5).

Son of God

We know that the Gospel story was constructed to show that the rabbi from Nazareth was God's promised Messiah, and that a major prior-ity of the Beloved Disciple in writing his Gospel was to strengthen his community's faith in Jesus as God's Christ. He is presented as God's only Son. One of the clearest indications of this is the way the Gospel records Jesus' use of 'I AM'. In John's Gospel 'I AM' has unmistakable echoes of the divine Name revealed to Moses in Exodus 3:13f.[100] When Jesus uses I AM, his Jewish hearers sometimes rightly understand this as a claim to divinity, and so as blasphemy meriting death. For exam-ple, 'Jesus said to them [the Judean authorities], "Very truly, I tell you, before Abraham was, I AM." So they picked up stones to throw at him' (8:58–59).

There are numerous times in John's Gospel when Jesus says of him-self, I AM (*ego eimi*). We have already referred to one of these when, in John chapter 6, Jesus calls to his terrified disciples in the boat, tossed by the storm: 'I AM: do not be afraid.' In other places, the concepts and symbols would have been very familiar with readers of the Hebrew Wisdom literature: I AM Bread, Light, Gate, Shepherd, Way, Truth, Life, Vine.[101]

In confrontation with the Pharisees, in dispute with the Judean au-thorities, in his healings, signs, in his closeness to and intimacy with God the Father, and perhaps particularly in his regular use of the di-vine Name, Jesus is revealed to the reader as God's Messiah, God's

---

100 'Moses said to God: "If I come to the Israelites and say to them, 'The God of your ancestors has sent me to you', and they ask me, 'What is his name?' what shall I say to them?" God said to Moses, "I am who I am."' This is the sacred name of God, often written in our Bibles as the Lord, or Yahweh.
101 For example: Bread (Sirach 29:21: 'The necessities of life are water, bread, and clothing, and also a house to assure privacy'; 24:21: 'Those who eat of me will hunger for more'); Vine (Sirach 24:17,19: 'Like the vine I bud forth delights ... Come to me, you who desire me, and eat your fill of my fruits'); Gate (Proverbs 8:34–35; 'Happy is the one who listens to me, watching daily at my gates, waiting beside my doors'); Way (Proverbs 3:17: Her ways are ways of pleasantness, and all her paths are peace'; Proverbs 8:32: 'Happy are those who keep my ways'; Sirach 6:26: 'Come to her with all your soul, and keep her ways with all your might'); Light (Wisdom 7:26; ' ... she is a reflection of eternal light'); Truth (Proverbs 8:7: ' ... my mouth will utter truth'; Wisdom 6:22: 'I will hide no secrets from you ... I will not pass by the truth'); Life (Proverbs 3:18: 'She is a tree of life to those who lay hold of her'; Proverbs 8:35: ' ... whoever finds me finds life'); Shepherd (Sirach 18:13: 'The compassion of human beings is for their neighbours, but the compassion of the Lord is for every living thing. He rebukes and trains and teaches them, and turns them back, as a shepherd his flock').

Word and God's Wisdom, God's Son.

Son of Man

Alongside the Gospel's demonstration of Jesus' divinity, however, there is another story being told. John's Gospel is also a celebration of Jesus' humanity – he is the Man. In fact, Jesus' preferred way of speaking of himself is not 'Son of God', but 'Son of Man' (e.g. John 1:51; 3:14). As such, he is the Mediator between God and humanity – even the ladder which connects heaven and earth (cf. 1:51). He is the Man from heaven. He is God's Word and God's Wisdom *made flesh*.

It may be that the Gospel (and perhaps, even more, the First Epistle of John) were written in part to underline the full humanity of Jesus to those people inclined so to emphasise his divinity that they tended to downplay his humanness. So 'we declare to you what was from the beginning, what we have heard, what we have seen with our eyes, what we have looked at and touched with our hands, concerning the word of life' (1 John 1:1). The Gospel shows us a Jesus who got tired on his journey through Samaria and asked for a drink of water (John 4:6–7), and was greatly disturbed and moved to tears at the grave of Lazarus (11:33–35). His soul was troubled at the festival in Jerusalem (12:27); he takes a servant's towel and bowl of water to wash his disciples' feet in the Upper Room (13:4–5). Jesus really died, his side was pierced with a spear, his body laid in a tomb. After the resurrection, it was a physical Jesus who invited Thomas to test out the wounds in his hand and side, and who later prepared breakfast on the beach for his disciples (20:27; 21:9). He is a man.[102]

3. Life in all its fullness

John's Gospel gives us several portraits of Jesus engaging with others, in which the life of God shines through his humanity. In this chapter, we will look at some of the encounters Jesus has during his ministry that illustrate the 'life in all its fullness' of which he spoke. It is to him that we look for answers to our question about what makes for human flourishing, what is authentic human life and well-being, how we are to live fully. Then, in a later chapter, we will look at other incidents in the

---

[102] In his book *In Search of Humanity*, John Macquarrie speaks of Jesus Christ as a 'transcendent humanity in which the image of God came fully to expression' (p.252). From a very different theological perspective, Thomas Torrance writes of 'the Son of God [who] comes to us as man ... God the Creator has come himself to us as a creature in the world he has made, and yet remains the Creator; ... God the creative and sustaining Source of all human being has come himself to us as a particular human being, yet without ceasing to be the divine Being he eternally is.' (*The Mediation of Christ*, p.67). To give a different example, when the Christian psychiatrist Frank Lake was searching for a psychological model for human personal development, the theologian Emil Brunner suggested that he should study the humanity of Jesus in relation to God his Father in the Fourth Gospel. Lake's study demonstrated to him that in Jesus Christ we see the Human One, the Authentic Human Being: that which God intended humanity to be. He is the Man (cf. *The Dynamic Cycle*, Lingdale Papers, 1986, referring to Lake's major work, *Clinical Theology*).

Gospel narrative which more clearly focus on the ongoing dispute in which Jesus finds himself in confrontation with 'the world', symbolized by his confrontation with Pharisees, and especially with the Judean authorities. In these, Jesus, the Man, struggles to overcome 'the world'.

4. Gospel relationships

Here, then, are some of Jesus' encounters in the Gospel story. But we begin with Jesus' relationship with his heavenly Father. It is this relationship that illuminates all the others.

(i) Being close to the Father's heart

The Gospel's portrait of the man Jesus – whom the disciples came to know as 'the Messiah', 'the Saviour of the World', 'my Lord and my God' – describes him as 'the Son of the Father', 'in the bosom of the Father' (1:18), that is, 'close to the Father's heart'.

If God the Father is the Fountain of all Fullness[103] – all goodness and love – it is 'from his fullness that we have all received, grace upon grace' (John 1:16), and that is mediated to us through Jesus Christ, in the power of God's Spirit. It is the intimacy of the relationship between Jesus and his Father that is the source of grace that blesses the disciples with fullness. 'I am come that they might have life in all its fullness.'

We are told that the Word was 'in the beginning ... with God' (1:1) and displays the 'glory as of the Father's only Son' (1:14). In him was life (1:4), and on Jesus God's Spirit remained (1:32). Jesus speaks of himself as 'from above' (3:31–32), and as one 'whom God has sent' (3:34). The Father loves the Son and has granted him authority in judgement (5:20,26). His will is to 'do the will of him who sent me' (5:30); he comes in the Father's name (5:43) and on him the Father has set his seal (6:27). He can even say 'the Father and I are one' (10:30).

We have seen how in the Gospel's Prologue, the references to 'the Word' give place instead to the relational language of 'Father and Son'. In the wondrous high priestly prayer of John chapter 17, that close intimacy of relationship between Jesus and the Father is transposed into a prayer that God will enclose the community of Jesus' disciples in that same intimacy, that they 'may be with me where I am'. (John 17:24). As we shall see, 'being where Jesus is' almost comes to define what discipleship means for the Gospel of John.

---

103 In *Jesus the Wisdom of God* (Wipf and Stock 1995), Denis Edwards quotes the medieval Franciscan Bonaventura as a key figure in the 'fecundity tradition' of the Middle Ages, that is: seeing God the Father as the bountiful source and fountain of all goodness and love – from whom all derives and to which all things go. Edwards describes the *fontalis plenitudo* as God's 'Fountain Fullness'.

It is the closeness of Jesus with his heavenly Father, which he longs for the community of disciples to share, that underlies and gives meaning to every aspect of Jesus' humanity as his portrait is painted through John's Gospel.

(ii) Including people on the margins (John 4:1–42)
Jesus' first conversations recorded in the Gospel are with men. First, some male Jewish disciples of John the Baptist, Andrew and Simon Peter, near the River Jordan. The next day in Galilee Jesus spoke with Philip and Nathaniel. The next extended conversation is with another man, Nicodemus. Then in John chapter 4 there is an unexpected turn. Jesus, resting by Jacob's well at Sychar, a city in Samaria, took the initiative to speak with a woman of Samaria whom he had not met. This broke all the rules. It was unusual for men and women to have conversations with each other in public. It was even more unusual for people from different cities, let alone for a Jewish man to speak with a foreign woman – and a Samaritan at that! The Samaritans were a national group with a long history of conflict with Jews from Israel. No wonder the disciples who had gone into the city to buy food, 'were astonished' (4:27). Jesus was breaking all the cultural taboos in order to speak to this Samaritan woman about 'the gift of God', 'eternal life', 'living water', and lead her to the point of discovery that Jesus is the expected Messiah (vv. 25–26), the 'Saviour of the world' (v.42) – a title normally used for the emperor! Jesus, in whom God's Word and Wisdom is embodied, is bringing the fullness of God's life to someone on the edges of society: the despised Samaritans, the low-status women. Extraordinarily, later on Jesus even seems to accept being called a Samaritan himself – in a term of abuse from the Judean authorities (8:48).

Another astonishing fact about Jesus' encounter with the woman at the Samaritan well was that this was the first time in this Gospel that Jesus uses this symbolic divine Name, I AM. 'Jesus said to her, "I AM he, the one who is speaking to you' (*Ego eimi, ho lalon soi*) (4:26).

The fullness of life that God offers through Christ in the Spirit is offered first to the marginalized and the outsider, to those despised and of low social status. It is a grace that is inclusive and equalizing, even though it breaks all the rules.

(iii) Celebrating creation: health and the Sabbath (5:1–24)
In John chapter 5 water is associated with healing. At the spa of bubbling water at Bethesda near the Sheep Gate in Jerusalem, which had once been a pagan healing shrine, a paralyzed man – one of a large

crowd of invalid people – was approached by Jesus. Jesus asked: 'Do you want to be healed?' The paralyzed man's lifetime of rather fatalistic self-pity ('I've got no one to help me; everyone else gets help first'), probably reinforced by pagan customs, is challenged by a word from Jesus that gives him the freedom to take some responsibility: 'Rise, take up your pallet and walk.' The hearing of the healing Word places the person under an obligation to respond. In his case, it was a healing response of faith and obedience.

The primary focus of this sign, as reported in the Gospel, is that it happened on a Sabbath. Sabbath was – with the Torah and the Temple – one of the foundations of contemporary Jewish faith.

'Sabbath' holds together the biblical concepts of 'creation' and 'covenant'.[104] The whole creation 'project' (to use Colin Gunton's phrase) is God's covenanted intention to bring the whole created order to its perfection. The kingdom of God is 'creation healed'. This intention – God's promise and God's faithfulness – is expressed in God's covenant with his people and with 'every living creature'. The Sabbath is one of the connecting links between God's promise both to people and at the same time also to the whole created order. God 'rested' we are told from the work of creation and 'was refreshed' (Genesis 2:3; Exodus 31:17). Sabbath was given for God's people to refrain from work, to be refreshed, and to keep the Sabbath day holy to remember God's creative work (Exodus 20:10), and also to remember their deliverance from slavery (Deuteronomy 5:15). Sabbath links creation and redemption. So a good Sabbath leads to 'delight in the Lord' (Isaiah 58:14), rather than 'pursuing your own interests' (Isaiah 58:13).

In the passage in John 5:1–24, the picture painted of Sabbath observance kept by the Pharisees is of a very legalistic sort. By contrast, Jesus demonstrates the fullness of his life by very deliberately challenging the paralysis of the old legalistic system, with the gift of renewed health. He even says (v.17) 'My Father is still working, and I also am working.' In other words, Jesus presents himself as the giver of the new creation. In so doing, he gives Sabbath a renewed meaning.[105]

A little later in John's Gospel, Jesus returns to the question of Sabbath observance to argue that it is not about keeping the letter of the law, but about making whole (7:22–24). It was on a Sabbath day that Jesus took earth and spittle to make clay with which to anoint a blind man's eyes and enable him to see (9:13–17). Earth and spittle are

104 As Karl Barth put it, 'creation is the external basis of the covenant, the covenant is the internal basis of creation', *Church Dogmatics III/I*, pp.42ff.,94ff.,228ff.
105 This point is cogently argued in George Browning, *Sabbath and the Common Good*, Echo Books, 2016.

both symbols of the natural order of creation. Jesus affirms the very material earth on which all life depends, and uses it for healing and personal well-being.

The Gospel of Luke makes explicit what is implied in John's Gospel text: it was on the Sabbath day that Jesus linked the prophecy of Isaiah to himself: 'The Spirit of the Lord is upon me, because he has anointed me to bring good news to the poor. He has sent me to proclaim release to the captives and recovery of sight to the blind, to let the oppressed go free, to proclaim the year of the Lord's favour' (Luke 4:18–19). This last reference ('the year of the Lord's favour') is to the jubilee laws of Leviticus 25, a 'Sabbath of Sabbaths' of 'complete rest for the land' (Leviticus 25:4). The Jubilee laws provided for regular refreshment for the land, as it was not to be sold in perpetuity; they were to guard against 'cheating', and to prevent capital building up in the hands only of a few. The reason given by God: 'for the land is mine' (Leviticus 25:23).

Far from being merely a law to be religiously observed, therefore, Sabbath is about the meaning of creation, the interconnectedness and well-being of the sacred created world.

The fullness of life which God offers through Christ in the Spirit includes the whole created order in which God delights, and our human place within it, our freedom to make our choices and exercise our responsibilities, and to walk in health.

(iv) Providing food

Of the many themes of 'practical wisdom' in John's Gospel, the need for food is one that occurs several times. One of the Wisdom writers of the Hebrew Scripture said: 'The necessities of life are water, bread, and clothing, and also a house to assure privacy' (Sirach 29:21). In other words, fullness of life includes sufficient food and drink, shelter and a sense of security.

Jesus' own life illustrated the need for food and drink. 'Give me a drink,' he said to the Samaritan woman at the well (John 4:7); 'I am thirsty' was his word from the Cross (19:28). The disciples go to buy food (4:8); he prepares a fish breakfast on the beach after the resurrection (21:9). But, as so often in John's Gospel, these ordinary basic necessities of life are used as symbols of something deeper.

Water
Jesus teaches about water at the Feast of Tabernacles (7:2), an autumn festival for grape and oil harvests during which Jewish people

lived in temporary tents as a reminder of their time with Moses in the wilderness. Two of the main symbols uses at that festival were water and light – two of John's Gospel primary images. The festival included prayers for rain, and a procession bringing water from the Pool of Siloam into the Temple to be poured out as a reminder of God's gift of rain. At the festival Jesus proclaims: 'Let anyone who is thirsty come to me, and ... drink ... "Out of the believer's heart shall flow rivers of living water"' (7:37–38). He had said much the same to the woman of Samaria: 'Those who drink of the water that I will give them will never be thirsty. The water that I will give will become in them a spring of water gushing up to eternal life' (4:14).

The abundance of water reminds the reader also of the abundance of wine provided at the wedding feast in Cana of Galilee, a sign of God's overflowing and abundant generosity.

Bread
Jesus also speaks of himself as The Bread of Life – the true bread which is the Father's gift from heaven (6:32). The context of the great saying 'I AM the Bread of Life' (6:35,48) is partly of the manna which God gave in the wilderness (6:31; Exodus 16:4,15,21) – a reminder of divine gift, but also of divine sufficiency. The manna provided was sufficient just for the day. The Gospel context is also partly the feeding of 5000 or more people on the hillside overlooking Galilee – sharing and multiplying to abundance the small gift of five barley loaves and two fish, sufficiently to satisfy a multitude. Jesus – as if offering a new Exodus – uses bread as an illustration of God's provision ('I have food to eat that you do not know about ... My food is to do the will of him who sent me', 4:32,34; 'work ... for the food that endures for eternal life, which the Son of Man will give you', 6:27). And by once again using the divine Name, I AM, Jesus is joining his divine nature with the produce of the earth (bread) over which he 'gave thanks' (6:11), just as in the Christian Eucharist, heaven and earth – God and humanity – come together in the central prayer of the liturgy, 'This is my Body which is given for you.'

The fullness of life that God offers through Christ in the Spirit includes the need for adequate food and drink as well as the gift from God's abundant generosity of divine food and rivers of living water that sustain God's people in 'eternal life'.

(v) Walking in the light of truth
The Feast of Tabernacles (7:2), a thanksgiving for the oil and grape

harvest, and God's gift of rain, was also a festival of light. Golden lamps were lit in the courtyard of the women (where the account of Jesus meeting a woman taken in adultery is set, John 8), and the people danced in remembrance of the pillar of fire that led their ancestors in the wilderness. It was here that Jesus not only proclaimed himself the Bread of Life and the Source of Living Water, but also the Light of the world. John's Gospel has a great deal to say about light. The Word (= Wisdom) is 'the true light, which enlightens everyone' (1:9). After Jesus' conversation with Nicodemus, the author explains the meaning of God's judgement by saying that 'people loved darkness rather than light' (3:19). 'All who do evil hate the light and do not come to the light' (3:20). So here at the Feast of Tabernacles Jesus says, 'I AM the Light of the World' (8:12).

Light, truth and freedom

As the teaching of John chapter 8 develops, the language moves to 'walking in the light', which then becomes 'continuing in Christ's word' – by which 'you will know the truth, and the truth will make you free' (8:32). Light, truth and freedom are all woven together. The Judeans who are criticizing Jesus are aghast that he should suggest that they were not 'free' – they are, after all, children of Abraham! But Jesus argues with them 'everyone who commits sin is a slave to sin ... if the Son makes you free, you will be free indeed' (8:34ff.), even saying, 'Your ancestor Abraham rejoiced that he would see my day' (8:56). The Judeans are not only slaves to the 'father of lies', but are blind to the truth that sets free. The next chapter in the Gospel is the story of a blind man whom Jesus healed. It gives an illustration of humanity's blindness to God's truth in the story of a man born blind from birth (9:1). But – as so often in the Gospel – it symbolizes something deeper. This blind man is presented as a picture of a true believer, who has come to believe in Jesus, and who – after a lifetime living in the dark – can now see. He, like the Christian community, suffers criticism and reproach from representatives of 'the world', but he holds fast to his faith. 'He said: "Lord, I believe." And he worshipped him' (9:38). This elicits Jesus' explanation, 'I came into this world for judgement so that those who do not see may see, and those who do [falsely claim to] see may become blind' (9:39).

Once again Jesus uses the divine Name: 'I AM the Light of the world' (9:5). The blind man is healed by Jesus. The Judeans are again unbelieving and critical. The effect of the Light is to give sight to the blind man, setting him free to live and walk in the true Light. It is also to blind those who wilfully refuse to open their eyes to the Light (9:39). The way of light and of truth is the way of following Jesus (8:12), continuing in his word (8:31), and *believing into* him (9:38). Jesus later says to a crowd who were surrounding him in Jerusalem, 'The light is with you for a little longer. Walk while you have the light, so that the darkness may not overtake you. If you walk in the darkness, you do not know where you are going. While you have the light, believe in the light, that you may become children of light' (12:35–36). And as he says to his disciples in the Upper Room, 'I AM the way, and the truth, and the life. No one comes to the Father except through me' (14:6).

The fullness of life that God offers through Christ in the Spirit includes following Jesus in the light of the true and living way that he shows to those whose eyes are open to his light.

(vi) Providing security and a sense of belonging (John 10:1–18)

Chapter 10 of the Gospel follows immediately after the discussion in chapter 9 about who Jesus really is. Jesus, who has been teaching in the temple, uses the parable ('figure', 10:6), of the shepherd and the sheep to provide a response. This conversation between Jesus and the Judeans was taking place during the Festival of Dedication (10:22), a time when the Jews celebrated deliverance from the tyrant Antiochus Epiphanes, and the rededication of the temple he had desecrated in the middle of the second century BC. Jesus draws on imagery used by the prophet Ezekiel and his vision of a renewed Temple in which God is the Shepherd King (Ezekiel 34, esp. vv.15–16). Other prophets, too, looked forward to the time when God would restore the fortune of God's people, coming to rescue the flock in the manner of great King David – the former good shepherd. The Wisdom of the Hebrew Scripture also uses this image. In Sirach 18:13, we read, 'The compassion of human beings is for their neighbours, but the compassion of the Lord is for every living thing. He rebukes and trains and teaches them, and turns them back, as a shepherd his flock.'

The Gatekeeper

Many themes are woven together here; the parable is told at a number of levels. Ezekiel's prophecy is against the Jewish leaders who had led their people astray: instead, God will be their Shepherd and lead them into security and good pasture. Jesus describes himself as the Gatekeeper for the Sheep: through him they enter into the safety of God's kingdom. He is the Way (cf. John 14:6). He is the genuine Shepherd (unlike the false guides of contemporary Judean leadership), who knows his sheep intimately, gives himself for them, and ensures that they know they belong.

The Shepherd
So Jesus is using this parable of the shepherd to claim that he is the true King of Israel. It is a kingship (to borrow themes from Ezekiel which Jesus applies to himself) of rescue (Ezekiel 34:10), of gathering together (34:13), of feeding with good pasture (34:14), of searching for the lost (34:16), of security and safety (34:25), of provision and sufficiency (34:29), of intimacy (34:30). The Good Shepherd will 'feed them with justice' (34:16). It is at this point that Jesus says that he brings 'life in all its fullness' (John 10:10, *GNT*). And not only to the Judeans: 'I have other sheep that do not belong to this fold' (10:16). In other words, just as the people of Israel were to be a 'light to the nations' (Isaiah 42:6), so the Good Shepherd's care extends worldwide, including others within the promise of abundant life – one flock, united around one Shepherd.

The fullness of life that God offers through Christ in the Spirit includes a sense of being provided for, protected, looked out for, known and loved, within an inclusive and united community.

(vii) Educating through word and deed
One of the characteristic marks of Jesus' time with his disciples is education. The little 'parable' in John 5:19 depicts Jesus as an apprentice in the workshop of his Father: 'Very truly, I tell you, the Son can do nothing on his own, but only what he sees the Father doing; for whatever the Father does, the Son does likewise.' And then Jesus seeks to train up his own apprentice disciples: 'the Son gives life to whomsoever he wishes' (5:21). Most of the disciples' learning comes through 'being where Jesus is', with him and following him. The First Letter of John puts it this way: 'Let what you heard from the beginning abide in you ... then you will abide in the Son and in the Father ... as his anointing teaches you about all things ... abide in him' (1 John 2:24–27).

Jesus' reputation as a teacher was widespread. Nicodemus, a member of the Jewish Sanhedrin who came secretly to Jesus by night began the conversation by saying, 'Rabbi, we know that you are a teacher who has come from God' (John 3:2).

And throughout the Gospel Jesus is described as 'teaching in the synagogue at Capernaum' (6:59); and apparently even more frequently, teaching in the temple (7:14,28; 8:2,20). There was anxiety lest he should spread his teaching to 'the Greeks' who had come to the temple for the festival (7:35). He claimed his teaching was from God (7:16; 8:28; cf. 6:45); but the Judeans rejected his teaching authority (9:34: 'are you trying to teach us?'). In Bethany, Jesus is referred to as the Teacher (11:28), and after the resurrection, Mary Magdalene recognized him as *Rabbouni* (20:16). Jesus' own statement at the Last Supper puts all this in focus: 'You call me Teacher and Lord – and you are right, for that is what I am' (13:13). The disciples will discover that when Jesus is no longer with them, the Holy Spirit 'will teach you everything, and remind you of all that I have said to you' (14:26). Even at his trial before the high priest, Jesus refers to his teaching: 'I have spoken openly to the world; I have always taught in synagogues and in the temple, where all the Jews come together. I have said nothing in secret' (18:20). Disciple means 'learner': education sheds light which enables understanding; it gives the liberating power of truth; it enables people to find their full potential.

The fullness of life that God offers through Christ in the Spirit includes a willingness to be taught, and a responsive obedience to God's word.

(viii) Serving with self-giving love (John 13:1f.)

Another image from the Hebrew Bible which Jesus applies to himself – this time in dramatic form – is that of the Servant. This was one of the names by which he was later known ('the God of our ancestors has glorified his servant Jesus', Acts 3:13). It was used of God's Messiah who represented God's people in the second part of Isaiah ('The righteous one, my servant, shall make many righteous' (Isaiah 53:11). And here in the Gospel it is linked to the washing of preparation for Passover, and to the commissioning of his disciples to faithfulness and love. The picture of Jesus laying down his garments (with echoes of the Good Shepherd 'laying down' his life for the sheep, 10:15), taking a towel and washing the feet of his disciples is not only a picture of God's humble engagement in the dust and earthiness of ordinary life, but is specifically a pointer to the coming engagement with the world's sin and suffering. The momentous week, for which this action of the Servant is just the start, ended at the Cross.

John chapter 13 begins with love: 'Having loved his own who were in the world, he loved them to the end' (13:1). It ends with love: 'I give you a new commandment, that you love one another. Just as I loved you, you also should love one another. By this everyone will know that you are my disciples, if you have love for one another' (13:34f.). And at its heart is this vivid drama: the Lord of Glory, the Word and Wisdom of God embodied in Jesus, engaging in the lowly dirty work of washing feet.

The fullness of life can involve the costly self-giving of lowly service.

(ix) Responding to rejection with love

The commandment to love comes in a chapter (13) that also speaks of the betrayal of Judas, and points towards the cowardice of Peter. Yet despite this, Jesus can also speak of his disciples as 'friends': 'You are my friends if you do what I command you ... I have called you friends, because I have made known to you everything that I heard from my Father' (15:14f.). As we read on in the Gospel, in chapter 18 Judas betrays Jesus; police from the chief priests and the Pharisees arrest Jesus; Peter swings his sword and cuts off the ear of the high priest's slave and, not too long afterwards, warming himself by a charcoal fire, three times denies knowing Jesus. Then Jesus himself in all his vulnerable humanity is not only abandoned by his friends, but arrested and bound (18:12), struck by a police officer in the chief priest's court (18:22) and handed over to Pilate who after questioning him had him flogged (19:1). Jesus was subjected to torture (19:2), mockery (19:3), false accusation (19:7), humiliation (19:17), crucifixion (19:23), defilement, shame and death (19:30).

As the Gospel leads to its climax in the death of Jesus on the Cross, his resurrection and gift of the Spirit, the point is pushed home. Life comes through sacrifice; God's gift comes through costly self-giving love. And in Jesus that is seen primarily in relation to those on the margins, the paralysed and blind, the hungry and insecure, those who do not belong to 'us'.

5. In summary

Life in its fullness is the life of God lived fully on earth, seen in Jesus, bringing heaven and earth together – a life which God intends to be shared out by the Holy Spirit. A fulfilled life is lived 'close to the Father's heart'. It is inclusive and equalizing, looking out to those on the margins whom others despise. It recognizes our human place within the whole of God's creation, our freedom to make choices and exercise responsibilities, the importance of health, worship, recreation and renewal. The fulfilled life recognizes in Jesus the light of the true and liberating way, and finds a sense of being provided for, protected, looked out for, known and loved, within an inclusive and united community of those who follow his way. It is concerned for education, a willingness to be taught, and a responsive obedience to God's word. It is expressed in loving, and sometimes the menial service of love to others, within a community of love that bears fruit for the father's glory.

6. Being where Jesus is

> *'Father, I desire that those also, whom you have given me, may be with me where I am.'* (John 17:24)

In a sermon preached in 2001, Archbishop Rowan Williams said:

> *Where Jesus is, there we shall be. That might serve to sum up the entire gospel of John: it begins by marking out the place Jesus occupies, the place 'in the bosom of the Father' or 'next to the Father's heart', the place of that eternal harmonic energy that is for ever 'in relation to God', pros ton theon, so profoundly and inescapably in relation that it is nothing but what God is; and then the story unfolds of how this life, lived in conversation with so many and so diverse persons, opens up that eternal place for human beings to inhabit. Following Jesus leads to this place, to his home: 'Rabbi, where are you living?' 'Come and see.'*[106]

As Williams makes clear, Christian calling is to follow Jesus: so all Christian calling is to find where he lives, where he is at home. And the Gospel of John shows unforgettably how he is at home simultaneously 'next to the Father's heart' and at the wedding feast, speaking in love and challenge to the woman of Samaria, arguing with the custodians of sacred words and places; on trial, on the Cross, calling Mary Magdalene by name. Next to the Father's heart – next to the heart of the reality in which he stands in his humanity. Our own journey to the heart of all things, the original love that grounds the universe, is by way of the realities in which we stand, the conversations into which we enter, seeking to bring to them that surrender to original love which burns in every act and word of Jesus. As we learn to drop our defences before God's love, so we learn to drop our defences against the reality of God's world; and vice versa. The call is always to that double truthfulness in which Jesus lives, true to God, true to creation: the Word made flesh, and what Williams calls 'the divine harmonic' embodied in the world of conflict and suffering.

Rowan Williams bases the calling to the Christian community on a phrase in the prayer given us in John chapter 17: 'Father, I desire that those also, whom you have given me, may be with me where I am, to see my glory.' Jesus' prayer that his disciples should 'be with me where I am' opens up ways of understanding our Christian role and ministry as an extension of his. For us to live fully is for us *to be with him, where he is.*

---

106 Used with permission.

7. Being where Jesus is today

So what might it mean for us to be 'where Jesus is', in an age in which we need sustainable development? Here are some examples:

Food

Jesus in the Gospel says, 'I AM the Bread of Life'; he provides food for the hungry and drink for the thirsty. One of the major anxieties of our time is where the food is to come from to feed future generations. To be where Jesus is, means to stand with the needs of hungry and thirsty people in our world now. Although the problem is as much about the greed of the richest countries as it is about population growth in the poorest, nearly half the world is currently undernourished – which requires action both in terms of food production and distribution, and also action to minimise environmental factors such as climate change and ocean acidification, which affect the food chain. From the use of pesticides in industrial agriculture to the over-consumption of red meat (which means more cows and more methane, more crops grown for animal feed and more deforestation), food security is a major question for today.[107]

Health

Jesus in the Gospel says, 'I AM the Light of the World'; he brings sight to the man born blind, as well as healing to others who are sick or paralyzed. Several of today's Sustainable Development Goals seeking to reduce extreme poverty relate to the provision of health care: for example, reducing child mortality and controlling epidemics of malaria or AIDS. The gap between health care in the developed and the developing worlds is enormous, and as Sachs demonstrates,[108] ill health and poverty go together. Part of the problem of achieving wider health care, he argues, arises from treating health care as if it were a free-market commodity. To be where Jesus is, means to shine his light on the needs of the sick, as well as the medical and nursing services who are seeking to alleviate suffering when life is at its darkest, and to work with the government departments who can decide on the allocation of resources.

Education

Jesus in the Gospel says, 'I AM the Truth', and much of his ministry

---

107 cf. Jeffrey D. Sachs, *The Age of Sustainable Development*, ch.10 and *passim*. cf. many of the publications from Christian Aid, Oxfam, Cafod, Tearfund etc. and particularly Tearfund's paper, 'The Restorative Economy', 2015.
108 cf. Sachs, op. cit. ch. 9. Note also in 2015 *The Lancet* established a Commission on Health and Climate Change, formed to map out the impacts of climate change, and the necessary policy responses, in order to ensure the highest attainable standards of health for populations worldwide.

is teaching and educating his disciples. Many of today's educational needs are on building the skills needed for what Amartya Sen calls capability-building,[109] on the availability of education from pre-school to higher education, and on education for what is needed to provide good health care across the life-cycle. To be where Jesus is, means to be with the primary school teacher, with the student in need of fees to pay for her course, with those who decide on political priorities.

Security

Jesus in the Gospel says, 'I AM the Gate of the sheepfold', providing safety and security for the sheep. He tells his anxious disciples not to let their hearts be troubled. He says to fearful disciples behind locked doors, 'Peace be with you.' And in the Gospel Jesus also says, 'I AM the Good Shepherd', a rich metaphor which covers many aspects of his ministry, but in particular that there are other sheep from other folds that he needs to find and bring in. His shepherding is a ministry of inclusion. Much of today's insecurity comes from social exclusions arising from, for example, inequality, the rising gap between the richest and the poorest, the change of employment prospects through the development of robots, the political commitment to free market economics without adequate constraints.[110] These need to be our concerns if we are to be where Jesus is.

Inclusion

Jesus in the Gospel includes the marginalized Samaritan women, saying to her, 'I AM he, the one who is speaking to you.' Much of today's world is marked by gender inequalities and by lack of empowerment

---

109 Amartya Sen, *Development as Freedom*, OUP, 1999. Amartya Sen is one key modern writer who has sought to reframe the concept of justice away from simply civic fairness and towards seeing that the justice of social arrangements is about the way those arrangements enable people to function better and to live well. Where social structures get in the way of human flourishing, they are unjust. When social arrangements help people develop the capability to fulfil their potential, they can be seen as just. Sen says we need the tools to address the issues people face in the lives they actually live, to enable them to live with more freedom to proceed justly within the constraints of ordinary life. He talks about 'maximising capabilities' for enhancing the quality of life. He is not interested is defining justice merely in terms of the distribution of wealth, but rather in terms of capabilities.

110 In *The Price of Inequality*, Joseph Stiglitz argues that 'capitalism is failing to produce what was promised, but is delivering on what was not promised: inequality, pollution, unemployment, and most important of all: the degradation of values to the point where everything is acceptable and no one is accountable' (xviii). And, he says, 'we are paying a high price for our growing and outsize inequality: not only slower growth and lower GDP, but even more instability. And this is not to say anything about the other prices we are paying: a weakened democracy, a diminished sense of fairness and justice, and even ... a questioning of our sense of identity (xxii). One of Stiglitz's primary points is that 'inequality is to a very large extent the result of government policies that shape and direct the forces of technology and markets and broader social forces. There is in this both hope and despair: hope because it means that inequality is not inevitable, and that by changing policies we can achieve a more efficient and egalitarian society; despair because the political processes that shape these policies are so hard to change' (82).

Will Hutton's *Them and Us*, written in 2010 in the aftermath of the financial crisis, underlines the importance of fairness in the growth of healthy societies and indeed civilization. Fairness is good to keep society together. And yet what the financial crisis of 2007–8 showed was that, in the UK at least, we sacrificed social and moral values for the sake of higher share prices and executive bonuses. Somehow we were all taken in by the thought that banks are too big to fail. We can now see the damage being done to social cohesion and human welfare by growing financial – and consequently social – inequality. And the problem is international. The structures of inequality are destroying social well-being. It is not possible for any of us to live well if those unlucky enough to be born poor are denied opportunity, and have their potential smothered.

and work prospects for women and girls in many cultures, as well as appalling patriarchal violence against women.[111] To be where Jesus is, means to be on the side of the poor, the marginalized, the excluded and those unjustly treated, and to work for gender equality and empowerment for women.

Two other examples in the Gospel, which we will look at in later chapters: Jesus in the Gospel says, 'I AM The Vine' – the 'vine' represents what true Israel, what true humanity, was meant to be. This picture is linked to his word to his disciples, 'You are my friends.' Jesus in the Gospel says, 'I AM the resurrection and the life'; he says it to mourning Martha, coping with the death of her brother, and giving her hope that this world is not all there is. To be where Jesus is, means to stand with the mourning and the dying, and also with all who seek to enable good and flourishing relationships of friendship and trust.

Jesus in the Gospel shows himself Lord of all creation in his stilling of the storm and the wind (I AM: do not be afraid). Food, health, security, friendship and hope are all aspects of our created being, of which Jesus is Lord. One of the places Jesus might well be today is alongside those who are seeking to mitigate and hold back the worst effects of climate change caused by human stupidity, selfishness and sin, and to work out in a systemic way how to relate equity, ecology and the economy.

Sustainable Development

It is worth emphasizing the resonance between some of these themes in the ministry of Jesus and the aspirations of the United Nations Sustainable Development Goals.[112] But in the Gospel it is much more

111 Note especially Elaine Storkey's important book, *Scars Across Humanity: Understanding and overcoming violence against women*, SPCK, 2016.
112 The United Nations Sustainable Development Goals (in which Jeffrey Sachs played a key part), were agreed in September 2015, and set an agenda for 'transforming the world' by ending poverty and hunger, protecting the planet from degradation, ensuring all human beings can enjoy prosperous and fulfilling lives, and fostering peaceful, just and inclusive societies free from fear and violence. Their stated intention is that this be fully implemented by 2030.
The goals covered:
- ending poverty in all its forms everywhere
- ending hunger, achieving food security, improved nutrition, sustainable agriculture
- ensuring healthy lives and promoting wellbeing for all at all ages
- ensuring inclusive and equitable quality education and life-long learning opportunities for all
- achieving gender equality and empowerment for all women and girls
- ensuring the availability and sustainable management of water and sanitation for all
- ensuring access to affordable, reliable, sustainable and modern energy for all
- promoting sustained, inclusive, sustainable economic growth, full and productive employment and decent work for all
- building resilient infrastructure, promoting inclusive and sustainable industrialization and fostering innovation
- reducing inequality within and among countries
- making cities and human settlements inclusive, safe, resilient and sustainable
- ensuring sustainable consumption and production patterns
- taking urgent action to combat climate change and its impacts
- conserving and sustainably using the oceans, seas and marine resources for sustainable development
- protecting, restoring and promoting sustainable use of terrestrial ecosystems, sustainably managing forests, combating desertification, and halting and reversing land degradation and biodiversity loss
- promoting peaceful and inclusive societies for sustainable development, proving access to justice for all and

than aspiration. As we shall indicate in chapter 12, it is within the community of Christ's people that we can learn not only who we are, and what is our destiny, but also how to live fully, following Jesus' Way of Wisdom.

building effective, accountable and inclusive institutions at all levels
These major goals were further expanded into 169 specific targets. The major challenges refer most obviously to Africa with very high fertility rates, and South Asia with its high population density, but these goals are intended for all countries, rich and poor, North and South, developed and developing.

Chapter Six

Glory: the Wisdom of the Cross and Resurrection

- One of John's great words is 'glory' – meaning God's presence with us.

- The Gospel speaks of the glory of Jesus Christ at the village wedding in Cana, displaying God's abundant generosity.

- It speaks of the glory of Jesus Christ at a village grave in Bethany, showing us God's deep compassion, as well as God's hostility to the power of evil.

- It demonstrates God's glory supremely in the loving self-giving of Jesus in his death on the Cross, confirmed as God's victory by the new Easter life of resurrection, when a new creation is born.

- Jesus draws together a community, energized by his Spirit to 'share his glory' and manifest God's presence in the world.

We have seen his glory (John 1:14)

One of the great theological words that the Beloved Disciple uses in John's Gospel is the word 'glory'.

> *'I don't know what you mean by "glory"', Alice said.*
> *Humpty Dumpty smiled contemptuously. 'Of course you don't – till I tell you. I meant "there's a nice knock-down argument for you!"'*
> *'But "glory" doesn't mean "a nice knock-down argument"', Alice objected.*
> *'When I use a word,' Humpty Dumpty said, in rather a scornful tone, 'it means just what I choose it to mean – neither more nor less.'*[113]

'Glory' has in fact come to mean more or less what we want it to mean in contemporary society. Virgin Trains, for example, had an advertisement for a high-speed journey from London to Manchester: 'Bound

---

113 Lewis Carroll, *Alice Through the Looking Glass.*

for Glory'. The words 'Death or glory' appear as titles in songs, heavy metal, military marches, punk rock, a Russian novel.

Much Christian art, most notably Graham Sutherland's magnificent tapestry in Coventry Cathedral entitled 'Christ in Glory', depicts the ascended Christ in heavenly splendour. In 2000, the National Gallery exhibition *Seeing Salvation* included Sutherland's first cartoon of the tapestry. The catalogue comments that the figure of the risen and ascended Christ on the tapestry shows Christ in glory above, rather than among, humanity, and as a king, rather than an 'ordinary' human being. Probably Sutherland's intricate designs had many multiple meanings, but the overall impression of 'Christ in Glory' is that he is not one of us. Yet, when John's Gospel uses the word 'glory' he is referring to Jesus the man – at a village wedding, at a village grave, on a criminal's cross.

In the thinking of many of the biblical authors, 'glory' has a very specific and sacred meaning. The writers of the Hebrew Bible take over a word that usually refers to 'honour' or 'splendour', and invest it with further and fuller meaning. Glory comes to refer to the revelation of God's presence among God's people – here on God's earth.

The fullness of life, seen in Jesus of Nazareth, which God offers through Christ in the Spirit to the community of Jesus' disciples, is a life that prompted those who were with Jesus to say they had 'seen his glory'.

The Word became flesh and lived among us, and we have seen his glory, the glory as of a father's only son, full of grace and truth. (John 1:14)

A former Archbishop of Canterbury, Robert Runcie, had a favourite quotation: 'The glory of God is a human being fully alive.' It is often quoted in this form, and is attributed to the great second-century theologian Irenaeus. Although it is wonderfully evocative, and true, and rightly celebrates human life in all its fullness, it is not quite what Irenaeus wrote. Irenaeus had John 1:14 in mind when he wrote, 'the glory of God is a living man.'[114] He was writing about Jesus. The disciples saw the fullness of God's glory revealed in the living human being – God's Word made flesh, Jesus the Man, present to us in all his weakness and vulnerability.

114 Irenaeus, Adversus Haereses (*Against Heresies*), 4. 34. 5–7. 'And for this reason did the Word become the dispenser of the paternal grace for the benefit of men, for whom He made such great dispensations, revealing God indeed to men, but presenting man to God, and preserving at the same time the invisibility of the Father, lest man should at any time become a despiser of God, and that he should always possess something towards which he might advance; but, on the other hand, revealing God to men through many dispensations, lest man, falling away from God altogether, should cease to exist. For the glory of God is a living man; and the life of man consists in beholding God. For if the manifestation of God which is made by means of the creation, affords life to all living in the earth, much more does that revelation of the Father which comes through the Word, give life to those who see God.'

God's presence with us

The background to John 1:14 is – as with much of the Gospel – the narrative of the exodus of God's people from slavery in Egypt. At the tent of meeting in the wilderness, the pillar of cloud would descend and God would speak to Moses (Exodus 33:9). When, later, the tabernacle was set up, 'the cloud covered the tent of meeting and the glory of the Lord filled the tabernacle' (Exodus 40:34–38). The 'glory' was God's presence on earth with God's people. And when John's Gospel says that the Word became flesh and 'tabernacled' among us, we are meant to understand allusions to the exodus.[115] Jesus is God's presence with us.

Many themes are coming together in this text in the Gospel: in Jesus we see a human being living in the fullness of God's life, God's presence among humanity, revealing to us who God is. He is the God of the exodus who sets people free – a God of liberation, of new beginnings, of new life, of new hope. Jesus embodies the hope not only of a new exodus, but of a new creation.

The times when Jesus is specifically said to show God's glory are few. The word is mostly used to refer to the glory Jesus had before the Word was made flesh: 'the glory that I had in your presence before the world existed' (17:5); and the glory to which Jesus would return after his death and resurrection: 'Father, I desire that those also, whom you have given me, may be with me where I am, to see my glory, which you have given me because you loved me before the foundation of the world' (17:24). But those few times are very significant. They occur after Jesus turns water into wine at Cana of Galilee; at the raising of Lazarus from the dead in Bethany; and especially with reference to Jesus' death on the Cross and his resurrection and ascension into heaven. We begin at Cana.

(i) Glory in Cana (John 2:1–11)

The story of the wedding feast at Cana of Galilee is told in John 2:1–11. It begins 'on the third day' – a phrase that resonates with another 'third day', namely Easter morning, 'the first day of the week' – the third day after Jesus was crucified (John 20:1). The wedding feast must have evoked in John's first readers the picture of divine blessing in Isaiah's vision of the Lord's banquet (Isaiah 25:6) where there was an abundance of wine.[116] In the prophet's mind, we are on Mount Zion. It is a

---

115 The Greek word for 'tabernacled' comes from the word translated 'tent' (*skene*), which has the same consonants as the Hebrew 'shekinah'. 'Shekinah' is the word used by later Rabbis to describe the glory of God's presence. It is linked to the word translated 'dwell' in the Exodus text 'I will dwell among the Israelites, and I will be their God' (Exodus 29:45). It signifies God's Word, Wisdom, Spirit, Presence without actually naming God.

116 'On this mountain the Lord of hosts will make for all peoples a feast of rich food, a feast of well-matured wines, of rich food filled with marrow, of well-matured wines strained clear' (Isaiah 25:6).

time when the whole earth is singing God's praise (Isaiah 24:16). It is a time of restoration, of salvation, of mercy through justice, of death being 'swallowed up' for ever (Isaiah 25:8), a day of gladness and rejoicing. Several of the prophets speak of the abundance of wine as a symbol of God's generous blessing (cf. Amos 9:13,14). And a wedding, of course, was used much later in Isaiah 62:4 and elsewhere as a symbol of God's healing of the relationship between God and the people, and God's delight in them at the time of their vindication and deliverance.

Abundant generosity
The six huge stone water jars were 'for the Jewish rites of purification', each holding 'twenty to thirty gallons'. So Jesus' action in providing an abundance of high-quality wine is both a demonstration of the superabundant generosity of God, and a sign that God is doing something new: Jewish ritual is being replaced with a messianic banquet; the old national identity is being transformed into a new community of believers in Jesus. At the end of the narrative we read 'Jesus did this, the first of his signs, in Cana of Galilee, and revealed his glory; and his disciples believed in him' (2:11). The text actually reads 'the beginning of his signs' – recalling the creation: 'In the beginning' of John 1:1. We are meant to see in Cana the sign of a new creation: a gospel of transformation from a religion of law to a life of grace for those who believe through the abundant generosity of God. It is in the ordinariness of a village wedding that God's glory is seen in Jesus.

For the community of the Beloved Disciple, this reminder of Jesus' 'sign' was a reminder of God's abundant generosity of grace, and that all that we have comes to us as gift. God is building a new community based on faith in Jesus, in which their 'joy shall be full' (John 16:24).

And yet, in the centre of this story, there is a reminder that 'the world' does not yet understand this divine generosity, nor experience this joy. 'They have no wine' (2:3). The mother of Jesus seems to be among those with Jesus who are enjoying the party. Her concern is for those without: they have no wine. The Christian life is never only about celebrating the grace of God for those within the Christian community: it is also about always looking with concern and action to those without, those with no wine.

(ii) Glory in Bethany (John 11:1–54)
We move from a village wedding to the ordinariness of a village grave, for the second example in John's Gospel of Jesus showing God's glory. The village is Bethany, a name that may mean 'house of figs' – or may

mean 'house of affliction'. The scene is certainly one of affliction. The dead man is Lazarus, brother of Martha and Mary, who in their different ways are overcome with grief. The story is told in John 11:1–54.

This amazing chapter moves from suffering and bewilderment to resurrection and hope, from surprise, fear and bereavement, to rejoicing and anger. In many ways a pivotal chapter in the Gospel, its themes spread much wider than our focus in this book. We will here concentrate primarily on the actions of Jesus. Through God's actions in Jesus, glory is given to God. It is not that, through raising the dead, Jesus does a mighty miracle for which people give glory to God – it is rather that, through facing death and demonstrating that he embodies God's life (I AM the resurrection), Jesus is signifying his own forthcoming death and resurrection through which God's saving presence and power in the world will be seen. Indeed, this narrative ends with a direct pointer to Jesus' own suffering (11:53). It is his Cross and resurrection which – as we shall see – are the supreme manifestation of God's glory.

Frustration

The context of Jesus' actions in Bethany is initially one of frustration. The message came to Jesus and the disciples that Lazarus was dead, and Jesus apparently did nothing, staying where he was for two days longer. Why did Jesus not respond to Mary's and Martha's messages by going straightaway? It was known that Jesus particularly loved Lazarus (11:3,36).

Then, when he eventually got to Bethany, Martha, and then later Mary also, expressed the universal human feeling, 'if only..': 'Lord, if only you had been here' (11:21,32).

Life restored

Another aspect of the context to this story was a common belief in a general resurrection: 'I know he will rise again in the resurrection on the last day', when God's people looked for a new heaven and a new earth (Isaiah 65:17f.). Jesus was to show them that resurrection was here, and now, in his Person.

A dominant feature of this story is grief and mourning. Mary and Martha needed 'consolation' (11:19). Mary and many Jews with her were weeping (11:33). Jesus himself wept with those who wept (11:35).

The story is full of questions, many remaining unanswered. But one explanation for Jesus' apparent lack of earlier activity was that he had been praying to his Father. So at Lazarus' grave he says, 'Father, I thank you for having heard me' (11:41).

The raising of Lazarus at the climax of the story is a triumphant, even defiant shout with a loud voice, 'Lazarus, come out', followed by, 'Unbind him and let him go.' God gives Lazarus back his life; the disciples are to play their part in removing the strips of cloth, and 'releasing' the new man.[117]

Compassion and anger

It is this action of Jesus through which the action of God is seen. For those who believed, it manifested God's glory (11:40). And that action deeply demonstrates the loving compassion, judgement and mercy of God. For at the heart of the dialogue between Jesus and the two women is a description of Jesus hardly found elsewhere. He is angry (11:33: 'greatly disturbed in spirit'). The verb describes the snorting of horses, and when used of human beings usually means 'angry'. More than that, he was 'deeply moved in his spirit' (11:33), and 'greatly disturbed' (11:38). Quite why this strength of emotion has been described in this way is not obvious. However, we know of Jesus' deep love for Lazarus, and of his empathetic weeping with Mary in her grief. The note of anger seems to connect this side of Jesus' compassion with a strong sense that there is something wrong. It cannot only be about Jesus' frustration with the unbelieving Judeans who have completely misunderstood his mission: they were focused on death; Jesus is the bringer of life. So what is the anger? Could it be, as Calvin suggested, anger at the intrusion of death itself into God's world? Or is it, as others suggest, the first round in the battle with the 'ruler of this world' (whom we meet in 12:31), and a realization of the deeper conflict to come in Jesus' own life? Lesslie Newbigin's comment is helpful: 'in the immediate presence of death, and of the hopeless unbelief of his friends in the face of death, Jesus was facing that power which he had come to destroy, a power which is met by the wrath of him who is the author of life, but which could only be "cast out" (12:31) when the author of life took the whole power of death upon himself.'[118] God is at work among the tears, the fear of a stench, the tomb, the stone and the strips of cloth. They also point powerfully forwards to Jesus' own death.

The glory seen at Bethany is the manifestation of the action of the living God through Jesus, prayerfully dependent on the Father, in deepest compassion, touching people with grace and tears in their affliction,

---

117 'Release' is the same word as 'forgiving' debts, or 'letting go' the donkey on Palm Sunday (cf. Matthew 21:2).
118 Lesslie Newbigin, *The Light has Come,* Eerdmans, 1982, p.144.

while at the same time standing firm in hostile combat with those forces of evil which destroy life.

(iii) Mary of Bethany: generosity, compassion, self-giving service

We pause at this point to take particular note of the way John's Gospel provides us with a lovely case-study of a disciple's response to the generosity, compassion and loving service of Christ in its depiction of Mary of Bethany, sister of Lazarus. Her story comes in John 12:1–18, soon after the narrative of the raising of Lazarus from the dead. She has seen the abundant compassion of God in Jesus, as well as his anger at evil in the world, and she offers him her gift of sacrificial love. It is a gift of great generosity, and it is offered with loving compassion. Her offering is with an eye to the coming suffering and death of Jesus. Maybe, also, the 'fragrance of the perfume' is mentioned deliberately to contrast with the reference to the 'stench' of the dead Lazarus about which Martha was so anxious at Lazarus' grave.

There are three characters alongside Jesus in this paragraph: Martha, Mary and Judas. Martha is serving the meal. In other Gospels she is portrayed as busy and anxious about getting the work done, while Mary is praised for sitting at Jesus' feet, listening, and here in John's Gospel for anointing his feet with expensive perfume and (coming shockingly close for a woman of those times) wiping them with her hair.

Sometimes, of course, that may be a salutary lesson – sometimes sheer busyness does get in the way of the personal, intimate, spiritual, relational, loving aspects to life, and in that sense Mary has chosen the better part (as other Gospels put it). But Martha's work has to be done, the dishes washed, the schedules completed, the church meeting agenda sent out, the budget balanced, the roof repaired – and then the contemplative life can seem rather an expensive luxury. So it seemed to Judas, who kept the moneybag, and complained about this expensive waste. In fact, to Judas, what for Mary was a costly and sacrificial gift was measured only in monetary terms.

Martha and Mary and Judas; they are sometimes all parts of us. We can think of Mary and Martha as different ways of relating to the world around us – perhaps different levels of engagement with the world. God gives gifts of active service – we thank God for those who can do things. We need activists. And we also need visionaries – those who keep alive the personal, relational, spiritual, meaning and purpose dimension, which can so easily get crowded out. Thank God for Mary and Martha, the pray-ers and the doers, the visionaries and the activists, the poets and the scientists – those who catch the vision for church growth, as well as those who ask 'who is going to pay for it?' Sometimes we need someone who keeps the moneybag as well.

But the focus of this section of the Gospel is on Mary. Lazarus died not long ago, and Jesus raised him back to life. At that point Mary, overwhelmed with grief, knelt at Jesus' feet and said, 'Lord, if you had been here my brother would not have died.' Even as Lazarus is raised from the dead, there is still death in the air: 'From that day the Judeans planned to put Jesus to death.' And here Mary seems to know that the end of the road for Jesus, and his own death, is only days away. So she takes this opportunity of using the expensive oils she has kept for the day of Jesus' burial, and responds to the abundant grace of God she has seen in Jesus, now offering him this gift of her sacrificial love. She takes some of the tokens of God's rich creation, and offers them back in generous thanksgiving and self-offering. And Jesus thanks her for it.

As the narrative of the Gospel unfolds, we realize that this is the first thing to happen in the final act of the drama of Jesus' life and death and resurrection – and that is why this reading is chosen for Passion Sunday in church lectionaries. Jesus is going to give his life in self-giving love; here he praises Mary for her sacrificial giving on her behalf. Here is faith and devotion richly given away.

Of course we need Martha to do the dishes. But Mary – says another Gospel – has chosen 'the better part'; her gift is of inestimable value. Judas interprets this costly, loving gift only in terms of a commodity with a price-tag. Why was this not sold, and the money given to the poor? Of course it was right to give to the poor. Their Bible told them there was a legal duty to give to the poor (Deuteronomy 15:11). But Jesus transposes that law into a gift of grace.

Judas misses the point. Mary and Jesus are relating in love, self-giving and sacrifice, not at the level of monetary value and legal duty. So much of our culture of consumption, monetary values and legal duties gets in the way of what is really important: loyalty, friendship, love. These are things that money cannot buy.[119]

And by saying 'you will always have the poor with you', I think Jesus is saying that the poor are not out there as people to whom good must be done; the poor are to be with you. Welcome the poor as people with you – not distant recipients of charity. Politically what this means in

---

119 cf. Michael Sandel, *What Money Can't Buy*, Penguin Books, 2012.

terms of the poverty of our world, the sustainable development goals, the management of the migrant crisis and so on is not easy to see. But one factor which must never be forgotten is that those who are poor are not numbers with a price-tag, not distant recipients of charity, but people who with all others are neighbours we are called to love. Mary kneels at Jesus' feet. She gives him her most costly gift. Mary is a representative of the devotion and self-giving found within the community of Christ's people. She sees before her not only her Lord, but also the Love that moves the sun and the other stars.

(iv) The glory of self-giving love

The abundant generosity of grace, that we have seen in Cana, and the deep compassionate love, anger and tears of God, which were evident in Bethany, come together in the glory of the Cross. Most of the references to 'glory' in John's Gospel come in the second half of the Gospel, which has led some commentators to describe this part of the Gospel as 'The Book of Glory' (as distinct from the first half of the Gospel which forms 'The Book of Signs').

There is a brief trailer back in John chapter 7, where in the middle of the festival of Tabernacles, Jesus speaks of himself as seeking the glory of the One who sent him. Later in that chapter the writer refers to the coming Holy Spirit, who was not yet given 'because Jesus was not yet glorified' (7:39). Further on, in chapter 8:50, Jesus says that he does not seek his own glory; rather, God seeks it, and He is the judge. But it is in John 12 that the Book of Glory really begins. One aside from the writer is instructive: 'His disciples did not understand these things at first; but when Jesus was glorified, then they remembered ...' (12:16). As becomes increasingly clear, this is a reference forwards to Jesus' death and resurrection. After the encounter with the Greeks who wanted to see him, Jesus says, 'The hour has come for the Son of Man to be glorified' (12:23), and then immediately speaks of those who lose their life in this world and keep it for eternal life. Accompanied by thunder in the heavens, Jesus then proclaims, 'Now my soul is troubled. And what should I say – "Father, save me from this hour"? No, it is for this reason that I have come to this hour. Father, glorify your name.' Then a voice came from heaven, 'I have glorified it, and I will glorify it again.' The glory is that God will be manifest to the crowd in the suffering and death of Jesus now that 'his hour' has come. The narrator soon returns to the 'glory' theme with a reference from the prophet Isaiah. He links Isaiah's words to Jesus, saying that Isaiah 'saw his glory and spoke about him'. Interestingly at that point in the Gospel it is noted that many people – even from the authorities and the Pharisees – believed in Jesus, but dare not say so for fear that they would be thrown out of the synagogue along with other Christian believers. They loved human glory, it was said, more than the glory that comes from God (12:43).

Self-giving service

Then follows chapter 13, with another strong statement from Jesus that 'his hour had come' (13:1), and by Jesus' self-giving service in washing his disciples' dusty feet. The Gospel goes on to speak of love – Jesus' love for them, and his new commandment that they love one another. It includes Jesus saying: 'Now is the Son of Man glorified, and God has been glorified in him ... Where I am going, you cannot come' (13:31–33). Jesus is speaking of his coming suffering, trial and death, and is looking onwards to Easter morning and the birth of a new creation.

It is predominantly in the long discourse to his disciples in the Upper Room, and then the great High Priestly Prayer recorded in John chapter 17, that Jesus speaks about glory. In the Upper Room discourses, it is a glory that – in this world – looks very much like suffering. The Father will be glorified in the Son (14:13) as he prepares for 'his hour'. The Father will also be glorified in the community of the disciples, as they share in the life of Christ, and 'bear much fruit', as branches do within a vine (15:8). The Father will take what belongs to the Son, and give it to the disciples – this will glorify the Son (16:14).

But it is in the great Prayer of chapter 17, that Jesus pronounces once again: 'the hour has come; glorify your Son, so that the Son may glorify you' (17:1); 'So now, Father, glorify me in your own presence with the glory that I had in your presence before the world existed' (17:5). The claim of this chapter is that the glory of the Son who shared the life of the Father before the creation of the world – that glory will be seen again in the self-giving service of the suffering, death and resurrection of the Son.

Strikingly it is in the garden at the time of Jesus' betrayal and arrest that John tells us three times that Jesus uses the divine name. He said:

> 'For whom are you looking? They answered, 'Jesus of Nazareth.' Jesus replied: I AM he.' Judas, who betrayed him, was standing with them. When Jesus said to them, 'I AM he', they stepped back and fell to the ground. Again he asked them, 'For whom are you looking?' And they said 'Jesus of Nazareth.' Jesus answered 'I told you that I AM he.' (John 18:4–8)

The fullness of life, seen in Jesus, displays the glory of God as it shows:

- God's abundant generosity and gracious gift;
- God's compassionate tenderness and love to those suffering, coupled with
- God's hostility to the destructive forces of evil; and
- God's sacrificial, loving self-giving service, even to Jesus' death on the Cross, and so the birth of a new creation on Easter morning.

(v) Easter

The incarnation of Jesus, the Word and Wisdom of God made flesh, is the beginning of the story of an abundant life that leads, by way of Cana and Bethany, to Gethsemane, to Good Friday, to Easter morning at the empty tomb, and on – as we shall elaborate in a later chapter – to Easter evening and Jesus' gift of Peace, Shalom, to his new community of disciples. Incarnation leads to what Celia Deane-Drummond rightly calls 'the Wisdom of the cross'.[120] Easter morning is the celebration of a new creation. It confirms the Cross as a victory, not a defeat.

Resurrection

Another of the Beloved Disciple's central themes is the life of God seen in Jesus, and in particular the life of the new creation born on Easter Day.

> *In him was life.* (John 1:4)
> *I AM the Resurrection and the Life.* (John 11:25)
> *I AM the Way, the Truth and the Life.* (John 14:6)

The Gospel presents Jesus as speaking to his Jewish critics about the Temple of his body: 'Destroy this temple, and in three days I will raise it up' (John 2:19). He was speaking about his resurrection from the dead.

After the healing of the paralyzed man at the pool of Bethesda, Jesus said 'Just as the Father raises the dead and gives them life, so also the Son gives life to whomsoever he wishes' (John 5:21). He goes on to speak about the destiny 'of those who have done good, to the resurrection of life, and those who have done evil, to the resurrection of condemnation' (John 5:29). Jesus is here teaching about the resurrection of believers. Then, as part of the lengthy discourse about the Bread of Life in John chapter 6, Jesus says 'This is the will of him who sent me, that I should lose nothing of all that he has given me, but raise it up on

---

120 cf. Celia Deane-Drummond, *Creation Through Wisdom,* T & T Clark, 2000, ch.2.

the last day. This is indeed the will of my Father, that all who see the Son and believe in him may have eternal life; and I will raise them up on the last day' (John 6:39–40).

There is an end-time dimension to God's gift of resurrection life, but in Jesus' resurrection, the end-time has burst through into the present. And for believers, 'eternal life' is life in God's Spirit here and now, as a foretaste of the life to come.

It is in John chapter 11 that all this comes to clearest focus. Martha speaks first about resurrection at the grave of Lazarus her brother. She shares the belief of many of her time (though not the Sadducees), in line with that of some of the Hebrew prophets (e.g. Daniel 12:3)[121]: 'I know that he will rise again in the resurrection on the last day' (John 11:24). To this Jesus replies, 'I AM the resurrection and the life. Those who believe *into* me, even though they die, will live, and everyone who lives and believes *into* me will never die' (John 11:25 – my emphasis and wording). Jesus is saying to Martha that here and now he embodies resurrection life: in him God's new creation has burst into the world; God's new world is born; the healing of creation is guaranteed. To underline the pivotal importance of the statement that in Jesus is resurrection and life, the Beloved Disciple underlines it three times in the next chapter: 'Jesus came … to the home of Lazarus, whom he had raised from the dead … the great crowd of the Jews … came not only because of Jesus but also to see Lazarus, whom he had raised from the dead …' Then there is reference to 'the crowd that had been with him when he called Lazarus out of the tomb and raised him from the dead' (John 12:1,9,17).

Then the climax, of course, comes in the narrative of Easter Day in John chapter 20. Tom Wright expresses this poetically by recalling the darkness and chaos before God's creation of the world, and then the coming of light and life. He reminds us of the Word made flesh, in whom God's life and light were made visible. And then: 'Flesh dies. Chaos comes again. Darkness descends on the little weeping group at the cross. Two men in the fading light do what has to be done. Then the long Sabbath, the rest in the cold tomb.' Then on Easter morning, there is again light and life. The Beloved Disciple, alongside Peter, arrives at the tomb – and 'he saw and believed'. Tom Wright again: 'Believed that new creation had begun. Believed that the world had turned the corner, out of its long winter and into spring at last. Believed that God had said "Yes" to Jesus, to all that he had been and done. Believed that

---

121 cf. N. T. Wright *The Resurrection of the Son of God,* SPCK 2003.

Jesus was alive again.'[122]

Then, beginning with Mary Magdalene, the message was spread. The message of Christ as the resurrection and the life itself came alive among the early believers. Jürgen Moltmann crosses the centuries with this comment in the prologue to his wonderful book, *The Living God and the Fullness of Life*: 'With Christ's resurrection, the horizon of the future, which is otherwise darkened today by terrorism, nuclear threat or environmental catastrophe, becomes light.'[123]

God's people of today, drawn into the life and light of Christ's resurrection, need to find ways of reiterating God's creative 'Yes' to the world, to life, to this earth, to its people, to all creation. This is the pivotal point of our study: fullness of life is God's gift to the world through the resurrection of Jesus Christ. In future chapters we explore what this means in the outworking of practical Wisdom in this world, within the Christian community drawn together by Christ's Spirit. It means an outworking of the abundance of God's grace, a sharing in God's deep compassion and God's antagonism to the evils that destroy and fragment, a proclamation of God's love and justice not only in words but in costly self-giving service. This becomes a vision of creation restored[124] through the life and death and resurrection of the Man who is so fully alive. God's creation 'project' has its origin in God's creative love, and goes by way of Cana, Bethany and the Cross to the kingdom of God's glory. Easter is the source and guarantee of Christian hope.

(vii) Glory in the Community of Christ's People

Remarkably, the new creation which came to birth in the death and resurrection of Jesus has its first focus in the community of disciples that Jesus has drawn together: 'All mine are yours, and yours are mine; and I have been glorified in them' (17:10). In Jesus, the God of the exodus sets people free – a God of liberation, of new beginnings, of new life, of new hope. And that new life is God's gift to the community of disciples. Their life is now to be marked, as was that of Jesus, with the abundance of divine generosity and grace that we see at Cana, with the divine compassion and love that we see at Bethany, and supremely with the gift of self-giving sacrifice and loving service that we see at the Cross – lived out in the resurrection power of God's life-giving Spirit. But here it is linked first of all with what seems most inglorious in this world's terms: suffering, persecution and death. The Gospel understands the

---

122 Tom Wright *John for Everyone Part II*, SPCK 2002, p 140–142.
123 J. Moltmann, *The Living God and the Fullness of Life*, WCC, 2016, p.x.
124 cf. Alan Galloway, *The Cosmic Christ*, Harper, 1951. Note also that both Elizabeth Johnson (*Ask the Beasts: Darwin and the God of Love*, Bloomsbury, 2014) and Christopher Southgate (*The Groaning of Creation*, John Knox, 2008) have extended discussions on the meaning of the redemption of non-human creatures.

martyrdom of Peter in exactly these terms: 'He said this to indicate the kind of death by which he would glorify God' (21:19).

Remarkably, Jesus indicates that the community of disciples will not only share God's glory, but also share the unity that the Son has with the Father 'The glory that you have given me I have given them, so that they may be one, as we are one' (17:22). This is spelled out in terms of the disciples 'being where Jesus is' so that they 'may see my glory' (17:24).

The whole earth is full of his glory

Centuries before Christ, the psalmist looking forward to the day of God's restoration and salvation, says: 'Faithfulness will spring up from the ground, and righteousness will look down from the sky. The LORD will give what is good, and our land will yield its increase.' On that day, he wrote, 'Steadfast love and faithfulness will meet; righteousness and peace [shalom] will kiss each other.' God's salvation is coming, he tells us, so that 'God's glory may dwell in our land.'[125]

As in Isaiah's vision of the holy presence of God in the temple, the angels cry out: 'the whole earth is full of his glory.'[126]

---

125 Psalm 85:9–13.
126 Isaiah 6:3.

Part III

Walking Wisdom's Way

Part III draws out some implications of following Jesus in the Way of Wisdom, and into a life which is 'fully alive'. 'Shalom' means well-being in all our relationships – with God, with others, with our environment, within ourselves. It is God's purpose to heal and renew all things, overcoming the 'darkness' of 'the world' with the light of truth. The conclusion of the Gospel in Jesus' death and resurrection leads into the gift of his Spirit who energizes a new community of disciples to continue the life of Jesus in God's world. It is within such a community that we discern the way of wisdom. This will give us some moral and social pointers to finding some Christian perspectives on equity, sustainability and economic justice. It will guide us in our Christian discipleship.

> *[God's] wisdom is made ours because it is the light in which we see light, and learn thereby to inherit all things; the exemplar and original of our wisdom, the fountain and pattern of all our joys, the author and inventor of all our delights, the end and sum of all our desires, the means of all our felicity, our very blessedness and glory.*

Thomas Traherne, *The Way to Blessedness*, 1675

Chapter Seven

Fullness: Shalom

- Jesus' incarnation, life, death and resurrection have opened up a new age, a new Way.

- Following Jesus is Wisdom's Way into a life that is 'fully alive' – described as 'eternal life' and 'knowing God'.

- There are many contemporary 'ways' offering fulfilment: the quest for material wealth, economic growth, welfare, beauty, virtue, happiness.

- The Way of Jesus includes much that is good in these, but offers something deeper and fuller. The biblical word is 'shalom': well-being in all our relationships – with God, with others, with our environment, within ourselves.

- Some examples of 'doing shalom'.

Wisdom incarnate changed everything

The incarnation of God in Jesus Christ changed everything. His birth brought heaven and earth together; his life and confrontation with 'the world,' culminating in his death, overcame all worldly powers. His resurrection inaugurated a new age, a new creation. His gift of the Spirit drew together a new community of believers to be with him and live his life in this world. This community of Christ's people, as we will explore in chapter 11, is God's gift to the world to share in God's mission to bring healing to the whole of creation. It is within such a community that we can discover who we are, what is our destiny, what it means to be fully alive and to find the resources to cope. Jesus has opened a new Way of living in God's world. His resurrection gives us hope.

Walking Wisdom's way: following Jesus

Many features of 'life in its fullness' are seen in practice in the human encounters of Jesus. Many reflect Wisdom themes: bread, light, gate, way, life, truth, vine. God's Wisdom, which means the rational ordering of things, is also the practical guidance needed for living and coping in this world.

This chapter explores further that practical Wisdom. We begin by looking at what John means by 'fullness'.

The word *pleroma* is used only once by John, in 1:16: 'from his *full-ness* have we all received, grace upon grace'. There it means something like completeness, sufficiency, having a full complement of grace. When, later in John 10:10, Jesus speaks about 'fullness' it means something further: 'I came that they may have life, and have it abundantly.' Here the text (using the word *perisson*) has the sense of abundance, even 'superfluity', of life: perhaps 'exceedingly, beyond measure'. Picture a children's party table full of food, and on a side table there is a chocolate fountain in which liquid chocolate is pumped to the top, to fill the topmost of several bowls, each lower bowl wider than the one above. Not only is the top bowl filled, the liquid chocolate overflows to fill the bowl below, and that one yet again overflows until the whole fountain is flowing with chocolate. Fullness to overflowing. Jesus uses the word *perisson* to speak about the sort of life that is not only full, but overflows in blessing to others. John's Gospel frequently refers to this as 'eternal life'.

Eternal Life

'Eternal life' is one of the Beloved Disciple's favourite phrases. It probably reminded his readers of the prophecy of Daniel 12:2:

> Many of those who sleep in the dust of the earth shall awake, some to everlasting life, and some to shame and everlasting contempt.

'Eternal life' carries the sense of 'the life of the age to come'. On Jesus' lips, that future hope also encompasses a present reality. 'Eternal life' now, an anticipation of the life of the age to come, is a gift in the present time, in this world, for those united with Jesus. Jesus speaks of giving 'springs of living water gushing up to eternal life' (4:13f.). He links eternal life both to his Word, and also to the Spirit: 'anyone who hears my word and believes him who sent me has eternal life, and does not come under judgement, but has passed from death to life' (5:24); 'the spirit gives life ... The words that I have spoken to you are spirit and life' (6:63). At one point, the disciples ask Jesus: 'To whom can we go? You have the words of eternal life' (John 6:68).

Eternal life is a gift. 'God so loved the world that he gave his only Son, so that everyone who believes in him may not perish but may have eternal life' (3:16; cf. 10:28).

'Eternal life' in John is rather like 'kingdom of God' in Matthew, Mark and Luke. We can be part of God's kingdom now: it is 'among us' in the presence of Jesus, but can be fully known when the kingdom comes in its fullness in God's future. Eternal life, then, is not only a matter of 'life after death', but of life before death: the reality of abiding in God's love, and living in God's joy now. It is knowing God in this way that holds us in all the uncertainties, struggles and conflicts of living in this anxious, still far from perfect world.

Knowing God
In his high priestly prayer, Jesus explains more fully what 'eternal life' means. It is a way of speaking about 'knowing God.'

> And this is eternal life, that they may know you, the only true God, and Jesus Christ whom you have sent. (John 17:3)

Once again, John's readers would realize the resonance with some of the Hebrew writings. The prophets warn the people: 'My people are destroyed for lack of knowledge' (Hosea 4:6), but also look forward in hope: 'The earth will be filled with the knowledge of the glory of the LORD, as the waters cover the sea' (Habakkuk 2:14). The writer of Proverbs said: 'by knowledge the righteous are delivered' (Proverbs 11:9). And again: 'Trust in the LORD with all your heart, and do not rely on your own insight. In all your ways acknowledge him, and he will make straight your paths. Do not be wise in your own eyes; fear the LORD, and turn away from evil. It will be a healing for your flesh and a refreshment for your body' (Proverbs 3:5–8).

John's Gospel builds on this when Jesus says: 'You will know the truth, and the truth will make you free' (John 8:32). He links knowledge of God with knowledge of himself: 'If you know me, you will know my Father also' (John 14:7).

Following Jesus: the Way
Another of the Beloved Disciple's themes is 'following Jesus'. It comes frequently throughout the Gospel. In chapter 1, two disciples were listening to John the Baptist as Jesus walked past, and 'they followed Jesus' (1:37). In Galilee, Jesus saw Philip and said to him, 'Follow me' (1:43). Later on, when Jesus is saying I AM the light of the world, he continues: 'Whoever follows me will never walk in darkness but will have the light of life' (8:12). The sheep 'follow' the Good Shepherd (10:4,5,27), knowing his voice. 'Whoever serves me must follow me' (12:26). And the Gospel ends with the risen Jesus saying to Simon Peter, now restored in love and friendship having earlier betrayed Jesus: 'Follow me' (John 21:19,22). Following Jesus is following his Way.

It was Thomas, confused by the warning that Jesus' time with the disciples was coming to an end, who said to Jesus, 'Lord, we do not know where you are going. How can we know the way?' This prompted the response from Jesus: 'I AM the way, and the truth, and the life. No one comes to the Father except through me' (John 14:5f.).

The word translated 'Way' usually means 'road' or 'journey', but sometimes means 'custom'. In some of the Wisdom literature it meant something like 'finding a direction in life'. 'The LORD gives wisdom ... preserving the way of his faithful ones' (Proverbs 2:6–8). 'It will save you from the way of evil' (Proverbs 2:13). Some Christians spoke about their faith as 'the Way' (Acts 9:2). Jesus' answer to Thomas probably means first that the way Jesus is taking, which leads him to suffering, death and resurrection, is the path which lies ahead for Jesus' followers. It also means that the direction in life, the 'way of life', the fullness of life seen in Jesus, can be God's gift to the followers of Jesus' Way, as they believe into him.

Following Jesus, receiving the fullness of eternal life he gives, and coming to know God through him, is Wisdom's Way into being fully alive in God's world. It is the Way of following Jesus in his suffering love, abundant grace, compassion and self-giving service.

Contemporary recipes for fullness of life

Before exploring further the Way of Jesus, we will take note of some of the ways to fulfilment and flourishing on offer in our contemporary culture. There are several.

Some seek it in material wealth.[127] Of course, in order to flourish, humanity needs the basic resources for sustenance, shelter, security – indeed a certain level of material well-being. There are parts of the world where these things are much more available than elsewhere – and parts of the world, including the UK, where human poverty is a shameful disgrace and its existence a judgement on the greed of many others of us. Yet there is a widespread assumption that over and above basic needs, more wealth inevitably leads to more happiness. Richard Wilkinson and Kate Pickett have demonstrated convincingly that this is not the case.[128]

Others assume that fulfilment depends on economic growth – a view

---

127 Critically discussed in Michael Sandel's prophetic book, *What Money Can't Buy*, Penguin Books, 2012.
128 Richard Wilkinson and Kate Pickett, *The Spirit Level: why equality is better for everyone* (Allen Lane, 2009), Penguin, 2010, p.43. Wilkinson and Pickett argue that while up to a certain level rising income corresponds to greater human health and well-being, raising incomes further does not have corresponding benefits. In fact, rising income above a certain level can lead to physical and mental ill health and many related social ills. Rather than it being the overall wealth of a society that determines its well-being, it is how that wealth is distributed within the society that matters. The more equally wealth is distributed, the more healthy the society is shown to be. There is a psychological factor in this: 'greater inequality seems to heighten people's social evaluation anxieties by increasing the importance of social status'.

helpfully dismissed by Tim Jackson in *Prosperity without Growth*,[129] in which he argued for a wholly fresh approach to economics.

Some describe fulfilment it in terms of 'welfare'. The humanist biologist E. O. Wilson called on evangelical Christians to join in 'saving life on earth'.[130] Wilson argued that despite the fundamental differences he sees between science and evangelical theology, 'human welfare is at the centre of our thought.'

Fiona Reynolds[131] is one of many recent writers who have commented on the fact that 'in the last fifty years we have been drifting towards an ever more materialistic and instrumental view of the world and our lives'. For her, fulfilment is found in the quest for beauty, justice and human values.

One common understanding of human flourishing is in terms of happiness. Richard Layard[132] draws on neuroscience, psychology, sociology and philosophy as well as economics, to explore what Jeremy Bentham called the Greatest Happiness principle – the policy of ensuring that the greatest number of people are in a state of feeling happy. He concluded that factors affecting happiness (family, finance, work, community, health, personal freedom) had to be set within an 'overall purpose wider than oneself'. Eric Lambin, in *An Ecology of Happiness*,[133] explored how environmental degradation affects human happiness, and showed a strong link between contented human beings, and a healthy environment. However, it is worth noting that some approaches which encourage mindfulness as a route to well-being refer to the 'happiness trap' in which, too often, the more we strive to be happy, the less happy we become[134].

Robert and Edward Skidelsky's *How Much is Enough: The love of money and the case for the good life*[135] argues that progress should be measured by such elements of 'the good life' as health, security, respect, personality, harmony with nature, friendship and leisure.

Some writers follow Aristotle's view of human flourishing in terms of virtue, emphasizing the importance of moral values to determine what is good.

Important as many, if not all, of the above approaches to human well-being and fulfilment may be, the Hebrew Scriptures provide a richer word – *shalom* – which describes the link not only between

---

129 Professor Tim Jackson served as Economics Commissioner with the UK's Sustainable Development Commission until it was sadly disbanded by the Coalition Government in 2011.
130 E. O. Wilson, *Creation,* Norton and Co. 2006.
131 Fiona Reynolds, *The Fight for Beauty,* One World, 2016.
132 Richard Layard, *Happiness: lessons from a new science,* Penguin, 2011.
133 Eric Lambin, *An Ecology of Happiness,* University of Chicago Press, 2012, p.160.
134 cf. Russ Harris, *The Happiness Trap* Robinson, 2007/8.
135 Allen Lane, 2012.

human welfare and the welfare of all God's creation, but does so in terms of the health and well-being of all our relationships – to God, to one another, to ourselves, to our natural environment, to all of God's other creatures.

Shalom: the ways of Wisdom

The Hebrew word 'shalom' is usually translated 'peace'. It is a word used at one point to describe the ways of Wisdom in the Book of Proverbs:

> *Happy are those who find wisdom ... her ways are ways of pleasantness,*[136] *and all her paths are peace.* (Proverbs 3:13,17)

'Shalom', translated 'peace', is used several times by Jesus in John's Gospel. Much of what is good in our contemporary quest for prosperity, health, beauty and welfare can find a home within 'shalom'. 'Shalom' is a word that carries a large weight of meaning. John's Gospel clearly assumes this weight of meaning when using the word 'peace'.

> *Peace I leave with you; my peace I give to you.* (John 14:27)
> *Jesus 'came and stood among them and said, 'Peace be with you.'* (John 20:19,20)

Getting our bearings on shalom

To get our bearings, we need to go back once again to the Hebrew Bible. Shalom is first of all something to do with the character of God.

The Lord *is* peace! So Gideon's altar to the Lord was built to testify (Judges 6:24). The Lord *brings* peace, as Isaiah's vision of the coming King makes clear.

> *For every boot of the tramping warrior in battle tumult and every garment rolled in blood will be burned as fuel for the fire. For to us a child is born ... and his name shall be called ... Prince of Peace. Of the increase of his government and of peace there will be no end.* (Isaiah 9:5ff., ESVUK)

The peace of the Messiah's kingdom is not simply the ending of hostilities, not simply the burning of the warrior's boot. The kingdom of peace is established and upheld '*with justice and with righteousness*' (Isaiah 9:7). 'Shalom' covers much more than the absence of war. Shalom is rather the absence of disorder at all levels of life and relationship, and includes *everything God gives for human well-being* in all areas of life. It means well-being in the widest sense of the word.

---

136 cf. 'like a honeycomb, sweetness to the soul and health to the body' (Proverbs 16:24).

When the Lord brings peace, there is *justice for all*. Shalom is linked inseparably with justice. The psalmist has a wonderful vision of the time when God's glory dwells in the land, heaven and earth come together, the land and its people flourish and 'justice and peace will embrace' (Psalm 85:9–13, paraphrase). The flourishing of shalom includes *prosperity for all and deliverance for the oppressed* – this is pictured in the opening words of Psalm 72 about a godly king:

> *Give the king your justice, O God, and your righteousness to a king's son. May he judge your people with righteousness, and your poor with justice. May the mountains yield prosperity for the people, and the hills, in righteousness. May he defend the cause of the poor of the people, give deliverance to the needy, and crush the oppressor ... In his days may righteousness flourish and peace abound, until the moon is no more.* (Psalm 72:1–7)

To do shalom means *living in justice and righteousness*.

Where there is shalom, there is *health* ('Peace, peace, to the far and the near, says the LORD; and I will heal them', Isaiah 57:19). Shalom describes *conciliation* (in Genesis 26:29), and *contentedness* (in Genesis 15:15 and Psalm 4:8). When the peace of the Lord is present, there are *good relationships* between nations and people (1 Chronicles 12:17–18). Shalom has a communal and community vision. God's shalom has both a personal and social aspect. 'Seek the welfare [shalom] of the city where I have sent you into exile, and pray to the LORD on its behalf, for in its welfare you will find your welfare' (Jeremiah 29:7).

Specifically, shalom is linked to the time when the Messiah comes, and all nations are brought to *enjoy God's justice and God's peace through walking in God's ways.*

> *In days to come the mountain of the LORD's house shall be established as the highest of the mountains ... all the nations shall stream to it. Many peoples shall come and say, 'Come, let us go up to the mountain of the LORD ... that he may teach us his ways and that we may walk in his paths.' For out of Zion shall go forth instruction, and the word of the LORD from Jerusalem. He shall judge between the nations, and shall arbitrate for many peoples; they shall beat their swords into ploughshares, and their spears into pruning-hooks; nation shall not lift up sword against nation, neither shall they learn war any more. O house of Jacob, come, let us walk in the light of the LORD!* (Isaiah 2:2–5)

So Shalom is part of the *good news of salvation under the kingly rule of God*:

> *How beautiful upon the mountains are the feet of the messenger who announces peace, who brings good news, who announces salvation, who says to Zion, 'Your God reigns.'* (Isaiah 52:7)

Indeed, the prophetic vision grows, in the whole of Isaiah chapter 61, to a celebration of the good news of God's deliverance, and the establishment of *liberty, joy, righteousness, sustenance, justice, flourishing.* And in chapter 65, he speaks of a 'new heaven and a new earth' in which that vision comes to its fulfilment.

The blessings of God's shalom are not only for people, however. God's covenant of shalom is a *covenant with the whole of creation*:

> This is like the days of Noah to me: Just as I swore that the waters of Noah would never again go over the earth, so I have sworn that I will not be angry with you and will not rebuke you. For the mountains may depart and the hills be removed, but my steadfast love shall not depart from you, and **my covenant of peace** shall not be removed, says the LORD, who has compassion on you. (Isaiah 54:9–10)

This recalls God's covenant with Noah, in which God speaks of 'the covenant that I make between me and you and every living creature that is with you, for all future generations' (Genesis 9:12).

Shalom includes a *healthy relationship with the natural environment, which also flourishes* under Messiah's rule:

> For you shall go out in joy, and be led back in peace; and the mountains and the hills before you shall burst into song, and all the trees of the field shall clap their hands. Instead of the thorn shall come up the cypress; instead of the brier shall come up the myrtle; and it shall be to the LORD for a memorial, for an everlasting sign that shall not be cut off. Thus says the LORD: Maintain justice, and do what is right, for soon my salvation will come, and my deliverance be revealed. (Isaiah 55:12–56:1)

In their book *Christianity, Climate Change and Sustainable Living,*[137] Nick Spencer and Robert White identify what they call 'the fullest vision the Bible has to offer of sustainable living' from these chapters (40–66) in Isaiah. They argue that social and environmental sustainability are closely linked, that the moral issue of seeking a sustainable way of living is rooted in the faithfulness of God, and the hope that faithfulness inspires. They show that sustainable living is a source of joy. And yet they rightly emphasize that shalom, indeed the wholeness of all creation, is achieved through self-sacrifice – and they point forwards to the cross of Christ.

Shalom, then, is about *being in right relationship*, but it is more even than that. Shalom includes also *the enjoyment and liberation, all-round health and satisfaction of being in right relationships* – with God and with neighbour, with oneself and with one's environment. Shalom is

---

137 Nick Spencer and Robert White, *Christianity, Climate Change and Sustainable Living*, SPCK, 2007.

peace with justice.

All this background is part of the heavy weight that the Hebrew concept of shalom carried, and to which the New Testament looks back. When Jesus begins his ministry, he not only models aspects of God's shalom by feeding the hungry, healing the sick, showing God's welcome to those whom others have excluded, and caring for all in a variety of needs. He is 'our shalom' as the writer to the Ephesians puts it: *Christ is our peace* (Ephesians 2:14).

Various places the New Testament pick up Isaiah's vision of a new heaven and a new earth in which God's justice dwells, and relates this to the life and death and resurrection of Jesus Christ. Human flourishing now for Christian disciples is to be caught up into the life of the risen Christ, who is the 'Lord of peace' (2 Thessalonians 3:16). It is to 'live in peace; and the God of love and peace will be with you' (2 Corinthians 13:11). It is to 'pursue what makes for peace' (Romans 14:19). And the Christian call, as we shall see, to love our neighbours, to seek for justice in all our affairs and to care for God's earth, means that we are *called to live in such a way that makes for the shalom of all people, and for all God's creation*. This does not imply that everything in the world is fine: far from it. We have discussed 'creation in jeopardy', and in our next chapter will note what John's Gospel means by 'the world', set over against the purposes of God. But even within the constraints of a broken world that has not yet become the kingdom of Christ's glory, there is a distinctive Christian vision of human flourishing captured by the word 'shalom'.

The flourishing described by shalom, then, includes: our attitude towards the natural world; the ability to love; to enjoy the respect of our peers; to contribute useful work; and to have a sense of belonging and trust in the community. It is seen in how we measure up in relation to health, security, personality, harmony with nature, friendship and leisure. It is damaged by an unequal distribution of wealth in society, and the consequent injustice and instability this brings. It is damaged by the pursuit of immediate wants instead of the satisfaction of genuine needs. Flourishing includes a recovery of a sense of human freedom, human values and an overall purpose that is bigger than we are. And it places all this within the context of a relationship with God, through Jesus Christ, and empowered by the life of God's spirit. Shalom is peace with justice.

Wolterstorff is right, therefore, when he says: 'Can the conclusion be avoided that not only is Shalom God's cause in the world, but that all who believe in Jesus will, along with him, engage in the world of Shalom? Shalom is both God's cause in the world and our human calling.'[138]

The Christian calling to follow the Way of Jesus, that is to love God and our neighbour, to seek justice in all our affairs and to care for God's creation on God's behalf, together with the gift of living within the wide-open space of God's joy, despite all struggle, suffering and uncertainties, brings another whole dimension to the meaning of human flourishing. We could call following this Way 'doing shalom'.

Shalom and the common good

Part of the calling to 'do shalom' is to work for what Pope Francis, in keeping with a long tradition of biblically based Catholic social teaching, called 'the common good'. His encyclical is subtitled 'On Care for our Common Home'. He describes the common good as 'the sum of those conditions of social life which allow social groups and their individual members relatively thorough and ready access to their own fulfillment'.[139] The common good involves respect for the human person, the welfare of society including the family, and a stand for basic human rights and against all injustice.

Two significant recent writers about the common good, Herman Daly and John Cobb, say that they believe 'that an economics for the common good is what ecological humanism calls for, and even more what stewardship of creation calls for'. Their major call for a paradigm shift in current economic thinking is entitled *For the Common Good: Redirecting the economy toward community, the environment and a sustainable future.*[140]

Daly and Cobb comment on the ancient distinction, drawn by Aristotle, between 'chrematistics' on the one hand, and 'oikonomia' and the other. The former is about the 'science of wealth' – about the management of money. This is more or less what the modern discipline of economics has become. The latter, 'oikonomia', however, is about the 'management of the household', which – if we include 'the larger community of the land', means 'shared values, resources, biomes, institutions, language and history – an "economics for the community"'.[141]

It is important, in the light of our earlier exploration of God's Creation, to underline that the concept of 'Common Good' must now refer not only to human society, but also to the well-being of all creation.

---

138 Nicholas Wolterstorff, *Until Justice and Peace Embrace,* Eerdmans, 1983, p.72.
139 Second Vatican Council, Pastoral Constitution on the Church in the Modern World, *Gaudium et Spes,* 26.
140 Herman E. Daly and John B. Cobb, Jr., *For the Common Good: Redirecting the economy toward community, the environment and a sustainable future,* Beacon Press, 1989.
141 Herman E. Daly and John B. Cobb Jr., op. cit., p.138.

This is why Pope Francis refers to 'Our Common Home'. We human beings need the whole of the rest of the created order within what Moltmann calls 'The Community of Creation' just as the rest of creation needs humanity to care for it in God's name. 'Common Good' must now be understood to include the whole of the created order.

Equity, ecology and economy belong together

'The words eco-logy and eco-nomy of course both come from the same root, *oikos*, which means – as we have seen – home or household, and, as many contemporary writers including Archbishop Rowan Williams[142] have emphasized, they belong inseparably together.

Shalom points us to an approach to human flourishing that is in the direction of community and of a sustainable future for the whole environment of God's earth. It recognizes the interplay of social, ethical, economic and spiritual factors, and understands that human well-being and the well-being of all God's creatures belong inseparably together. We and all God's creation are dependent on God for life and the means of life – and interdependent with each other. Human flourishing depends on, and is part of, the sustainable flourishing of all God's creation, our 'common home'.

'Doing shalom' in today's world

Shalom is God's gift to us in Jesus Christ. Doing shalom is following Jesus' Way of loving God and our neighbour, seeking justice in all our affairs and caring for God's creation. We will return several times to this theme in later chapters. It is worth at this point offering a few brief examples of what doing shalom implies in relation to our concerns for equity, for sustainability and for climate change.

(i) Shalom means restraining inequalities

To recapture the values of shalom, and healthy and health-giving relationships between ourselves and God, ourselves and others, and ourselves and our environment, means seeking what St Paul called 'concern for the interests of others'. This means a reshaping of all our values in both personal and corporate spirituality, so that they are to do with personal relationships – interpersonal and interdependent – rather than exclusively with self-interest.

Social inclusion is one of the primary ingredients of a sustainable social system, and yet today – although absolute poverty is thankfully diminishing – there are still many desperately poor people in the world: even in the UK, and elsewhere in the world. As I write this, people in

---

142 Rowan Williams, *Faith in the Public Square*, Bloomsbury, 2012, chapters 17–18.

Aleppo are dying of starvation. The gap between the most advantaged and the most disadvantaged people is growing at a depressingly high rate. Jesus' gift of peace, shalom, means that we cannot 'live well' until we have tackled poverty, exclusion and inequality.[143]

(ii) Shalom will need to build sustainable communities
Doing shalom is about the way we live corporately together in the world.

(a) Local communities
The Transition Town movement is one of a number of examples of local communities seeking to live sustainably. It began in Ireland, and now numbers hundreds of similar initiatives worldwide. It is helping large numbers of communities to think about the impact that their life-styles are having on the environment, and provides encouragement and incentives for local initiatives. The Transition Town of Totnes in Devon developed in 2005, to give one example, and sought to develop resilience through systems of local energy and food supplies. Some local communities are seeking to be wholly self-sustaining. Others, through developing farmers' markets, more effective local democracy, local currency, local renewable energy supplies and so on, are becoming increasingly sustainable. Many Christian communities are already involved in the transition movement.[144]

(b) Urban communities
The transition to sustainable living in large urban communities presents very different challenges. Many of our cities have over the last few decades become hugely dependent on automotive transport – from cars for work, to diesel trucks for delivery of goods – and the cost in air pollution has been enormous. Much urban development happened without planning for human needs such as open spaces, schools, churches, graveyards, community centres and so on, though in many places changes in good directions are now happening. To seek 'the shalom of the city' means planning urban centres to be resilient and sustainable communities with a proper relationship between city dwelling and rural food production, with a recognition that cities are often places of great inequality and where the gaps between rich

---

143 cf. Joseph Stiglitz's major work, *The Price of Inequality*, Allen Lane, 2012. The former Chief Economist at the World Bank illustrates the impact on inequality on societies in terms of higher crime, problems of physical health, mental illness, lower achievement levels and shorter life expectancy. He provides a strong critique of free-market economic theories that, he says, produce instability and tend towards wealth accumulating in the hands of only the few. He offers suggestions for a more just and more equal society that equates with a stronger and more stable economy.

144 cf. Timothy Gorringe and Rosie Backham, *Transition Movement for Churches: a prophetic imperative for today*, Canterbury Press, 2013.

and poor are most marked. For healthy living, issues such as pollution, waste disposal, congestion, adequate planning, affordable energy, health care and community provision have to be dealt with. As Jeffrey Sachs puts it: 'Sustainable cities are economically productive, socially (and politically) inclusive, and environmentally sustainable. In other words, they must promote efficient economic activities, ensure that all citizens can benefit from them, and must do so in a way to preserve the biodiversity, safe air and water, and physical health and safety of the citizens.'[145]

(iii) Restraining population growth
To live well and sustainably on a finite planet raises questions about how many people there are and where they live.

Some people argue that worries about population are overblown: technology will ensure enough food for everyone. Others, despairingly, say the opposite: we are on course for major global catastrophe, mass starvation and increasing violence in the struggle for diminishing resources. In his book, *Population 10 Billion: The coming demographic crisis and how to survive it,* Professor Danny Dorling gives a more measured view.[146] He says that it looks as though we are on course for an increase in population to between 9 and 10 billion people by 2100, for which current food production and energy supplies cannot cope. As Dorling rightly says: 'If greed prevails, we're probably doomed.' The problem is much more about over-consumption by the rich in the world than it is about over-population in the poorer parts of the world.

We should not immediately think that reduction in fertility rates solves our environmental crisis. The link between fertility and climate change is complicated. The lowest fertility areas of the world tend to be the wealthiest, with highest consumption of fossil fuels, and other resources, and highest impact on climate change. High fertility areas tend to be the poorest, causing least damage to the climate. We cannot make an easy equation, therefore, between population change and environmental impact.

However, even if population growth were to stabilize in decades to come, there is still an urgent problem about the present and immediate future: the problem of justice, of equality, of equitable sharing of the earth's resources. Though rightly opposed to any coercive approach to contraception, many Christians argue for the importance of campaigns for reproductive health and for voluntary family planning.

---

145 Jeffrey Sachs, *The Age of Sustainable Development,* Columbia, 2015, p.366.
146 Danny Dorling, *Population: 10 Billion,* Constable, 2013.

This is right, not only because of population size in the future, but as part of 'doing shalom' in the quest for sustainability, equity and justice now.

(iv) Responding to the threat of damaging climate change: clean energy

There is a very great deal, at personal, local, national and global levels, needed in response to the necessity of mitigating for and adapting to climate change. Climate justice is part of shalom. We mention just one factor at this point: the need to work for clean energy.

We have for a very long time been getting our energy from the sun by way of coal, oil and gas – fossil fuels which have lain in the earth for millennia, having derived initially from photosynthesis and then the death of plants and animals. This has been of inestimable benefit to human civilization, and has enabled the development of industrialization across the world, and the alleviation of extreme poverty in many places.

The downside of burning fossil fuels, we all now know, is that this is a primary driver of climate change, and if we are to achieve the internationally agreed targets for reduction in carbon emissions, we have to stop burning coal, stop drilling for oil and gas, stop fracking for shale gas – and do so urgently.

If poorer parts of the world, and future generations, are to be 'fully alive', and the richer parts of the world are to continue to have the possibility to live well, a low- or zero-carbon energy supply is crucial, and becomes a question of justice/shalom. If the rich West has taken generations to develop and achieve its present economic level, the poorer parts of the world need their opportunity equally to grow and achieve, but to do so without causing the damage that we in the West have caused. It is urgent both that we move quickly to renewable energy supply, and also that the West takes a major share of the global costs of doing so.

Thankfully there are very encouraging signs – at least in industry, if not yet in government circles. There is a faster than predicted fall in the cost of renewable energy, especially solar, and lower installation costs than feared. There is growing interest in electrical energy storage, as new manufacturing capacity develops, removing problems of intermittency. Smart grids can apparently be made to work effectively with renewable energy, supported by storage and greater connectivity.[147]

147 A major report for the European Union was published in 2010, examining the economic, environmental and social benefits of their vision of a 100% renewable energy system for the EU by 2050. And the potential for one region in the UK was explored in a report commissioned from The Resilience Centre by the MEP for the South West, Molly Scott Cato: 'How to meet the region's energy needs through renewable energy generation.' cf. http://ec.europa.eu/clima/consultations/

Climate justice is part of 'doing shalom'.

(v) The question of Eco-system services

There is one recent academic approach among ecologists in trying to think 'ecology, economy and equity' systemically together. It is the concept of 'Eco-system services,' and it is controversial. The project began in the year 2000 when the UN Secretary General, Kofi Annan, called for The Millennium Ecosystem Assessment to study the benefits which nature provides for human well-being. Numerous studies and reports have contributed to an assessment which recognizes how much nature provides for us for free: such provisions as food, water, fuel; such supportive resources as nutrient cycling and soil function; regulatory provisions for climate, floods, disease, water purification and so on – and also cultural benefits: aesthetic, spiritual, educational and recreational. These are some of the benefits that human beings receive for free from eco-systems.

One of the huge positive results of this Millennium Assessment has been the education of policymakers to understand something of our human dependence on nature, and the importance of natural resources for our security, health and other aspects of living a good life. The concept becomes controversial, however, when related to economic values, and the assumption that 'the environment' needs somehow to be understood as part of 'the economy.' There are positive dimensions to this, of course, as policymakers – so frequently operating wholly within an economics framework – are enabled, by 'putting a price on nature' to make judgments between competing priorities for limited resources. What would be the financial cost of losing bees and other pollinators by cutting down hedgerows and wild-flower meadows, with corresponding loss of flowers, seeds, fruit, compared to the economic benefit to industrial agriculture? How do we work out the balance in nature between protection of bird species and the resultant effects on insects? The increase of attention being given to Natural Capital[148], that is 'what nature gives us for free', is based on the belief that ultimately the value of nature is its usefulness for people. This sort of approach is given short shrift by commentators such as George Monbiot who argued in a lecture in 2014 that 'putting a price on nature' is a 'neoliberal road to ruin'[149] because this whole approach is to 'harness the natural world to the economic growth that has been

docs/0005/registered/91650013720-46_european_renewable_energy_council_en.pdf and http://mollymep.org.uk/wp-content/uploads/The-power-to-transform-the-South-West_FINAL1.pdf
148 See, for example, Dieter Helm *Natural Capital: Valuing the Planet,* Yale 2015
149 The speech was reported in *The Guardian,* 24 July 2014.

destroying it.' Furthermore, what would we think of the rest of nature that does not present any clear benefit to us humans – does that cease to have value? Would we only protect biodiversity that benefits human beings?

From our earlier reflections on God's creation and our human role within it, we would argue not that the environment needs to be understood as part of the economy, but rather the other way round: the economy (now understood in terms primarily of finance) is essentially part of the environment, understood as the fundamental economy on which all God's 'household' depends. Further, rather than believing that nature is there primarily for us – a return to Francis Bacon's mistake – we argue that nature, and we ourselves as part of nature, are there primarily for God. We have several times stressed the interdependence we humans share with all other creatures under God. One of the positive points about Eco-system services is the stress on cultural benefits: educational, recreational, aesthetic and spiritual, on which, of course, it becomes in many cases incongruous to try to put a price on nature. We may value the beauty of a view over the Moors that would be lost by the development of fracking, for example, but not be able to quantify it. However, the anthropocentric direction of much of the work on eco-system services needs to be replaced by the recognition these eco-systems are reciprocal. God calls us to serve nature's well-being as well as providing nature to serve our own. We must not be limited by an economic framework that loses the transcendent values of beauty, truth, justice and love. We are called to a systemic relating of environmental and economic concerns within the calling to do shalom: peace – well-being in all our relationships – with justice and equity.

Alive in God's world: 'eternal life' both now and yet to come

Shalom describes what it is to be fully alive in God's world: the enjoyment of peace with justice. To be alive in God's world, that is, to know the fullness of eternal life by knowing God in Jesus, is to walk the way of God's Wisdom. It is the way of shalom in which equity, economy and ecology are thought through together, in which the environmental agenda and the developmental agenda are not separated. It is closely related to the quest for sustainable living in God's world, and to what a long Christian tradition has called 'the common good'.

The enjoyment of the freedom that shalom with justice brings can be substantially if not fully found even in a world of injustice, disappointment, ill-health and pain. It is grace that, we shall see, holds on to us in all uncertainties and through suffering and sacrifice sometimes, yet in which there is strengthening joy. It is the 'life in its fullness' of which John's Gospel speaks, the 'eternal life' of God's kingdom through knowing God, that can be experienced in some measure now and fully in the life to come. It is the fullness of God's life that we see in Jesus, the only Son of God the Father. It is the fullness of life that the crucified and risen Jesus gives in the power of God's Spirit to the community of disciples he has drawn together to further God's 'creation project'. It can be lived now on earth in the light of what will be eternal, and includes struggles and uncertainties as well as the wide-open space of God's joy. It can lead to the path of both crucifixion and resurrection. It is summed up as wholeness: peace with justice.

Peace I leave with you; my peace I give to you. (John 14:27)

Chapter Eight

The Darkness of 'The World'

- The Way of Jesus Christ is a way of struggle with 'the World', that is humanity living without reference to God. 'The World' neither acknowledges God nor Jesus, the Son and Word and Wisdom of God. John's Gospel describes 'the World' as 'darkness' that has rejected Christ's 'light'.

- The Gospel depicts Jesus' confrontations with various representatives of 'the World' such as Judeans, Pharisees, Pontius Pilate.

- Behind these struggles is a confrontation with 'the Father of Lies', the 'ruler of this World'; that is the Devil – which we can perhaps discern in our current networks of 'lord-less Powers' (the 'Domination System').

- The Christian communities of the first century were not immune to confrontation with 'the World'. The community of the Beloved Disciple had its own struggles – so does the Christian Church today.

He was in the world, and the world came into being through him; yet the world did not know him. (John 1:10)

The Way of Jesus Christ is fraught with difficulties. For him, it was a road of conflicts leading to crucifixion. For the community of the Beloved Disciple it was a road of division on the inside and persecution from the outside. For both there was opposition from what the Gospel calls 'the World.'

'The World'

We need to be careful here, because some people wrongly think that John's Gospel teaches a very negative approach to 'the World'; so much so that they think the spirituality of the Gospel is primarily about with-drawal from the world into an individual sort of mysticism.[150] This is

---

150 Paul Santmire's classic study of ecology in Christian tradition, *The Travail of Nature,* Fortress Press, 1985, identifies two major motifs: he contrasts the 'ecological motif' of 'nature-affirming' metaphors in the theology of Irenaeus, later Augustine, Francis of Assisi, parts of Calvin and so on, with what he calls the 'spiritual motif' of those whose understanding

what seems to be in mind in Iris Murdoch's novel *The Green Knight*, where we meet Bellamy who had decided in the middle of life's journey 'to abandon the world and become some sort of religious person'. Bellamy draws a contrast between 'living in the world' and being 'some sort of religious person'. The Gospel of John does not make this mistake.

It is true that John's Gospel operates with a sort of dualism, but not a dualism between mind and matter, nor between 'being religious' and 'living in this world'. It is rather a distinction between what the author calls 'this world' and 'the world above.' Both these 'worlds' exist in the same time, both now and in the life to come. We could describe these as 'the world from above' (that is 'from God') and the other as 'the world from below' (that is 'not from God').[151]

However, and rather confusingly, John's Gospel does use *kosmos* in different ways. Sometimes by *kosmos* he means the whole creation, the world of all people, the world God loves ('God so loved the world'). More frequently he means the 'worldliness' of 'the World', which needs to be resisted and overcome. In this more frequent second sense, 'the World' means 'humanity living without reference to God'.[152] And the Gospel tells us something else as well: 'this World', which does not know God, the world to which Jesus' disciples do not belong, is under the power of 'the ruler of this world' (John 12:31). It is that 'ruler' who, the disciples are told, will be 'driven out' (John 12:31) by Jesus. And Jesus encourages his disciples with the words, 'Take courage; I have conquered the world!' (John 16:33).

A hostile 'World'

One significant aspect of the life of Jesus, as John's Gospel tells it, is the increasing opposition that he faces. It culminates in his suffering and death before his resurrection and 'going to the Father'. The community of the Beloved Disciple knew a lot about what striving to live for God in a hostile world was like – and this no doubt significantly influenced John's selection of material for his Gospel. The Gospel itself shows us the struggle of the early Christians against persecution, and the pressures on those within the Christian community to fall away from their faith in Jesus as the Messiah. This is referred to explicitly in 9.22: 'the

---

of the spiritual journey towards God was a journey away from nature. Santmire suggests that the Fourth Gospel falls clearly into the latter category. I want to argue that Santmire is not wholly correct – at least in relation to the Prologue.

151 So Jesus says to the unbelieving Judeans, 'You are from below, I am from above; you are of this world, I am not of this world' (John 8:23). The 'world below' does not know the gift and love of God. By contrast, Jesus' disciples are 'in this world' but not 'of this world'. In Jesus' prayer in John 17:16 he says of his followers, 'They do not belong to the world, just as I do not belong to the world.'

152 It is this contrast to which Rudolph Bultmann refers when we writes of 'the perversion of "creation" into "the world"'. Bultmann, *Theology of the New Testament*, SCM, 1965, 2 vols.

Jews had already agreed that anyone who confessed Jesus to be the Messiah would be put out of the synagogue'. That would be more than enough to tarnish hope. The context from which the Gospel is written includes fear of expulsion from the worshipping community. As David Rensberger put is: 'It was within this situation of conflict, crisis and alienation that the Fourth Gospel was written, and against this background it must be understood.'[153] The concentration later in the Gospel on the importance of mutual love may also indicate that there were divisions within the community, getting in the way of God's mission, which the Beloved Disciple believed he needed to address. Perhaps this is why – even more than the other Gospels – John portrays Jesus' ministry as a confrontation with 'the World' – and gives encouragement to the community in their own struggles: 'Take courage; I have conquered the world!' (John 16:33). The writer often describes 'the World' in the stark contrasts of good and evil, and especially light and darkness.

> *And this is the judgement, that the light has come into the world, and people loved darkness rather than light because their deeds were evil. For all who do evil hate the light and do not come to the light, so that their deeds may not be exposed. But those who do what is true come to the light, so that it may be clearly seen their deeds have been done in God.* (John 3:19–21)

If the Gospel of John, as some have suggested, depicts a sort of trial scene in which Jesus is being defended against the accusations of 'the World', then this chapter brings together some voices for the prosecution. Here, then, are some of the voices of those who stand for the darkness of 'the World'.

Judeans
The Gospel often portrays Jesus in terms of his own confrontation with the Judeans, and sometimes more specifically with the Pharisees. Following some other writers, I translate '*Ioudaioi*' as 'Judeans' rather than 'Jews',[154] to make clear that – despite some claims to the contrary – this Gospel should not be read as anti-Semitic (after all, Jesus himself was a Jew). The 'Judeans', who first appear in John chapter 2 at the Temple, are Jewish people who adhered to the religion of Judea, whether or not they lived there. They would have thought of the Christian community from which John's Gospel was written as one of many dissenting religious groups around Palestine at that time. We

153 David Rensberger, *Overcoming the World*, SPCK, 1988. p.28.
154 There is a huge literature on this point. I am drawing on John Ashton, *Understanding the Fourth Gospel*, Clarendon, 1991, and also Stephen Motyer, *Your Father the Devil*, a new approach to John and the Jews, Paternoster, 1997, and Ruth Edwards, *Discovering John*, SPCK, 2003.

do find some 'Judeans' in Galilee (6:41), so we are not so much talking about where people come from, but more about their political and spiritual allegiance. The 'Ioudaioi' seem primarily to refer to a strict, orthodox 'temple-party' with significant political clout among the people of Judea. The Temple was at the heart of the community, and of the economic life of the nation. Its leaders were important political figures.

The Judeans, it becomes increasingly clear as the Gospel progresses, were against Jesus, and 'looking for an opportunity to kill him' (7:1). For the most part, throughout the Gospel, the Judeans can be taken as representative figures – to stand for 'the World'. The Judeans, then, and the Pharisees among them, are a symbol for 'the World' in which society is organized without belief in Jesus as God's Word, God's Christ: those who live in the darkness of 'the World' rather than in the light of Christ.

Pharisees

The conflict with the Pharisees seems mostly about authority. On whose authority, they ask, is Jesus speaking and acting? Jesus poses a threat to their authority (1:24; 4:1; 7:32f.; 8:3,13; 9:13ff.) and a threat to their security ('if we let him go on like this, everyone will believe in him, and the Romans will come and destroy both our holy place and our nation' 11:46f.; 12:19,42).

So the Gospel story is told as a conflict between Jesus, who claims to speak God's Word with God's authority, and the Judeans and Pharisees, who think they hear God's word through their Scriptures, or their traditions through Moses – which they need to safeguard – or through prophets like John the Baptist, although they do not recognize the authority of God's Word in Jesus (5:33,39–40): 'You search the scriptures because you think that in them you have eternal life; and it is they that testify on my behalf. Yet you refuse to come to me to have life.' Their ultimate understanding of power and authority is not with the Word of God, but with the Roman authorities. There are some, like Nicodemus, a Pharisee, a ruler of the Jews, who seem half-persuaded that Jesus has been sent from God. But he comes to Jesus 'by night', in the dark (John 3:2; the night-time is emphasized again in 19:39). It is in response to Jesus' words to Nicodemus that the Beloved Disciple comments: 'the light has come into the world, and people loved darkness rather than light' (3:19).

'Overcoming the world' is something to do with the questions of power and authority – whose it is and how it is to be exercised. All human relationships are embedded in social structures and therefore engage in the dynamics of power. The question is how to use power in a way that reflects God's character, God's wisdom and God's ways. 'Overcoming the world' is also something to do with bearing witness to the truth, and speaking truth to power.

Persistent murmuring against Jesus
As the Gospel story develops – through the conversation with Nicodemus, Jesus' meeting with the woman of Samaria, healing of the official's son and of the man with the long-term illness by the pool of Bethesda, his feeding of the crowds in Galilee, the calming of the storm on the lake, and teaching at the Festival of Tabernacles in Jerusalem – the murmuring of Jesus' opponents becomes louder and more determined. The opposition to his ministry becomes more obvious and more violent.

The murmuring against Jesus seems to gather momentum from John chapter 6 onwards. It is because he said (in one of his uses of the divine name): 'I AM the Bread of Life', that the Judeans began to complain against him (6:41). The disturbances get louder in chapter 7, where we are told that by then, '[Jesus] did not wish to go about in Judea, because the [Judeans] were looking for an opportunity to kill him' (7:1). In fact, it is at the Festival of Tabernacles in chapter 7 that 'no one would speak openly' about Jesus, for fear of the Judeans (7:13). Quite soon, upset by the crowd's positive reaction to Jesus by their believing in him, and even saying so, the Pharisees sent temple police to arrest Jesus (7:32). Unfortunately for the Pharisees, the temple police seem to have been persuaded by the testimony of the believers, because when the Pharisees complained that they had not in fact arrested Jesus, they replied 'Never has anyone spoken like this!' (7:45–46). Even Nicodemus gets nearer to nailing his colours to the mast by standing up for Jesus on a point of law: 'Our law does not judge people without first giving them a hearing to find out what they are doing, does it?' – but this did not cut much ice with the other Pharisees (7:51). By the time we reach the end of chapter 8, the Judeans pick up stones to throw at Jesus (8:59), and in chapter 10 the same thing happens: 'The Jews took up stone again to stone him' (John 10:31).

The long section of the Gospel between chapter 7 and chapter 10 is marked by reference to Jesus' authority over against that of the Judeans, and by Jesus' claim to be bearing witness to truth. So Jesus spells out his authority: 'My teaching is not mine but his who sent me' (7:16). By contrast, the people of Jerusalem wonder why 'the authorities' do not seem to know that Jesus is the Messiah (7:26). The Gospel is increasingly told as a story of a confrontation between the authority of God revealed in Jesus, and the authorities of 'the World' who 'do not know him'. Jesus' claim to speak the truth provokes another hostile reaction: 'If you continue in my word, you are truly my disciples; and you will know the truth, and the truth will make you free' (8:31–32). Who are you – say the Judeans – to talk about freedom? We are children of Abraham! This leads Jesus to respond that the *true* children of Abraham are those who accept Jesus' word.

Judas

One of the saddest and most poignant lines in the whole Gospel comes towards the end of the story of the gathering of Jesus with his disciples in the Upper Room: 'And it was night.' Jesus has washed the feet of his disciples, including Judas. He has broken bread with the disciples, including Judas. And yet all the while the heart of Judas had been given to 'the ruler of this World' (John 13:2). Jesus understood this, and – without the other disciples realizing what was going on – told Judas to do quickly what he had to do. The others thought that because Judas was the keeper of the common purse, Jesus was perhaps telling him to go and buy what was needed for the festival, or to give some money to the poor. But Jesus had discerned Judas's heart, and the darkness within it. Judas 'immediately went out. And it was night.' Judas misses out on Jesus' teaching to the other disciples of love, of the encouragement to them not to let their hearts be troubled, of his gift of the Spirit, and the gathering together of a community of friends. The next time we hear of Judas is after the great high priestly prayer of Jesus that his followers may 'be with me where I am' – it comes in the garden across the Kidron Valley to which Judas, in betrayal, brings the police and the religious leaders, with lanterns and torches to light their way.

Jesus and Pilate

The clearest example that the confrontations Jesus has with 'the World' are about power and about truth is found in the narrative of Jesus' conversation with Pilate. After Jesus' words with the community of disciples in the Upper Room, and the high priestly prayer given to us in chapter 17, the story moves across the Kidron Valley to a garden, and from there to the courtyard of the high priest and then to Pilate's headquarters, where – early in the morning – Pilate came out to meet Jesus and his accusers. Pilate, Governor of Judea, is another representative figure in the Gospel. Here he stands, as do all the Judeans who were opposed to Jesus, for 'the World': human experience organized and lived without reference to God. Pilate embodies the 'domination system' of the Roman Empire, with its expectation of allegiance, and the worship of Caesar as Lord.

Pilate's first question is 'Are you the King of the Jews?' This takes us to the heart of what Jesus' message has been throughout the Gospel, though not usually expressed in the language of 'the kingdom of God'. Jesus has made clear that he comes from God, speaks from God, acts from God and brings generous, compassionate, sacrificial and loving healing and redeeming grace from God. Jesus is not 'from' this world, but is very much 'in' this world. If his kingdom were 'from this world', then it would show the characteristics of a this-worldly kingdom, and his followers would take up arms to fight for him (18:36). But Jesus' kingdom is not from this world, but from the Father.

The reason Jesus was born and came into 'this world' was, he says, continuing the conversation with Pilate, 'to testify to the truth'. The Prologue describes Jesus as 'the true light, which enlightens everyone' (1:9). He describes himself as the truth: 'I AM the way, and the truth, and the life' (14:6). It is, as we have seen, that by following in Jesus' Way, his disciples will know the truth, and the truth will make them free (8:31f.). 'Everyone who belongs to the truth', continues Jesus in reply to Pilate, 'listens to my voice' (18:37), which prompts the piercing question, 'What is truth?' In a sense, the whole of the Gospel up to this point has been the answer to Pilate's question: the life, teaching, service and testimony of Jesus to the Father's love, grace and compassion and to the Messiah's rule of God's justice and peace and renewal. All this – and all that these huge themes entail – is the truth of Jesus' kingdom.

Then, after an altercation between Pilate and the Judean authorities, Pilate returns to speak to Jesus again: this time about power. 'Do you not know that I have power to release you, and power to crucify you?' (19:10). Jesus' reply is that all power comes from God. We have seen God's power in the gift of new wine in Cana, the healing of the official's son and of the paralyzed man at Bethesda, in feeding the crowds, in stilling the storm on the lake, in the reminder of the provision of manna in the wilderness, in the giving of sight to the blind and the raising of Lazarus from the dead. And we have also learned that such power of God is not seen in dominion or coercion, but in service; not in robes of purple but in a towel and a basin. The power of God is loving service, healing and life-giving – both for people and for Galilean storms. For this is the power of the Creator, before whom Pilate now stands

(19:10f.). Within the fallen world symbolized by Pilate, all power is corrupted and is – as James D. Hunter put it – 'infected by the same tendencies toward self-aggrandizing domination. The natural disposition of all human power is to its abuse. It is this power and the spirit that animates it whose sovereignty Christ came to break.'[155]

Pilate, representing 'the World' organized without reference to God, represents a world lived without God's order and God's Wisdom. It demonstrates in full colour what the Gospel has been saying in many different ways. Although it is possible to live in this world without reference to God, the fullness of human life in this world, and the flourishing of all creation belong in 'another kingdom', with 'another king named Jesus' (Acts 17:7). Supernature and nature together. The earthing of heaven.

James D. Hunter refers to a 'fundamentally different kind of social power' seen in Jesus in his intimacy with and submission to the Father, his rejection of status and reputation, his love for humanity and for creation, and the non-coercive way he dealt with those outside the community of faith – by blessing. 'In contrast to the kingdoms of this world, [Christ's] kingdom manifests power to bless, unburden, serve, heal, mend, restore, liberate.'[156]

'The father of lies'
Behind all the confrontations between Jesus and individual people or groups, there is a deeper, spiritual conflict going on. The fact that the confrontations Jesus faces are about truth and about authority and power is made crystal clear when the Gospel speaks about the devil.

Jesus refers to 'the ruler of this world', the 'father of lies', 'the evil one', as a usurper of authority. He says 'the ruler of this world will be driven out' (12:31). It was 'the devil' that put it into the heart of Judas to betray Jesus, and 'Satan' who 'entered into him' (13:2,27). And it is the 'ruler of this world' who is 'coming' (14:30), Jesus says, as he moves from the Upper Room on the way to Gethsemane. Yet 'the ruler of this world has been condemned' (16:11). Whatever we are to understand by 'the devil', Jesus is clearly indicating an alien power that can confront the authority of God both in people's hearts and in institutional life.

The 'Domination System'
The Dutch theologian Hendrik Berkoff wrote a book in 1953,[157] which

---

155 James D. Hunter, *To Change the World*, Oxford, 2010, p.188.
156 Hunter, op. cit., p.193.
157 Hendrik Berkoff, *Christ and the Powers*, 1953; translated from Dutch for Herald Press, 1962.

has become a classic, referred to by Karl Barth, Walter Wink and John Howard Yoder to name but three significant theologians of the past few decades. He called the book *Christ and the Powers* and it is primarily an exploration of the apostle Paul's handling of what he called 'the powers', 'the rulers of this age', 'the prince of the power of the air', and other similar titles. Berkoff argues that Paul is drawing this terminology from contemporary Jewish apocalyptic writing, but by it he means two things. 'The Powers' are personal, spiritual beings, and they influence events on earth, especially events within nature. In the great text in Romans chapter 8, Paul writes that 'neither death, nor life, nor angels, nor rulers, nor things present, nor things to come, nor powers, nor height, nor depth, nor anything else in all creation, will be able to separate us from the love of God in Christ Jesus our Lord' (Romans 8:38f.). 'Obviously Paul means to name a number of realities, which are a part of our earthly existence, and whose role is one of domination' (Berkoff, p.18). These experienced realities are unmasked and disarmed, Paul argues, by the Cross. 'When the Powers are unmasked, they lose their domination over men's souls, and the jubilant exclamation arises: "Nothing can separate us from the love of God in Christ Jesus!" Yet this rejoicing is also broken, ambiguous. The believer is still but a man' (Berkoff, p.48). He or she is a sinful human being in a world still infected by the domination systems of 'the Powers'. Walter Wink[158] calls the network of Powers in the world 'the Domination System'. 'It is characterized by unjust economic relations, oppressive political realities, biased race relations, patriarchal gender relations, hierarchical power relations, and the use of violence to maintain them all' (Wink, p.39). In other words, behind all these oppressive institutionalized systems there are spiritual powers at work.

'Lordless powers'

In Karl Barth's discussion of the prayer 'Your kingdom come',[159] he refers to what he calls 'lordless powers' to describe the nature of the evil in the world which Christians call upon God to set aside. Sinful humanity, alienated from God, tries to become his own 'lord and master' ('You will be like God', Genesis 3:5). But misused capacities become 'spirits with a life and activity of their own, lordless indwelling forces' (214). 'World history, being the history of man and humanity, of Adamic humanity which has fallen from God, is also the history of innumerable absolutisms of different kinds, of forces that are truly and properly

---

158 Walter Wink, *The Powers that Be*, Doubleday, 1998.
159 Karl Barth, *The Christian Life*, Church Dogmatics, IV.4

man's own, but that have won a certain autonomy, independence, and even superiority in relation to him' (216). Barth lists among the 'lord-less powers', the misuse of government when power breaks loose from law. He refers to Mammon: the material possessions, property and re-sources that have become idols. He comments on various ideologies to which humanity gives loyalty and which then come to possess him. And then Barth lists (for the1960s) the very earthy forces that can be-come dominating powers, such as: technology; the power of 'fashion'; the commercialization of sport; the insatiable quest for pleasure and entertainment; and even the field of transportation which makes life such a rush that we fly past so many things of real value. Today, 50 years later, we might particularly add the growing and unaccountable power of corporate institutions in a globalized world, such as the fossil fuel industry with its grip over humanity's use of natural resources, or the gun lobby in American politics. We might add the idolatry of the free market when it is accorded a power over which we humans are said to have no control. Or the ambiguous effects of a growing social media which can do good, but also very much harm.

When John's Gospel refers to 'the ruler of this world' – or in some places 'the devil' – I think we are to understand the power behind this 'Domination System' or the 'lordless powers' that Wink and Barth de-scribe.

Jesus first refers to the devil in the conversation with the Judeans about children of Abraham. He says to the critical Judeans who are denying Jesus' claim to speak the truth, 'You are from your father the devil ... he is a liar and the father of lies. But because I tell the truth, you do not believe me' (8:44–45).

Whose side are you on?
Jesus' word ('your father, the devil') to the Judeans seems a very harsh statement, one that has too often been used to support the thesis that this Gospel is anti-Semitic. However, as Stephen Motyer has convinc-ingly argued,[160] the way the writer of the Gospel introduced arguments *against* Jesus' Messiahship as well as *in favour* of it, suggests that a significant part of the purpose of the Gospel is to open up a debate – or even a court-room trial scene – with the Judeans. The hope was to con-vince the Judeans about Christian faith. Here is one Jew (Jesus) trying to persuade others (Judeans) of the truth of God. In this chapter of the Gospel, the question for the Judeans was this: 'Is Jesus a false proph-et?' Jesus is making a prophetic appeal about 'true freedom'. First, he

---

160 Stephen Motyer, *Your Father the Devil? a New Approach to John and 'the Jews'*, Paternoster, 1997.

speaks about freedom from slavery (8:34–38), and then about freedom from the devil (8:39–47). In other words, this section is really
about whether or not the Judeans in their confrontation with Jesus are
on the side of God's truth or not. In this moment of confrontation – and
choice – the Judeans are speaking 'out of' a power other than the love
of God and obedience to God's truth. The harsh statement ('your father
the devil') is not then at all about the ultimate judgement of God on
all Jews (as some have wrongly argued), nor is it a criticism of Jewish
religion as such. It is a calling, in the Gospel's context, to the Judeans to
respond to the truth of God as it is in Jesus. It is part of the evangelistic
purpose of the Gospel. It is yet another illustration of the words of the
Prologue 'He came to what was his own, and his own people did not
accept him' (John 1:11). And 'people loved darkness rather than light'
(John 3:19).

The community of disciples in the darkness of 'the World'

Division within the Christian community
It is because of this spiritual conflict, that the Gospel writer emphasizes Jesus' words to his disciples not only that 'the ruler of this world
is coming' (14:30), but also that 'the ruler of this world has been condemned' (16:11). And also, significantly, 'Take courage, I have conquered the world' (16:33).

The Christian community, followers of Jesus, are also nonetheless
themselves to expect hostility from 'the World'. The Gospel was written to encourage them when they too experience conflict in the world.
Jesus said to them: 'In the world you face persecution' (16:33), and
even that they would indeed be put out of the synagogue (16:2), but
this leads to Jesus' strong statement in the Upper Room: 'Be of good
cheer; I have overcome the world.' (16:33, ESV). Again and again Jesus
tells his followers: 'Do not be afraid' (6:20, on the lake); 'Do not let
your hearts be troubled' (14:1,27, in the Upper Room); 'Your hearts
will rejoice' (16:22); 'I have said this to you, so that in me you may have
peace' (16:33).

The Christian community is to find their courage in the face of persecution, their hope in the face of many uncertainties, through Christ's
Word and his presence and the promise of his Spirit. In his prayer to
the Father, Jesus explicitly does not ask God to take his followers out of
the world: 'I am not asking you to take them out of the world, but I ask
you to protect them from the evil one' (17:15). The Christian calling is
rather to be 'sanctified in the truth' so that they may be 'sent into the

world' just as Jesus was sent into the world (17:18). In other words, they 'do not belong to the world' (17:16), but they are 'sent into the world' so that 'the world' may believe that Jesus was sent by the Father (17:21). Yet, after Jesus' death, the disciples still met behind locked doors 'for fear of the [Judeans]' (20:19).

We will explore more in chapter 10 how in John's Gospel the light of Jesus bursts into the confusions of 'the World', scattering the darkness, and bringing light, truth and freedom to the Christian community. First, we will pause to try to identify more clearly some of the 'darknesses' of our contemporary culture.

Chapter Nine

'Keep Yourselves from Idols'

- The First Letter of John ends with a warning against idolatry: the worship of false gods.

- This chapter selects some of the 'false gods' of contemporary culture, which are pointing in a different direction from the Way of Jesus Christ.

- The idolatry of the Market; of autonomous individualism; of misplaced faith in technology; of the consumer culture; of post-truth.

The First Letter of John, most probably written by the author of the Gospel for the same Community of the Beloved Disciple, and likely within the same decade, concludes with a strong affirmation of Christian identity and distinctiveness, but also with a strong warning against idolatry: the worship of false gods.

> We know that we are God's children, and that the whole world lies under the power of the evil one. And we know that the Son of God has come and has given us understanding so that we may know him who is true; and we are in him who is true, in his Son Jesus Christ. He is the true God and eternal life. Little children, keep yourselves from idols. (1 John 5:19–21)

Before looking further, in our next chapter, at the way John's Gospel celebrates the Light of Christ, breaking into the darkness of 'the World', it is perhaps appropriate to pause to reflect on the contemporary 'idols' which, so it seems to me, represent something of the 'darkness' of our world. We need to identify these in Christian response to the calling to walk hopefully the Way of Jesus, the Way of Wisdom, the Way described by shalom as 'peace with justice'. We argued earlier that shalom requires us to think about economy, equity and ecology systemically together. Economy (working for the priority of human and environmental values, and primarily the interests of others and not only our own), equity (the quest for justice, especially for those on the edges and the margins), and ecology (thinking about the health of the environment understood as priestly service and stewardship of God's creation) all belong together under the lordship of God.

Today's idols include bowing down to the priority of financial market controls, and to selfish greed, in place of an economy based on human and environmental values, and the interests of others. They include the exaltation of the false gods of autonomous individualism in place of the quest for equity. They celebrate the worship of human technological power, as we see ourselves as 'lords and masters' over the environment, instead of creation's servants. They include the new religion of the consumer culture, and the lure of 'post-truth'.

For John, the idols may have been the pagan idolatries of local communities, or false teachings that were leading believers astray. It may have been any ideology that was taking the place of God in their beliefs or their ways of life. The writer may well have had in mind the ways in which a 'Wisdom' paragraph from the prophet Isaiah, written centuries before, had cautioned God's people against the lure of false gods. Referring to those who take some wood and use part of it for fuel, and then turn part of it into a god to bow down to and worship, Isaiah says, 'They do not know' what they do. The worshipper 'feeds on ashes; a deluded mind has led him astray, and he cannot save himself or say, "Is not this thing in my right hand a fraud?"' (Isaiah 44:18ff.). A false god is a delusion, a fraud, and cannot save anyone.

It is powerful language, then, for Pope Francis, in his Encyclical Letter *Laudato Si*, to refer to the market in terms of 'idolatry' – 'the interests of a deified market, which becomes the only rule' (para.56).

Restraining the idolatry of the Market
Why does the Pope refer to the market in terms of idolatry? We need to distinguish between the proper use of 'the markets' by which the fruits of human labour are shared, and 'the Market', which the Pope criticized as 'deified'. To avoid making the market into an idol means bringing the market back to its primary purpose in the service of human values and the well-being of all creation, and not the service only of the rich and greedy. As Karl Polanyi[161] argued seventy years ago, 'markets' in the sense of exchange of commodities are of ancient origin. By contrast, 'the Market' as the primary organizing principle of society, originated in the 'great transformation' from feudalism to capitalism. When the Pope refers to the idolatry of 'the Market', he is criticizing the 'mindset of those who say: "Let us allow the invisible forces

---

161 Karl Polanyi, *The Great Transformation: The political and economic origins of our time*, Boston, Beacon Press, 1944.

of the market to regulate the economy, and consider their impact on society and nature as collateral damage"' (para.123). This is very close to Polanyi's formulation: 'the control of the economic system by the Market is of overwhelming consequence to the whole organization of society: it means no less than the running of society as an adjunct to the Market. Instead of economy being embedded in social relations, social relations are embedded in the economic system.'[162]

We have for too long thought about 'the economy' as though it were a science governed by the laws of mechanics (called 'supply and demand'). And, of course, if there is some sort of natural law (or 'invisible hand') by which the economy functions, we can understand why 'governments must not interfere'. Thankfully more and more people are realizing that economics is not a physical science, but is constructed by human beings to serve certain goods and values – and so can be altered, undone and rethought by human beings if we have the wit and the will, and – as Karl Polanyi put it – can be 'embedded in social relations'.

There are a growing number of voices in today's world calling for a different sort of economy, from Kate Raworth's *Doughnut Economics*,[163] to David Marquand's *Mammon's Kingdom*,[164] and Paul Mason's *Postcapitalism*[165] from one political viewpoint, to Roger Scruton's plea for a capitalism which 'thinks seriously about the planet' in *Green Philosophy*[166] from another. A bit longer ago, Jonathan Porritt[167] pleaded for a *Capitalism as if the World Matters*. Eve Poole[168] seeks to redefine 'next generation economics' which hopefully will avoid *Capitalism's Toxic Assumptions*. Together they say: neo-liberal capitalism has failed; the environmental costs are devastating; the social costs are unjust; we must find another approach in which economy, ecology and equity are held together and thought through systemically.

What is clear is that if we are to change the way we think, we need incentives to do so. These might be philosophical and spiritual incentives,

---

162 Polanyi, p. 57. This sort of social critique is not new. As long ago as 1920 R. W. Tawney wrote *The Acquisitive Society*, so called because the 'whole tendency and interest and preoccupation is to promote the acquisition of wealth'. Tawney contrasted this with what he called a 'Functional Society', in which money is not an end in itself, but a means to social good and human creativity. We can think of a society, he says, which aims at putting the acquisition of wealth into the service of a sense of social obligation. Money would then help encourage the performance of functions that serve the wider society. Our focus would be not so much on what we can get, but how we can serve – money would find its place within a culture of service.' However, modern societies are not like that, he says (Tawney is writing in the 1920s, but it could have been 2008). Modern societies are acquisitive societies, because they aim at protecting economic rights, while leaving economic functions to fulfil themselves. Tawney concludes that 'the appeal of this conception must be powerful, for it has laid the whole modern world under its spell'. R. W. Tawney, *The Acquisitive Society*, Harcourt Brace, 1920, p.30.
163 Kate Raworth, *Doughnut Economics*, Random House, 2017.
164 David Marquand, *Mammon's Kingdom*, Allen Lane, 2014.
165 Paul Mason, *Postcapitalism: A guide to our future*, Allen Lane, 2015.
166 Roger Scruton, *Green Philosophy: How to think seriously about the planet*, Atlantic Books, 2012.
167 Jonathan Porritt, *Capitalism as if the World Matters*, Earthscan, 2005.
168 Eve Poole, *Capitalism's Toxic Assumptions*, Bloomsbury, 2015.

such as suggested by Charles Eisentein in *Sacred Economics*.[169] Or they might be financial incentives, such as taxes and subsidies like those discussed in relation to climate change in different ways by Nicholas Stern[170] and by William Nordhaus.[171] Part of our Christian mission will include addressing the changes in public opinion needed to persuade governments to alter direction and think through economy, ecology and equity together in fresh ways, so that the economy is more firmly rooted in the needs and values of the environment and of people.

Restraining greed

Michael Northcott has a comment[172] on the greedy consumption which is a major driver of climate change: Nature 'calls time on the freedom of the human species to continue to raid the planet for resources to sustain industrial civilization', while there is a struggle for access to diminishing food and water resources. Naomi Klein's book, *This Changes Everything* is subtitled *Capitalism verses the climate*[173]. She argues that we now have to choose either the attempt to avert environmental catastrophe or to continue with the illusion of limitless economic growth. 'Climate change detonates the ideological scaffolding', she argues, on which our contemporary economic and political ideology rests.

In the then Mayor of London's 'Margaret Thatcher Lecture' (2013) Boris Johnson – even allowing for his rhetorical flourish – seemed to celebrate greed: 'I don't believe economic equality is possible. Indeed, some measure of inequality is essential for the spirit of envy and keeping up with the Joneses that is, like greed, a valuable spur to economic activity.' We are, he implied, a 'market-led' economy in which something called 'the Market' rules; finance trumps every other consideration; everything, including the environment, becomes a commodity to be desired, or given a price-tag. Lesslie Newbigin[174] gave his response to that sort of idolatry:

> When the free market is made into an absolute; outside of rational control in the light of ethical principles, it becomes a power that enslaves human beings ... The idea that if economic life is detached from all moral consideration and left to operate by its own laws all will be well, is simply an abdication of human responsibility ... If Christ's sovereignty is not recognized in the world of economics, then demonic powers take control.

The Christian task here is to confront the principalities and powers

169 Charles Eisenstein, *Sacred Economics: Money, gift and society in the age of transition*, Evolver, 2011.
170 Nicholas Stern, *Why are we Waiting: The logic, urgency and promise of tackling climate change*, MIT Press, 2015.
171 William Nordhaus, *The Climate Casino: Risk, uncertainty and economics for a warming world*, Yale, 2013.
172 Michael Northcott, *A Political Theology of Climate Change*, SPCK, 2014, p.167.
173 Naomi Klein, *This Changes Everything*, Allen Lane, 2014.
174 Lesslie Newbigin, *Truth to Tell: The gospel as public truth*, SPCK, 1991, p.77.

of the free market economy, and try to recover a sense of sufficiency in God's provision, and the obligation to work for equity and justice throughout the world.

The Gospel narrative tells its own story: not of overconsumption, and greed, but of generosity and self-giving service in the interests of others. It is about equity and justice.

Restraining the idolatry of autonomous individualism

In their critique of neoliberal economic theories, calling instead for an economics redirected towards community, the environment and a sustainable future, Daly and Cobb refer to the assumptions about human nature made by modern economics. 'The chief feature of *Homo economicus* ... is extreme individualism'.[175] The view of *Homo economicus* in current theory, 'still breathes a good deal of the air' of eighteenth-century rationalism and Deism – such as expressed by the father of economics, Adam Smith. 'The view of *Homo economicus* derived from that anthropology and still underlying the existing discipline is radically individualistic. Society as a whole is viewed as an aggregate of such individuals. We want', say Daly and Cobb, 'to replace this with an image of *Homo economicus* as person-in-community ... The world that economic theory normally pictures is one in which individuals all seek their own good and are indifferent to the success or failure of other individuals engaged in the same activity. There is no way to conceive of a collective good.'[176]

One damaging feature of the 'enlightenment' thinking that we can trace back to the sixteenth century is the growth of what we may call an 'autonomous individualism'. Of course, 'the individual' is vital in Christian understanding. God calls us all individually by name. We are baptized one by one, person by person. So we need to be careful how we express this, because in some senses 'the individual' was a Christian discovery. It was the Christian thinkers of the Middle Ages, building on the insights of the early Christian Church, who pioneered beliefs in individual liberty and the equality of individual people before the law.[177] This rests on a fundamental moral insight of Christianity – our individual moral responsibility before God. However, what we are arguing against here is the sort of 'individual*ism*' which so focuses on the individual person and his or her choices and preferences, that this forces a split in our culture, dividing person from person, and opening a chasm

---

175 Daly and Cobb, p.87.
176 Ibid., p.159.
177 cf. Larry Siedentop, *Inventing the Individual: The origins of western liberalism*, Allen Lane, 2014.

down which we lose words like fellowship, society, community, communion, neighbour-love. Any sense of concern for 'the interests of others' gets crowded out.

'There is no such thing as society'

The comment from Margaret Thatcher which provoked the most controversy in her whole 10 years as Prime Minister was made during an interview with *Women's Own Magazine* in 1987: 'There is no such thing as society.'[178] Of course, Margaret Thatcher was right that individual responsibility is important. However, the Thatcher decade was also marked by a growth of 'autonomous individualism' – a radical assertion of individual rights and powers irrespective of the needs of others. Margaret Thatcher was seeking to empower the individual. Her mentor was Friedrich Hayek, who wrote of the 'autonomous spheres in which the ends of the individuals are supreme'.[179]

The book which stood next to the Bible on the bedside tables of many American Republicans was Ayn Rand's 1957 novel, *Atlas Shrugged*. Rand became the prophet of radical individualism, egoism, and 'rational selfishness'. The route from Thomas Hobbes' *Leviathan* leading to Ayn Rand goes by way of F. Nietzsche. It also leads to Richard Dawkins' *The Selfish Gene*.[180] Our culture has become increasingly individualistic. It is often assumed that the 'social atomism' that splits human society into separate, isolated individuals, is somehow an inevitable aspect of Darwinian evolutionary competition. It is taken to be a sort of natural law of the universe. However, even Darwin himself pointed out 'how much friendly order and cooperation' there is in the evolutionary story. There is cooperation in nature even more than there is competition.[181] Daly and Cobb themselves argue that the *social* character of human existence is primary ('in the real world, the self-contained individual does not exist'). The individualistic assumptions of modern economic theory have lost touch with justice, fairness and the well-being of the community as a whole.[182]

However, it was radical individualism that Mrs Thatcher's advisors promoted. Everyone's priority is to look to his or her own interests

---

178 Mrs Thatcher was actually referring to the proper importance of individual responsibility. 'I think we've been through a period where too many people have been given to understand that if they have a problem, it's the government's job to cope with it: "I have a problem, I'll get a grant," "I'm homeless, the government must house me." They're casting their problem on society.' It was at that point she said, 'There is no such thing as "society". There are individual men and women, and there are families. And no government can do anything except through people, and people must look to themselves first. It's our duty to look after ourselves and then after our neighbour. People have got the entitlements too much in mind, without the obligations.'
179 F. A. Hayek, *The Road to Serfdom*, Routledge, 1944, p.60.
180 cf. Mary Midgley, *The Solitary Self*, Acumen, 2010.
181 cf. Brian Goodwin, *How the Leopard Changed its Spots: The evolution of complexity*, Scribners, 1994; cf. also Martin Nowak and Sarah Coakley (eds), *Evolution, Games and God: The principle of cooperation*, Harvard, 2013.
182 Daly and Cobb, p.161,89.

first and foremost. This became a basic assumption of the neoliberal approach to economics that the Thatcher decade promoted so power-fully.

Persons in relation

The air that is breathed by a reader of John's Gospel is very different. The whole Gospel has a corporate flavour to it. Even the very individual conversation between Jesus and Nicodemus in John chapter 3 depicts Nicodemus as a representative figure: 'Rabbi, we know that you are a teacher who has come from God' (v.2). And the author gives Jesus' re-ply also in corporate, representative terms, as though this is the voice also of the community of Christ's people from which the Gospel au-thor comes: 'we speak of what we know and testify to what we have seen; yet you do not receive our testimony' (v.11). The early chapters of the Gospel keep pointing us towards the difficult situation of that Christian community at the end of the first century. This comes much clearer in chapters 13 to 17. No radical individualism here, no 'rational selfishness', but a community of interpersonal relationships in which, as John Macmurray put it in *Persons in Relation*, 'the Self is constituted by its relation to the Other'.[183]

The interests of others

And the 'other' includes the personal encounter that the self has with other people, with God, and with our natural environment. We are in a network of interdependent interpersonal relationships. By the same sacramental action in which we are baptised as an individual person, we are also by that action incorporated into 'the family of God', the 'household of faith', or (as the *Book of Common Prayer* calls it) 'the ark of Christ's Church.' As we have discovered throughout our reflec-tions on John's Gospel, human flourishing is a corporate endeavour: working together for the common good. We have already referred to Joseph Sittler's vision, drawing on Colossians 1, of the Cosmic Christ 'in whom all things hold together' which provides Sittler with what he calls a 'life-affirming Christology of nature'. The triad of God, human-ity and nature, is the basis, he says, for our calling to unity with one another and with all creation. As Pope Francis wrote in his Encyclical *Laudato Si*, subtitled 'On care for our common home', 'A sense of deep communion with the rest of nature cannot be real if our hearts lack tenderness, compassion and concern for our fellow human beings ... Everything is connected. Concern for the environment thus needs to

---

183 John Macmurray, *Persons in Relation*, Faber, 1961.

be joined to a sincere love for our fellow human beings and an unwavering commitment to resolving the problems of society' (para.91). St Paul put it succinctly: 'Let each of you look not to your own interests, but to the interests of others' (Philippians 2:4).

Restraining a misplaced faith in technology and in human ability

From Francis Bacon onwards our Western culture developed a view of nature as a mechanism that we, 'nature's lords and masters', can control for our own benefit. We autonomous humans stand over and above the world, which is there for our good. We are the masters, the 'God species' – using the world to provide for all our wants, so we exploit it, and extract it, and damage it without thought for the future. We can manage. By doing the right research, by asking the right questions and pushing the right buttons, we can manipulate nature to yield her secrets, and to produce whatever we want to fulfil all our desires. We find this sort of thing in Nigel Lawson's book about global warming.[184]

The message I take from Lawson's book is: 'the earth is very resilient; technological discovery has always come to our rescue in the past; we can manage the world for our benefit; it makes no economic sense to take any action to change energy policy; just go with the flow – there is no need to worry about others, or about the future. We need to focus on looking after ourselves.'

From a Christian perspective, the primary difficulty with Lawson's approach is its individualistic anthropocentrism: the assumption that the rest of the world is there to serve human needs and human desires – more particularly, *my* needs and *my* desires. There is no concern for the well-being of the rest of God's creation, nor of our human interdependence with the oxygen, plants and animals which provide our nutrients, energy and livelihood. There is little interest in the well-being of future generations: the economy will have grown, technology will have developed; let the future look after itself.

As we have noted, Christian theology has itself sometimes contributed to an anthropocentric view of the world. What is needed is a recovery of a God-centred perspective, and of the covenant of relationships

---

184 Nigel Lawson, *An Appeal to Reason*, Duckworth, 2008, 2009. Lawson set up the Global Warming Policy Foundation to promote sceptical views about climate change; many of their more recent publications take forward the position taken by Lawson's book in 2008. His appeal to reason is welcome, and he rightly argues that global warming is not just about science but also about economics, politics and ethics. Unfortunately, in each of these areas I think his book is wrong or seriously misleading. In his review of Lawson's book, Sir John Houghton, former Director of the UK Met Office and first chair of the science panel of the Intergovernmental Panel on Climate Change, said it showed 'a surprising ignorance of elementary statistical analysis'; it was 'misleading' about the reality and impacts of climate change, trivializes the threat of sea-level rise, and refuses to acknowledge that there are likely to be loss of resources, livelihood and land for millions of people; and is wrong about the need for and cost of mitigation. He urges Lawson to do his homework.

– rooted in the promise, gift, grace and loving faithfulness of God – between God, the earth and humanity. We are not 'lords and masters' of Nature. We are God's priests and creation's servants.

The Gospel narrative is not of individualism, management and control, and looking only after ourselves, but rather a story of interdependence, cooperation and fellowship. It is a story of neighbour-love.

Restraining the idolatry of our consumer culture

Individualism and competitiveness, coupled with our technological skills, are primary drivers of the consumer culture that so dominates our age. Our consumer culture is the new religion – a new idol.

The Pope[185] rightly notes that human beings have constantly intervened in nature 'but for a long time this was in tune with and respecting the possibilities offered by the things themselves.' In other words, we received from nature what nature allowed. 'Now, by contrast, we are the ones to lay our hands on things, attempting to extract everything possible from them while frequently ignoring or forgetting the reality in front of us.' The Pope argues that this has made it easy 'to accept the idea of infinite or unlimited growth, which proves so attractive to economists, financiers and experts in technology'. But the idea that unlimited economic growth is possible in a finite planet is a nonsense. Archbishop Rowan Williams commented[186] on the Pope's Encyclical: 'Measureless acquisition, consumption, or economic growth in a finite environment is a literally nonsensical idea; yet the imperative of growth remains unassailable, as though we did not really inhabit a material world.'

Yet this consumerist view of human beings persists – so much now that we are realizing, all too late, that we as a species are exceeding the carrying capacity of the planet if not only we, but all people – and God's other creatures – are to live well. Sallie McFague wrote,[187] 'Consumerism is a cultural pattern that leads people to find meaning and fulfillment through the consumption of goods and services. Thus the well-known comment that consumerism is the newest and most successful "religion" on the globe is not an overstatement.'

The inevitable consequence of the consumer culture – and the desire to acquire more and more goods – is to treat the earth's resources not only (nonsensically) as unlimited, but (selfishly) as there only for our use, however reckless we may be. The plundering of rain forests to

185 *Laudato Si,* esp. paras 106,144.
186 Rowan Williams, 'Embracing our Limits', *Commonwealth Magazine,* 23 Sept 2015.
187 Sallie McFague, *Blessed are the Consumers,* Fortress Press, 2013, p.x.

make space for crops (either for food or for energy supplies), the development of industrial agriculture with its loss of hedgerows, its use of pesticides with consequent damage to biodiversity, and especially the extraction and burning of coal, oil and gas for energy, are significant factors in the rapid growth of human-induced climate change. So, as Sallie McFague put it[188]: 'Increasingly the issue of how to live well has become one of *how to change from how we are living now to a different way.* As our crises worsen, more and more people are questioning the reigning anthropology of insatiable greed, and they are coming to the conclusion that the prospects of the consumer culture have been greatly overrated and that serious change at a fundamental level – of who we think we are and what we must do – is necessary.'

The need to challenge consumption

If a habitable world is to survive, such that all people can discover something of the open space of God's joy within which fullness of life can be experienced, I believe we need urgently to reduce consumption, particularly in the Western world, and bring together the scourge of inequality, the need for inclusiveness, and the imperative for a new approach to the financial economy.

Of course an expanding global economy has done a very great deal to enhance the lives of many people, and significantly to reduce extreme poverty, which has been falling worldwide. The downside is, however, increasing consumption, particularly of damaging fossil fuels and other resources – which is increasingly making the planet a more difficult place in which to live and flourish – and a marked increase in inequality, which leads to social unrest and increasing injustice. We have already argued that 'economy', 'equity' and 'ecology' have to be thought through together. Consumption has to be reduced if a fragile planet is to have a liveable future. As John Taylor put it 'enough is enough'.

In our reflections on Jesus' ministry we noted the opposition to which he was exposed, and to which he predicted that his followers would likewise be exposed. He was called on to speak truth to power, to bear witness to truth, and to 'do the truth' in a 'World' which was organized without reference to God. Jesus 'overcame the world' by removing sin's alienations, shining God's light into the world's darkness, embodying the truth of God's gracious provision, and the liberating power of forgiveness and suffering love, and by victoriously calling

---

188 op. cit., p.xi.

together a community to follow his Way. In our world of deified markets, and a rampant consumer culture, living well will require us to find ways of bearing witness to truth which is life-giving and liberating, rather than idolatrous.

The lure of 'post-truth' (and of untruth)

A new adjective joined the Oxford English Dictionary in 2016: 'post-truth'. It describes circumstances 'in which objective facts are less influential in shaping public opinion than appeals to emotion and personal belief'. The word came to prominence after aspects of the 2016 Brexit campaign in the UK, widely criticized for emotionally promoting untruths and half-truths as the basis for decision-making, and after Donald Trump's campaign for the Presidency in the USA. 'Post-truth' is not quite the same as 'lies'. It is about exercising power and control, and manipulating public opinion. The liar may know the truth, but the post-truth politician does not care what is truth and what is not. In 'post-truth' politics, people pick and choose between 'alternative facts', the phrase once used by one of President Trump's aides when defending the White House's statements concerning the numbers who attended the presidential inauguration.

'Truth' as wishful thinking is illustrated by Odd Ball, Donald Sutherland's character in the film *Kelly's Heroes,* who responds to a fellow soldier's complaint that a bridge might have been blown up again by the enemy: 'it's a beautiful bridge... think it will be there, and it will be there.' It is possible to be drawn into a fantasy land where, through our own determination, we can come to believe whatever we wish to be 'true.' It is increasingly possible, also, for example through social media, to belong within a bubble of like-minded people who continually reinforce each other's views of the world whether or not that has any true relationship to reality.

For post-truth politicians and journalists — and, indeed, for many users of social media — 'truth' no longer carries the transcendent quality that it does in the Bible. The traditional understanding of 'truth' as 'being in accord with reality' has become more and more relativized in 'my truth and your truth', 'truth for me'; indeed, 'post-truth'. If the Way of Jesus Christ is 'the true and living way', then pathways dependent on untruth, half-truth, or post-truth lead directly to the worship of the 'father of lies'.

Here are some examples.

Advertising

One of the clearest examples of the power of untruth in our culture is in a misuse of the world of advertising. A comment from the psychologist David Smail illustrates one misuse: 'However banal it may seem, nothing holds up to us the nature of our aspirations better than television advertising.' He says that, however sophisticated we may feel about them, advertisers confront us almost remorselessly with ideals we can never live up to. Smail pictures 'the happy loving family eating their cornflakes against views of waving wheatfields, eagerly awaiting the joys of the day to unfold'. He describes the 'slim beautiful women whose smooth and unblemished limbs slide effortlessly into blue denim skins, later to catch the strong and approving gaze of confident young men who will cherish them with just the right amount of lust'. He comments on the 'unwrinkled middle aged couples, with lovely children', 'tough men in a man's world'; clever 'wielders of power tools' and many other stereotypes. His point is to underline the despair that such an idealized world creates in many people who cannot live up to it. This is his conclusion: 'It is my contention that the ideal world in which we profess belief is riddled with myth, and that the secret world of anxiety and pain in which we actually live our lives is the real one which we truly share.'[189]

Advertising is, of course, an important asset in any functioning society. It is an essential tool of a consumer society. However, another serious misuse of advertising is its commitment to the goal of limitless economic growth, because then we have constantly to be persuaded that we need to consume more and that we have more and growing needs. Both the goal and the advertising it creates are lies that enslave rather than liberate.

Selling doubt

The power of untruth in the political world was documented recently by Naomi Oreskes and Erik Conway in their book, *Merchants of Doubt*.[190] They illustrated how, in the 1950s, tobacco companies – perhaps in part to try to reduce punitive government taxes – sought to undermine scientific evidence that cigarette smoking causes cancer. Their strategy was to use a group of scientists to sow doubt. 'Doubt is our product' ran the infamous memo written by one tobacco industry executive in 1969, 'since it is the best means of competing with the "body of fact" that exists in the minds of the general public' (p.34). A

189 David Smail, *Illusion and Reality – the Meaning of Anxiety*, J. M. Dent, 1984.
190 Naomi Oreskes and Erik M. Conway, *Merchants of Doubt: How a handful of scientists obscured the truth on issues from tobacco smoke to global warming*, Bloomsbury, 2011.

group of scientists – many the same people – also became 'merchants of doubt' about Star Wars, nuclear winter, acid rain, the ozone hole, all the way to global warming (p.35). Many of the doubts sown about climate change have originated from the Heartland Institute, with its strong programme to undermine climate science. Naomi Klein refers to the 'thought crimes' of what she calls 'the Heartlanders'. She affirms that many of the global warming sceptic scientists actually know the truth, but realize that if they were to admit it, they would lose the 'central ideological battle of our time', namely the battle for free market capitalism[191].

Another recent example of living in untruth comes from the oil giant ExxonMobil. A paper from David Hasemyer and John H. Cushman Jr in *Inside Climate News*, October 2015, claims that ExxonMobil have sought to sow doubt about climate science for decades. According to a report in the *The Guardian* of 27 May 2016, 'the company knew of climate change as early as 1977, but spent the next 30 years and at least £30m promoting climate-change denial and blocking action. While telling shareholders there was too much uncertainty about global warming to take action, it was building exploration facilities that allowed for the sea level rise it knew was on the way.' As a result, as I write the company is under investigation by attorneys general from 17 US states. Oreskes and Conway conclude their book with a quotation from Shakespeare. They rightly say that for human society to function at all in the modern world, there has to be some degree of trust in our designated experts. Otherwise life is reduced to 'a tale told by an idiot, full of sound and fury, signifying nothing'.[192]

The disappearance of truth
Michael Polanyi, the scientist/philosopher, whose quest for truth in science and in society was deeply motivated by the lack of respect for truth in Stalin's Russia, made a similar point in 1975:

> When a judge in a court of law can no longer appeal to law and justice; when neither a witness, nor the newspapers, nor even a scientist reporting on his experiments can speak the truth as he knows it; when in public life there is no moral principle commanding respect; when the revelations of religion and of art are denied any substance; then there are no grounds left on which any individual may justly make a stand against the rulers of the day. Such is the simple logic of totalitarianism[193].

---

191 Klein, op. cit. p.40.
192 Macbeth Act V. Scene 5.
193 Michael Polanyi and Harry Prosch, *Meaning*, University of Chicago Press 1975, p.19.

A story of doom

One further area of contemporary untruth, even post-truth, are the fatalistic stories of doom which are being told by serious commentators as much as by Hollywood blockbuster movies. We began this book with the story of a lady in a Norfolk village unable to cope with the likelihood of coastal erosion destroying her home. She is not alone in telling a story of fear, uncertainty and despair at our ability to cope. We are impotent, some people say, in the face of Nature's power: look at the tsunamis and at the Zika virus. Nothing we do can make any difference. We are essentially part of 'Nature', which is living, developing and therefore unpredictable. There is very little point in thinking we can do anything to change it. We simply have to be part of what happens.

Some academic writers are more forthright about the damage we are causing to the earth, and that we are right to be fearful. But when this is coupled with despair, we need to be careful. They say that the earth system is very fragile and sensitive to climate change; we are seriously damaging the environment. In fact, we human beings have probably gone beyond planetary boundaries too often already. Many species – perhaps the human species itself – are living on borrowed time. Be afraid, be very afraid. In his book about population trends, *Ten Billion*, Stephen Emmott's verdict[194] – in strong Anglo-Saxon – is, 'I think we're f****d.' How does a Christian respond to fatalism or to overwhelming despair?

Underneath all this is a fear of our own human vulnerability and apparent powerlessness. How does Christian faith, with its conviction that the decisions we make for good or ill do have a great effect on God's earth, enable us to uncover and deal with our fears and vulnerabilities?

We need first to take fully on board the need to live within limits. Recognition of our own place within God's creation, as we have said, challenges the presumption of our human domination of nature. It also challenges the fear that we have no place at all. 'The Lord is gracious and merciful, slow to anger and abounding in steadfast love' (Psalm 145:8). 'I am convinced that neither death, nor life, nor angels, nor rulers, nor things present, nor things to come, nor powers, nor height, nor depth, nor anything else in all creation, will be able to separate us from the love of God in Christ Jesus our Lord' (Romans 8:38f.)

Understanding God's Wisdom as holding all things together, and all

---

194 Stephen Emmott, *10 Billion*, Penguin, 2013.

things ultimately being renewed and redeemed within the love of God, holds out the promise of hope in God's purpose for God's world. Our calling is to relearn that our place is to live within the limits of a finite planet, and within the moral and social limits of God's ways of Wisdom.

> *The Gospel narrative gives us a different story: not of fatalism nor doom and despair, but of compassionate love and mercy, of trust in the truth and faithfulness of God. It is about joy in creation, the promise of life in all its fullness, resurrection and a renewed and healed creation. It is a story of hope.*

The Christian community

As we shall explore further in chapter 11, Jesus bequeathed to the world a group of believers, some half-believers, some troubled with doubts, whose initial fear kept them behind closed doors. But as the truth of the resurrection dawned, and Jesus breathed his Spirit on them, the time came when even the doubter Thomas could affirm of Jesus: 'My Lord and my God' (John 20:28). But although confidence in the faith grew in many different ways, by the time John's Gospel was written, the hostility and persecution from the Pharisees in particular was deeply troubling the Christian community. How could they follow their Teacher and Lord in testifying to the truth? How could they keep themselves from idols? How could they demonstrate the power not of domination but of service? Not of control, but of love? Not of despair, but of hope?

That is still a question for today's Church. Can today's Christian community continue in our time to bear witness to the Christ who overcomes the world? Hunter offers a very sobering assessment: since the conversion of Constantine in AD 313, 'rather than challenging the principalities and powers, the people of God became united with the powers; rather than proclaiming peace, the church embraced an ethic of coercion, power and, thus, violence; rather than resisting the power of the state, the church provided divine legitimation for the state, which has invariably led to the hubris of empire, conquest, and persecution; rather than modelling a new kind of society, the church imitated the social structures of hierarchy and administration; rather than being a servant to the poor and the oppressed, the church has been complicit in wielding economic and political power over the poor and the oppressed'.[195]

This poses a huge question today for Christian discipleship. Are we in fact following Jesus in his self-giving love, especially on behalf of the

---

195 Hunter, op. cit., p.153.

marginalized and the poorest communities? Or are we as a Church still caught up in the power struggles that display 'coercion, power and, thus, violence' rather than 'being a servant to the poor and the oppressed.' So one major question for today's Christian community in the context of a quest to think through economy, equity and environment together, and in response to God's calling to us to care for God's world, is to find a way of bearing witness to God's truth as it is in Jesus, and which follows the Way of Jesus in doing shalom, even when that – as it inevitably will – provokes hostility from 'the World'.

To summarise: The story that the followers of the Way of Jesus has to tell is different from the various stories being told by 'the world'. Instead of a story about over-consumption, and greed, the Way of Jesus speaks of generosity and the power of self-giving service in the interests of others. It is about equity and justice. Instead of a story about autonomous individualism, management and control, it is rather, a story of interdependence, co-operation and fellowship. A story of neighbour-love. Instead of a story marked by fatalism, doom and despair, the Way of Jesus is rather about compassionate love and mercy, trusting in the truth and faithfulness of God. It is about joy in creation, the promise of life in all its fullness, resurrection and a renewed and healed creation. It is a story of hope.

Chapter Ten

Light, Truth and Freedom

- The Light of Jesus Christ breaks into the darkness of the world.

- John's Gospel gives us various light-giving examples: Jesus is the Lamb of God who takes away the sin of the world; Jesus cleanses the Temple; Jesus is to be 'lifted up' on the Cross to bring healing; Jesus brings peace in the darkness of the storm; Jesus gives sight to the blind beggar; Easter morning is the dawn of resurrection.

- The Gospel often links 'light' with 'truth'. It speaks of 'bearing witness to the truth'; it recognizes that speaking truth to power is costly; it makes clear that truth is personal (I AM the truth).

- The links between truth and freedom can be seen in the personal story of Simon Peter, and more widely in the concept of the free society.

Two more of major themes from the pen of the Beloved Disciple are light and truth. The Wisdom and Word of God, made flesh in Jesus is the 'true light that enlightens everyone' (John1: 9). Jesus describes himself as 'the Light of the World', and 'The Truth' (John 8:12; 14:6). The Gospel links both light and truth with the giving of freedom. This chapter explores further some of these great themes.

After acknowledging the darknesses of our 'world', the 'lordless powers' which confront us, and the temptations to idolatry in our individualised consumer culture with its greed, self-interest and too often despair, it is a relief to turn to the way John's Gospel points to the Light, with its life-giving, liberating message of hope.

1. Light
Come to probably any carol service at Christmas time, and one of the first readings from Scripture will almost certainly say:

> *The people who walked in darkness have seen a great light; those who lived in a land of deep darkness – on them light has shined.* (Isaiah 9:2)

The hope-filled image of the coming of the light to scatter the darkness of the world is deep in the writings of the Hebrew prophets. In the sixth century before Christ, Isaiah of Jerusalem had a vision of a coming royal Messiah, of the line of great King David, who would establish a kingdom of justice and shalom. He speaks of this royal coming in terms of the shining of a great light.

We are recalled to the creation narratives at the start of the Bible: 'God said, "Let there be light"' (Genesis 1:3). We also find light used as a symbol in the Wisdom literature: 'The path of the righteous is like the light of dawn, which shines brighter and brighter until full day' (Proverbs 4:18). This comes in a section of Proverbs which contrasts those who live in darkness, and constantly stumble, and 'those who begin life's path at daybreak and walk it in sunlight that "shines ever brighter"' illuminating the obstacles of the path ahead.[196]

Unsurprisingly, light is a major theme for John. The First Epistle declares that 'God is light' (1 John 1:5). The Prologue to the Gospel announces: 'The light shines in the darkness, and the darkness did not overcome it' (John 1:5).[197]

John the Baptist, we are told, 'came as a witness to testify to the light, so that all might believe through him. He himself was not the light, but he came to testify to the light. The true light, which enlightens everyone, was coming into the world' (John 1:7–9). To the Judeans and Pharisees who were critical of him, Jesus said, 'I AM the light of the world. Whoever follows me will never walk in darkness but will have the light of life' (8:12). At the time of the visit of some Greeks seeking to see Jesus, described in John chapter 12, Jesus says to them, 'While you have the light, believe in the light, so that you may become children of light' (12:36). In other words, walking in the light of Christ, believing into Christ, doing the truth and continuing in Christ's word are all part of the freedom that belongs to the disciples of Christ, the children of light. As the Gospel underlines, Jesus says, 'I have come as light into the world, so that everyone who believes in me should not remain in the darkness' (John 12:46).

With different images, symbols, encounters, healings and teachings,

196 David A. Hubbard, *The Communicator's Commentary: Proverbs,* Word Books, 1989, p.85.
197 Our English translations sometimes use the same word to convey different Greek words. In the Prologue we read that 'the light shines in the darkness, and the darkness did not overcome it.' In that verse (1:5), 'overcome' is a word meaning 'seize, grasp, master, suppress, makes one's own'. When Jesus later says to the disciples, 'Take courage; I have overcome the world' (16:33, NASB), the word he used, also translated 'overcome' means 'gain the victory'. Where the forces of darkness seek to seize the world by suppressing the light, Jesus the Light conquers the world through his victory over the power of darkness.

the Gospel makes clear that the coming of Jesus is a wholly new thing. The incarnation of the Word/Wisdom of God changes everything. God's light is shattering the darkness and idolatry of 'the World', bringing instead words of judgement, healing, truth, liberty, and a kingdom of shalom with justice.

We will look some of the ways in which God's light, which enlightens everyone, shines out in some of the Gospel scenes, and brings God's light into the world.

(i) Jesus is the Lamb of God who takes away the sin of the world.
We begin with John the Baptist, whose first word of witness, pointing to Jesus, is, 'Here is the Lamb of God who takes away the sin of the world.' Why does John the Baptist use this surprising phrase? Why not 'Here is your Teacher' or even 'Here is your Messiah'? Why 'the Lamb of God who takes away the sin of the world'? By 'sin', the Gospel means alienation from God, walking in darkness rather than in the light of God's truth. So much is fairly clear. But why 'lamb'? There are a number of places in the Hebrew Bible where a lamb plays a very significant part in the story – any or all of these[198] could have been in mind in John chapter 1 when John the Baptist points to Jesus and says, 'Here is the Lamb of God who takes away the sin of the world' (John 1:29,36). It is worth pausing to look briefly at these.

Abraham
The story of Abraham and Isaac on Mount Moriah, in which God tests Abraham's faith by asking him to forego his future by sacrificing his son, is a story that rightly causes us significant moral unease. It may have been written precisely to counter the practice of child-sacrifice. Whatever its origin, the symbolism is profound. Father and son together are at the place of sacrifice when a ram is substituted as a victim. It becomes a symbol of God's surprising initiative of grace, and of God's provision. Abraham called the place 'The Lord will provide' (Genesis 22:14). Jesus, Lamb of God, is here *God's gift of unexpected grace and provision.*

Passover night
The lamb also plays a prominent part in the story of the exodus from Egypt (Exodus 12). On Passover night, the instruction to the people was to choose a lamb that was exactly to meet the needs of the family; it was to be without blemish; its blood was to be daubed on the doorposts and lintel of the house. And when the angel of death passed

---
198 cf. C. H. Dodd, *The Interpretation of the Fourth Gospel*, 1953.

over the land of Egypt in judgement and in liberation, those who were sheltering in the place marked by the blood of the lamb were safe, and could start their pilgrimage to their promised land. It was a night of judgement and death, of mercy and freedom from slavery. Passover became a festival of liberation, and its symbolism was kept alive throughout the whole history of the people of God. Jesus Christ was described by St Paul as 'Christ our Passover, sacrificed for us' (see 1 Corinthians 5:7). And in John's Gospel, there are several Passover festivals referred to during Jesus' ministry, culminating in his last week with his disciples. In John's chronology of that week, Jesus dies at the moment the Passover lambs are being sacrificed in the Temple. Jesus, Lamb of God, is *the Passover lamb of liberation*, overcoming the bonds of slavery from sin, setting God's people free.

Sacrifice
The whole sacrificial system described in the book of Leviticus, in which lambs play a key part, keeps alive in the memory of God's people, the liberating grace of God, particularly in relation to the forgiveness of sins and the removal of guilt. The whole burnt offering of a lamb symbolized the consecration of the whole person to God's service, as well as a willingness to allow God's forgiveness to enter one's life in a transformative way. The Letter to the Hebrews in the New Testament is among the clearest illustrations of how Jesus, the Lamb of God, opens for us a *way to receive God's forgiveness and cleansing* (Hebrews 10:19–25).

Suffering servant
Moving forward to the prophet Isaiah, the suffering lamb of Isaiah chapter 53 could also have been in John the Baptist's mind. Isaiah, a prophet quoted more than once in John's Gospel, refers to 'a lamb that is led to the slaughter' (Isaiah 53:7) to describe the Servant of the Lord who suffers with and on behalf of the people. There are allusions to Jesus as Suffering Servant in John's Gospel, notably when washing his disciples' feet (John 13), and especially in his *self-giving love* on the Cross. Jesus, the Lamb of God, is the Servant King of Isaiah's prophecy, 'by whose wounds we have been healed' and on whom the Lord has 'laid the iniquity of us all' (Isaiah 53).

Victory
One further allusion may be to the Hebrew Book of Enoch, where a great horned ram leads the people to victory. Maybe this refers to the time of Judas Maccabeus' revolt against the Seleucid invaders of

Palestine. But the image is picked up in the Book of Revelation, where, in the vision of the throne, there stands a vulnerable Lamb, 'as if it had been slaughtered' (Revelation 5:6), a vision which becomes, in a series of images, the victorious Lamb who is the Judge ('the wrath of the Lamb', Revelation 6:16), the Shepherd (7:17), the Bridegroom (Revelation 21:9), and the One to whom the world is coming and *whom all God's people follow* (Revelation 14:4: 'these follow the Lamb wherever he goes').

Jesus, the Lamb of God, overcomes the world by removing sin's alien-ations, shining God's light into the world's darkness, embodying the truth of God's gracious provision, and the liberating power of forgive-ness and suffering love, and victoriously calling together a community to follow his Way 'wherever he goes'.

(ii) Jesus cleanses the Temple

A further vivid illustration of the new light that the Gospel shines on the tradition of the Judeans is Jesus' cleansing of the Temple. Probably this occurred, as the other Gospels describe, towards the end of Jesus' ministry. John is placing it at the start, in chapter 2 of the Gospel, to set the scene for what is to follow: a gradual demonstration of the new life of the good news of Jesus' provision, healings, teaching, service, suffering, death and resurrection. We are in the Temple in Jerusalem. As Margaret Barker and others have shown, the construction of the Temple – and the wilderness tabernacle before it – were demonstrably in seven stages, which later writers linked to the seven days of cre-ation described in Genesis 1. The Temple, in other words, became a visual aid, even a microcosm, of God's creation, and the Holy of Holies – symbolizing God's presence – was the place from which the priest, once a year, would emerge with the gift of God's blessing. The Temple was to be a place of worship, of God's blessing on the fruitfulness of all creation, a sign of the divine gift. It was to be a place of unity, and inclu-sion[199], for all people. However, over time the meaning of the Temple had been lost, or overshadowed with other things. So much so that the prophet Malachi said that God's messenger will come to the Temple, refining and purifying it 'until they present offerings to the LORD in righteousness' which will be 'pleasing to the Lord as in the days of old and in former years' (Malachi 3:1–4).

The Temple described in John chapter 2 was apparently pre-dominantly a market place, a place of industry and commerce and

---

199 cf. Isaiah 56.6–8.

money-changing, a place with birds and animals ready for sacrifice at the festival. Perhaps this mostly happened in the Court of the Gentiles, which was separated from the inner Court of Israel into which only Jewish males were allowed.[200] The Judeans, we have said, stand for the Temple authorities – the people of political and economic power in Palestine: the centre of national life. When Jesus takes a whip of cords and starts his protest, the disciples recall the Messianic psalm, 'zeal for your house ... has consumed me' (Psalm 69:9). But that same Psalm is quoted again in the Gospel at the time of the crucifixion, 'for my thirst they gave me vinegar to drink' (Psalm 69:21, cf. John 19:28–30). The Gospel is telling us not only that Jesus is confronting an ideology which had lost touch with God, but that in doing so this will lead to his own death. This event happened near Passover time, when God's people recalled their liberation from oppression. Jesus explains his symbolic action: 'Stop making my Father's house a place of trade.' This is not only the action of God's messenger, refining and purifying a religion that has gone stale. It is a major confrontation with 'the World' of a consumerism that has lost sight of God's gift and generosity. It is an action of exorcism (*exebalen* means he 'cast them out'), and an action of cleansing. The light of God's blessing shines again from the Holy of Holies for the whole of creation – including the world of politics, economics and religious power. The section ends with Jesus speaking about a renewed temple: the temple of his risen body, after the resurrection, the body of the new world order into which Jesus' disciples are incorporated, the place of God's post-Easter presence in the world. We notice that Jesus' confrontation with 'the World' is here in part action against ungodly power and in part shining the light of truth that he came to bring.

(iii) Jesus is to be 'lifted up' on the Cross to bring healing
The symbol of the British Medical Association, and indeed a number of other medical organisations around the world, features a serpent on a pole. Some people relate this to the mythology of the Greek God Asclepius who was sometimes denoted by a staff, sometimes by a serpent. The BMA refers back to the narrative of Numbers 21:4–9, which is quoted by John's Gospel in 3:14. God's people in the time of Moses in the wilderness became ill from bites by poisonous snakes. Moses

200 And of course, the inner heart of all was the Court of the Priests, within which the Holy of Holies was curtained off by a veil through which only the high priest was allowed, and that only once a year. The Temple had become a place of division and separation. How powerful the symbolism, then, referred to in Matthew's Gospel, of the 'veil of the Temple being torn in two from the top to the bottom' at the moment of Jesus' death on the cross. It could not be more powerfully said: 'the separations are ended, the barriers broken down, the divisions healed: all are welcome in the presence of God' (cf. Matthew 27:51).

made a serpent of bronze and put it on a pole. Whenever a poisonous snake bit someone, that person would look up to the bronze serpent and live. It was not the serpent that brought healing, but 'the uplifted serpent drew the hearts of Israel to God for their salvation'.[201] It is the 'uplifting' to which John's Gospel refers when it says, 'Just as Moses lifted up the serpent in the wilderness, so must the Son of Man be lifted up ... (John 3:14). The lifting up of Jesus on the Cross, the Gospel goes on to demonstrate, is not only Jesus' exaltation to glory, but, as the text goes on to say, brings healing (salvation) to the world: '... that whoever believes in him may have eternal life' (John 3:15).

The work of inaugurating that 'other kingdom', of which Jesus spoke in conversation with Pilate, took Jesus to the suffering of the Garden, the indignity of the crown of thorns, the agonizing death of the Cross. All the story of the Gospel leads to the Cross. The moment of God's immersion to the depths of broken humanity in suffering, humiliation, defilement and death, is the moment by which supremely 'the World' is overcome. Jesus died under the banner, written by Pilate, 'The King of the Jews'. His words were 'It is finished.' These words prompt us to recall that at the end of the creation narrative in the opening of Genesis, 'God finished the work that he had done' and creation was set forth on its project towards the kingdom of God's glory, to be brought to its perfection through God's Spirit. It is on this day at Golgotha that Jesus' work of testifying to the truth of God's kingdom was 'finished' in his death, and the way opened for the dawning light of Easter morning and the birth of a new world. The story of the Cross becomes the story of the world's redemption. The light that enlightens everyone has come to the world.

(iv) Jesus brings peace in the darkness of the storm

A further symbolic incident in the Gospel narrative is set in a boat on the Sea of Galilee. It was dark and the disciples were alone. The wind was blowing; the water was rough; the disciples were terrified. This paragraph comes in the middle of John chapter 6 with its many references to bread from heaven – which recalls for the disciples and the readers the Exodus story of the rescue of God's people through the water of the Red Sea. The sea, in parts of the Hebrew Bible, particularly some of the Psalms, stands for what is chaotic and frightening and destructive of God's ordering of things. Just as Moses leads the people through the sea to their liberty, so John's Gospel is making the same point about Jesus. For the disciples – terrified to see Jesus,

---

201 C. K. Barrett, *The Gospel according to St John*, SPCK, 1958, p.178.

though not at first knowing who he was – the light dawns when they hear his voice: 'I AM; do not be afraid.' Once again, there are many layers of meaning caught up by the author in these few lines: Jesus brings calm to troubled minds; Jesus is the new Moses leading God's people to liberty; Jesus commands the chaos of disorder in God's creation and makes peace.

To a troubled Christian community at the end of the first century, this paragraph also had many hope-filled layers of meaning. Jesus is your peace. The Way of Jesus is the way of freedom. Jesus speaks with the authority of God the Creator to bring order out of chaos, and light into darkness. Do not be afraid.

(v) Jesus gives sight to the blind beggar

In David Rensberger's approach to John's Gospel, Nicodemus stands for the half-believer who needs shaking into commitment. By contrast, the beggar, blind from birth, who receives his sight from Jesus in John chapter 9, stands for the authentic disciple. He starts with nothing, he receives Jesus' gift – first of sight, then of a growing realization of who Jesus is – and this develops into a commitment of belief into Jesus, the Son of Man. 'He said "Lord, I believe." And he worshipped him' (John 9:38). The majority of this long chapter 9 in the Gospel is about Jesus serving a blind beggar – Jesus on the side of the outsider, the marginalized, the poor. And it is also about not only the growth to faith of the blind man, but the growing antagonism of the watching world, represented by the Pharisees and the Judeans.

This episode follows the Feast of Tabernacles (ch.7) which is about water and light. It is introduced by these words of Jesus:

> I AM the Light of the World. (John 8:12; 9:5)

Rensberger's point in choosing to place the blind beggar alongside Nicodemus as a representative figure is to suggest that this blind man is the representative believer in the Christian community. He does not hide like Nicodemus does, but stands up in front of the world to display his faith in the man who had brought him light – and provokes opposition and consternation among those who find this puzzling or offensive. Referring to the altercation between the blind man and the Pharisees, Rensberger comments, 'The blind man's God does not live in a book, not even the book of the law itself, but in the act of mercy that has been done to him.'[202] Describing the Christian community of the Beloved Disciple, Rensberger points out that the believers in that

202 Rensberger, op. cit., p.45.

setting had either to suppress their experience, or defy 'those who in their society are in charge of communal norms and their interpretation'. 'Johannine Christianity', he goes on, 'is thus not merely a subculture but a counterculture within at least the local Judaism wherein it has precipitated so painful a conflict. The Johannine Christians have experienced God anew in Jesus, and from their perspective to be told that their confession of Jesus is illegitimate is to be told that they must confine their experience of reality itself to what the ruling authorities define as acceptable. This they cannot do.'

It is not the rich and influential Nicodemus, but the poor, blind beggar who has nothing, but whom Jesus finds and heals, who is the role model for the Christian believer in this community. He is the one who understood Jesus to be the Light of the World.

(vi) Jesus is alive! The new dawn of resurrection

Easter morning opens 'while it was still dark'. As the sun comes up in the eastern sky, so the light dawns in the hearts and minds, first of Mary Magdalene, then of Peter and of the Beloved Disciple, and then most of the others, that the empty tomb and the appearances of the risen Jesus means one thing: Jesus is alive. 'I have seen the Lord.'

The point of discovery – the light of truth dawning – in the resurrection narrative in John chapter 20 is when Jesus turns and calls Mary Magdalene by name. Peter and the other disciples had seen and believed and then gone home. But Mary, who was with others at the foot of the Cross, was waiting and searching and weeping; and Jesus calls her 'Mary'. From then on everything changes in her relationship with Jesus – and in that of all Jesus' 'brothers' also: his Father is now also her Father and theirs, his God, now their God. Mary is commissioned to announce to them the good news. Jesus' words, 'Don't touch me', say, 'There is something new.' Something new about Jesus' resurrection body; something new about Jesus' ongoing relationships with his brothers and sisters; something new about the Garden – now there are angels there (perhaps an echo of the cherubim who had a very different role guarding Adam's way in a different garden); something new, in fact, about the whole world. Easter says to the whole of creation: 'The light of God's new world has dawned.'

Throughout the Gospel, the presence and actions of Jesus – the Lamb of God, the cleanser of the Temple, the healer, the stiller of the storm, the Suffering Servant – illustrate the shining of God's Light for the world. In his life, death and resurrection, the Light has come. The true light that enlightens everyone has come into the world. Therefore there is hope.

2. Truth

After the dialogue with Nicodemus referred to in John chapter 3, the narrator makes a link between 'living in the light' and 'doing the truth'. *'This is the judgement, that the light has come into the world, and people loved darkness rather than light because their deeds were evil. For all who do evil hate the light and do not come to the light, so that their deeds may not be exposed. But those who do what is true come to the light, so that it may be clearly seen that their deeds have been done in God'* (3:19ff.).

In several places 'light' and 'truth' belong together for our author. And so do truth and freedom. To repeat what we said earlier, 'walking in the light of Christ', 'believing into Christ', 'doing the truth' and 'continuing in Christ's word' are all part of the freedom that belongs to the 'children of light'.

It is time now to focus more on the importance of truth, and of bearing witness to truth, in John's Gospel, and the way the Beloved Disciple links together truth and freedom.

The Meaning of 'truth'

There are, of course, many minefields in philosophical discussions about truth – correspondence theories, coherence theories, existential approaches, and so on. Most of these concentrate on what it means to say that a statement is 'true'. In the Bible, the emphasis is much more practical. In the Old Testament, 'truth' can mean faithfulness or reliability. It is about 'doing the truth', acting with integrity. It points to God's 'steadfast love and faithfulness.'

In the New Testament, truth is contrasted with hypocrisy when words do not match deeds. In Jesus, whose 'word is truth' and who embodies 'the truth', we see personal integrity, trustworthiness, being in touch with reality. The antithesis of truth is not error, so much as lies or deception. Although 'truth' can mean 'a true statement', it more often refers to 'moral and personal integrity'. 'Truth' thus means more than simply 'factuality' – parable may be true, though not factual. Truth encompasses integrity, reliability and faithfulness in the discerning, interpreting and recounting of 'facts' in accordance with reality. 'Truth' points to something transcendent, something universal, described by the Gospel in terms of the trustworthiness of God.

To speak of truth – or indeed justice, love or beauty – as *transcendent* is to say that truth confronts us with its own masterful objectivity and ultimate authority. Truth stands above us and beyond us as a reality that we reach out to but never control, as a navigator before the pole star reaches towards it and sets his course by it. Truth places us under an obligation to respond appropriately. Our statements about truth refer beyond themselves, and so are not themselves ultimate and final, but always open to correction as further truth is disclosed to us in our discoveries. Our statements have their own truthfulness by reference to an ultimate Truth. In Christian understanding, Truth is always related to the faithfulness of God, who is the source of all Truth, and is revealed as personal Being in Jesus Christ.

For us to live in the light of Christ means bearing witness to Christ's truth.

(i) Bearing witness to the truth

The true light, which enlightens everyone, was coming into the world. (John 1:9)

The Prologue to John's Gospel refers to John the Baptist. He came to 'bear witness' to the true light which enlightens everyone and which was coming into the world (1:6–9; 5:33). Jesus himself at the end of the Gospel says to Pilate 'For this I was born, and for this I came into the world, to testify to the truth' (18:37), eliciting the famous response from Pilate: 'What is truth?'

As the Gospel makes clear, knowledge of truth is God's gift. The glory of the Father's only son was seen 'full of grace and truth' (1:14). Living in the light of the truth as it is in Jesus is the same as doing 'what is true' (3:21). True worship is 'in spirit and truth' (4:24). The 'father of lies' who is behind the opposition that 'the World' makes towards Jesus, and who creates slavery in those who 'choose to do' his desires (8:44) is described as not standing 'in the truth' (8:44). By contrast, the truth to which Jesus bears witness, 'will make you free' (8:32).

By the time we reach the Upper Room discourses in the second part of the Gospel (chapters 13–17), it becomes clear that the truth is ultimately personal: 'I AM ... the truth' (14:6), Jesus says to Thomas. And the risen Jesus describes the Holy Spirit, a gift from the Father to Jesus' new community of disciples (14:16), as the Spirit of truth who will live among them (14:17), who will bear witness to the truth as it is in Jesus (15:26), and who will guide the community of Christ's people into all the truth (16:13).

We thus find that John's Gospel's understanding of truth is that it is a gift of God the Father, is manifest in the personal relationship between God the Father and Christ the Son, and is discovered in the shared journey of discipleship within the Christian community led by God's Spirit, as the personal love of God the Holy Trinity is discovered and shared in the fellowship of Christ's people. Jesus prays that this community will be dedicated to the service of God 'in the truth' (17:17), just as for their sakes he was dedicated to the service of the Father (17:19). They are to be sent 'into the world' just as Jesus himself was 'sent' into the world (17:18). In other words, bearing witness to the truth, which was the basis of Jesus' own mission, now becomes the mission of the community of Christ's people.

The calling to live 'in the truth' and to 'do the truth' is also a calling to bear witness not only to 'the truth as it is in Jesus', but more generally to truth wherever it can be discerned in God's world. We look now more closely at what is meant by saying 'truth is personal', and then at the links between truth and freedom, drawing particularly on the Gospel's story of Simon Peter.

(ii) Truth is personal

I AM the Way, and the Truth, and the Life. (cf. John 14:6)

I recall a very severe winter when I was a child. A neighbour's water pipe cracked because of the frost, and water flooded down the wall in a sheet of water, which promptly froze into a sheet of ice from gutter to ground. It was cold, rigid and brittle. It was the nearest I have got to seeing a frozen waterfall. That is the image – a frozen waterfall – that the German theologian Emil Brunner used to describe some approaches to truth. He describes some aspects of the sort of Protestant orthodoxy that developed in the period following the Reformation in these words: 'a hoar frost has fallen; a splendid growth has suddenly become as though cut off and benumbed. The age of orthodoxy appears like a frozen waterfall – mighty shapes of movement, but no movement. What happened? The paradoxical unity of Word and Spirit fell to pieces; the Scriptures became a gathering of divine oracles, the essence of divinely revealed doctrine. Men *have* God's Word.'[203]

Brunner was contrasting the sort of 'objectivist' approach to truth which he found in some aspects of both Catholic and Protestant post-Reformation churches, in which 'truth' became understood as a rigid

203 Emil Brunner, *Truth as Encounter*, 1938; 2nd ed. 1945, ET SCM, 1963, p.77.

and brittle doctrinal system, with the 'subjectivist' reaction of later pietism, where 'the experience of the individual moves commandingly to the center of attention' and 'pious feeling' becomes of chief importance. Then 'truth' becomes merely 'truth for me', as many today who call themselves post-modern are also prone to say.

The contrast between 'objectivist' and 'subjectivist' approaches to truth can also be illustrated from today's world. Richard Dawkins is fond of saying that religious faith 'means blind trust, in the absence of evidence, even in the teeth of evidence'.[204] Although no one I know holds such a view of faith, it points up the contrast between, on the one hand, the evidence of sense experience in the supposed 'real' objective world out there and, on the other hand, the supposed 'private' inner world of personal morality and religious faith. For Dawkins, truth is about the evidence that is discovered by scientific methods of exploration. St Augustine, by contrast, says that he believes in order to understand (*credo ut intelligam*), and that phrase has been picked up by some scientists, such as Michael Polanyi, to describe their approach to scientific knowledge.[205]

For Polanyi, knowledge of truth comes to us as a 'gift of grace', but it arises in the relationship of the knowing subject and the reality that is being sought in the context of a shared commitment of faith and of the will. Knowledge of truth, he says, always has an irreducibly personal dimension. Faith is generally understood by Christian people to mean trust in the promises and faithfulness of God, involving a conviction of the mind based on sufficient evidence, coupled with a confident trust and the consent of the will. Truth arises in the 'intersubjective' realm, within the context of a believing and exploring community – of science, or of religious faith – and is put 'out there' for testing by others and open to correction if new insights are found.

To return to Emil Brunner, he argues that to approach the question of truth on the basis of an objectivist/subjectivist antithesis 'is a disastrous misunderstanding' (p.69). Such an antithesis completely misses the biblical approach to truth, which is that truth is always relational. It is a 'happening' between what God gives and what we receive. Following Polanyi's lead, we can say that ultimately *truth is personal*. Knowledge of the truth in the Bible is essentially knowledge of God mediated by God's Spirit through personal encounter with Jesus

204 Richard Dawkins, *The Selfish Gene*, OUP, 1989 edn., p.198. cf. *The God Delusion*, Black Swan, 2006, p.232.
205 Michael Polanyi writes: 'We must now go back to St Augustine to restore the balance of our cognitive powers [that is to avoid 'objectivism' on the one hand and subjectivism on the other]. In the fourth century ad St Augustine brought the history of Greek philosophy to a close by inaugurating for the first time a 'post-critical philosophy'. He taught that all knowledge was a gift of grace, for which we must strive under the guidance of antecedent belief: *nisi credideritis, non intelligitis* [unless you believe, you will not understand] (*Personal Knowledge*, Routledge, 1958, p.266).

Christ, the divine Wisdom, and the true and living Way. Jesus said 'I AM the truth.'

(iii) Speaking truth to power is costly

As we saw in the previous chapter, 'the World' into which Christ's disciples are sent in mission is a world perverted from God's good creation, a world in which sin and alienation from God distort and damage and suppress the witness to truth.[206] For Jesus, speaking truth to power led to the Cross. Believers seeking, as best they may within a fallen world, to speak the truth of Christ to the principalities and powers of this 'World', also find themselves under persecution and oppression. Jesus says, 'If the world hates you, be aware that it hated me … Because you do not belong to the world, but I have chosen you out of the world – therefore the world hates you … If they persecuted me, they will persecute you … In the world you face persecution. But take courage; I have conquered the world' (John 15:18–20; 16:33).

One of the costly aspects of being a disciple of Christ 'in the world' is the responsibility of speaking truth to power. Jesus' time before Pilate was in the context of crucifixion. The 'father of lies' is unmasked and disarmed at the Cross, but is still a power to be reckoned with. The community of Christ's people now live in the tension and ambiguity of seeking to live in the wisdom of God's will and God's ways in a disordered and ungodly world.

(iv) The truth sets free: Simon Peter discovers forgiveness

Encounter with Jesus sets free. This is Jesus' word to some of the Judeans who had come to believe in him:

> *'If you continue in my word, you are truly my disciples; and you will know the truth, and the truth will make you free'* (John 8:31f.).

One of the character studies of John's Gospel illustrates this from painful experience: Simon Peter. Earlier we looked at the example of Mary of Bethany in her heartfelt devotion to our Lord – a piety we would often find it hard to emulate. But Simon Peter is very different. He is someone we can identify with. Early picked out by Jesus as a key follower (1:42), he comes over as impetuous, zealous, getting the wrong end of the stick, cowardly, out of breath, teachable, willing, and ultimately admirable. The community of Christ's people certainly includes people like that.

206 St Paul says as much: 'The wrath of God is revealed from heaven against all ungodliness and wickedness of those who by their wickedness suppress the truth … though they knew God, they did not honour him as God or give thanks to him, but they became futile in their thinking, and their senseless minds were darkened … they exchanged the truth about God for a lie and worshipped and served the creature rather than the Creator' (Romans 1:18,21,25).

In the Upper Room, Jesus, the Lord and Master, takes the servant's towel and basin and washes his disciples' feet. 'He came to Simon Peter who said to him, "Lord, are you going to wash my feet?" Jesus answered, "You do not know now what I am doing, but later you will understand." Peter said to him, "You will never wash my feet." Jesus [facing him with an unwelcome truth] answered, "Unless I wash you, you have no share with me." Simon Peter [who only half understood] said to him, 'Lord, not my feet only but also my hands and my head!" Jesus said to him, "One who has bathed does not need to wash, except for the feet, but is entirely clean"' (John 13:6–10).

Eventually, through misunderstanding, bluster and protest, Simon Peter – already 'cleansed' through Jesus' word (15:3) – now accepts and receives the routine, daily cleansing water as gift from Jesus, and through being made clean is reaffirmed in his 'share' in the community of Christ's people. Baptism – and the once-for-all gift of God's gracious welcome – is not repeated but the daily requirement for cleansing and forgiveness needs to be. Peter learns of the ongoing need to be washed – to allow Jesus to serve him – in order that he may be of service to others.

After the meal, when Peter wants to go with Jesus, and boldly affirms his willingness to lay down his life for his Master, Jesus says, 'Will you lay down your life for me? Very truly, I tell you, before the cock crows, you will have denied me three times' (John 13:37f.)

The next major episode involving Peter is in the Garden of Gethsemane. Appalled at Judas' betrayal and Jesus' arrest, he impetuously lashes out with his sword and cuts off the ear of the high priest's slave, Malchus (John 18:10). No doubt he wants to defend Jesus' honour, though Jesus tells Peter to put his sword back in its sheath. As we discover in Jesus' confrontation with Pilate, Jesus' Way is not the way of violence – Jesus' kingdom is not from this world. If Jesus' kingdom did follow the ways of this world, then his followers would fight (John 18:36). But Jesus' Way, the Way of Wisdom, all of whose paths are shalom, is not the violent way.

Peter, suitably subdued, then followed Jesus into the high priest's courtyard, where his nerve gave way. Warming himself by the charcoal fire, he is put on the spot and lies his way out. 'The woman [who guarded the gate] said to Peter, "You are not also one of this man's disciples, are you?" He said, "I am not"' (John 18:17). The same thing happens a bit later on; once again, 'I am not.' Then a slave, one of Malchus' relatives, asked, '"Did I not see you in the garden with him?" Again Peter denied it, and at that moment the cock crowed' (John 18:25–27).

Our last glance at Simon Peter is at breakfast on the beach after the resurrection, beside another charcoal fire. He has led the way in deciding to go back fishing. Now the stranger on the beach calls to the disciples in their boat. Jesus had come to find the disciples, who had gone back to their old ways, and he comes with characteristic abundant generosity of gift – too many fish to handle. And Jesus' gentle, persistent questioning of Peter, and facing him with the truth about himself – three times – gives Peter the chance – three times – to reaffirm his love for Jesus. Peter, 'ransomed, healed, restored, forgiven', not only three times receives Jesus' forgiveness, but also a fresh commission for service. The Good Shepherd commissions his under-shepherd to carry on the good work. The Good Shepherd, as we have said, gathers together, nourishes, searches for the lost, provides security and safety, food and sufficiency, an intimacy of belonging and being known. The Good Shepherd's care extends worldwide, including people of all sorts within the promise of abundant life within an inclusive and united community. That is now the under-shepherd's commission: 'Feed my lambs; tend my sheep; feed my sheep' (John 21, esp. vs.15–19).

Peter has discovered that the truth as it is in Jesus sets free. And Jesus' word which commissioned him extends to all within the community of Christ's people who respond to the liberating light of truth as it is in Jesus, and they also hear the Good Shepherd's voice: 'Follow me.'

(v) Truth is the basis for a free society (Michael Polanyi)

One writer whose philosophy of science very consciously linked truth and freedom was Michael Polanyi. We have referred briefly to him earlier. The reason for considering his work in a little more detail now is the link he made between the processes of discovery in science in its search for truth, and the role of truth in what he called a 'free society'. Polanyi's work on the nature of scientific discovery led to his understanding of what he called 'personal knowledge'. He was strongly opposed to the detached approach to science that he called 'objectivist', in which the scientist is supposed to keep himself/herself out of the process of discovery, and in which supposed scientific facts are entirely separate from moral values. On the contrary, Polanyi argued, all knowledge has an inescapably personal dimension. The scientist, with tacit awareness of certain clues, strives forwards to find their joint meaning at a higher level of understanding. Scientific discovery involves the personal commitment of the scientist, believing that there is some reality there to be discovered, weighing and making judgments about the evidence, using skills he or she has learned through apprenticeship, and striving forwards towards some greater truth that had hitherto not been realized. All science, says Polanyi, shows this inescapably personal dimension. That is why he is so opposed to supposedly 'detached' understandings of science. 'No scientist is ever concerned with producing the most convenient summary of a given set of facts. This is the task of the editors of encyclopaedias and telephone directories. It is of the essence of a scientific theory that it commits us to an indeterminate range of yet undreamed consequences that may flow from it. We commit ourselves to these, because we believe that by our theory we are making contact with a reality of which our theory has revealed one aspect.'[207] Notice the key words: 'we commit ourselves ... because we believe ...' Polanyi draws on the saying of St Augustine (which refers to Isaiah 7.9) : 'we believe in order to understand.'

To avoid the misunderstanding that Polanyi is advocating a wholly subjective approach to knowledge, he very clearly underlines the fact that the scientist works within a tradition of beliefs and understandings, and puts his discovery out into the public realm of the scientific community for scrutiny, correction or corroboration. There is a conviviality, an 'inter-subjective testability' within the community of science. Polanyi evocatively calls the community of scientists 'a society of explorers.'

One of the primary motivations which drove Polanyi – a secular Jew from Hungary who later acknowledged Christian faith – from his professorial chair in chemistry, first in Berlin and then – when the Nazi's came to power – in his new home in the UK in Manchester, and into his new work in social science and philosophy, was his outrage at the way Stalin's Russia handled the question of truth. For the Marxist society of the mid 1930's, truth was what the party defined it to be. Research scientists were free to follow their own interests, but 'owing to the internal harmony of socialist society, they would inevitably be led to lines of research which would benefit the current Five Year Plan.'[208] Polanyi was having none of this. Just as science is a 'society of explorers', committed to the belief that there is some transcendent reality to discover, so – by analogy – a free society, Polanyi says, also needs to hold fast to transcendent values of truth, love, justice, beauty and law, and be de-

---

207 Michael Polanyi, 'Scientific Outlook: its sickness and cure', *Science,* Vol.125. p.480f.
208 Polanyi, *Science, Faith and Society,* Chicago 1946, p. 8

termined to work together in the light of these values. The Hungarian Revolution of 1956 was a striking example of a society refusing the Communist definitions of truth, and demanding instead the freedom to write the truth, write about real people, report truthfully on events. 'The free society', says Polanyi, 'can be defended only by expressly recognizing the characteristic beliefs which are held in common by such a society and professing that these beliefs are true'. He goes on: 'the ideal of a free society is in the first place to be a *good* society: a body of men who respect truth, desire justice and love their fellows.' [209] Or again: 'a general respect for truth is all that is needed for society to be free.'[210] There is no place for 'post-truth'.

Polanyi's approach to 'personal knowledge' and a free society committed to transcendent values stands in opposition to much 'objectivist' science which seeks to promote detachment between the scientist and his or her objects of study. Unfortunately, some aspects of conservation science today work with an 'objectivist' ideal; whereas the reality is that we human beings and other creatures are subjects together within God's creation. The objectivist approach, like that of Francis Bacon and Descartes, when the covenant with the Creator God was fractured, feeds the notion that we are 'masters and possessors' of nature, rather than fellow subjects under God's creative love and care. Today's approach to economics also too often assumes the detached rational individual, and a mechanistic approach to economic theory, instead of one rooted in transcendent values of love and justice and other human values. A free society working for the common good will seek not only equity amongst human beings, but the common good of all God's creatures, and will seek to understand the financial economy within the wider framework of the transcendent values of God's creativity.

The truth of Christ that sets an individual such as Simon Peter free through love and forgiveness also lies behind the sort of approach Polanyi takes to the free society. His discussion of personal knowledge underlines the importance of the human person in all knowledge, which cautions against a relapse into Baconian objectivism, and so against treating other people and other creatures simply as commodities with a price-tag. But 'personal knowledge' points also to those transcendent values to which a society needs to be committed if it is to avoid the road to various sorts of totalitarianism, the values of love, justice, beauty and law, expressed so fully in shalom, which are

---

209 Polanyi, *The Logic of Liberty* (Chicago 1951) Liberty Fund 1998, pp. 35, 36.
210 Polanyi, *Science, Faith and Society*, p. 19.

essential pointers to Wisdom's Way, and which motivate a Christian's concern for the wellbeing of the whole environment of God's creation.

Chapter Eleven

The Community of Christ's People: Jesus' Friends

- The Church is the Christian community brought into being by the risen Jesus, and energized by the Holy Spirit.

- In John chapters 13–17 we explore various features of the community around the Beloved Disciple.

- Jesus describes his followers as his 'friends'.

- It is a community given life by the Holy Spirit; a community marked by self-giving service and good works; called to be courageous and persistent under persecution, patient and hopeful under suffering. It is a community marked especially by love and the quest for justice; a community sent out in mission, and held together by prayer and worship.

To all who received him, who believed in his name, he gave power to become children of God. (John 1:12)
You are my friends. (John 15:14)

Throughout all our reflections on John's Gospel, we have constantly been pointed forwards to the establishment of a community of Christ's people, a fellowship of Jesus' followers who believe 'into' him, receive his gift of 'eternal life', come to know God through him, live his Way of Wisdom by doing shalom in the light of his truth, and so continue his work of bringing God's healing love to the world and the whole of creation. The second part of the Gospel, especially chapters 13–17, fills out some of the marks of this community, and will be our focus in this chapter.

'The Church is the Christian community'
One of the huge and joyous privileges of my ministry was being for some years Fellow and Chaplain of Corpus Christi College, Oxford. My study overlooked the exquisite main quadrangle. In the centre of the quad, the pelican sundial stood as a reminder of the medieval use of

the pelican, believed to feed its young by plucking blood from its own breast, as a symbol of the Body of Christ. Across the quad I could see the library, the hall and the gateway to the chapel – the three main public buildings which the founder (Bishop Richard Foxe, in 1517) had put together at the centre of the college. These three main buildings were to represent the fullness of human life, sustained in body and mind, and all given to God in worship. The chapel, with its Rubens' altarpiece, memorials to previous Presidents of the College, and its rather fragile ceiling bosses, was a small, quiet space for prayer and worship. At least it was in my day. One of my predecessors not too long before me had had to face a difficult question, put to him by some Fellows who saw no need for a chapel, but did see a great need for an enlarged library. How would he feel about closing 'the church', and turning it into a library extension? His wise answer was: 'The Church is the Christian community, not where it meets.' Thankfully, other ways were found for handling the library's needs, and the chapel is still in use as the place where the Christian community meets – now with a refurbished ceiling.

'The Church is the Christian community' is a thought that would have been familiar to the author of John's Gospel, though he does not use the word often translated 'church'. He speaks instead of a community of 'children of God' ('To all who received him, who believed in his name, he gave power to become children of God', John 1:12). Later, he speaks of Jesus' friends ('You are my friends', John 15:14).

The Gospel, as we have reminded ourselves more than once, was written 'that you may come to believe that Jesus is the Christ ... and that through believing you may have life in his name' (20:31). This has an evangelistic flavour – suggesting that the concern of the Gospel writer is to help someone to come to faith in Jesus as the Christ, and no doubt that is true. But this text could also mean 'that you may *continue* to believe', which is more a word of encouragement to struggling Christians to hang on and keep on in their faith. Perhaps we are meant to read both.

The focus of John's Gospel moves from the early chapters ('The Book of Signs'), which bear witness to the truth as it is in Jesus, to the later chapters (13 onwards, sometimes called 'The Book of Glory'), with their primary focus on the new community of disciples that Jesus calls together. In particular, John's Gospel chapters 13–17 is sometimes called the 'Upper Room Discourses', which precede the Garden of Gethsemane and Jesus' trial, crucifixion and resurrection.

Three sets of 'last words'

John chapters 13–17 are complicated chapters. One way we can understand them is in terms of three farewell discourses, that is three sets of 'last words', followed by a whole chapter (17) of Jesus at prayer.

- The first discourse (13:31–14:31) says a lot about coming and going, about Jesus' presence and forthcoming absence. Jesus prepares his disciples for his departure by saying much about his own relationship with God his Father.
- The second discourse (15:1–27) is mostly about Jesus' relationship with his 'friends'.
- The third discourse (16:1–33) covers various topics, especially the strengthening work of the Holy Spirit in the new Christian community.

For our purpose in this chapter, we are going to select a few of the themes from these complicated chapters. This is not an exposition of all that the Gospel says – rather a selection of some of the features that marked the community of the Beloved Disciple. We find that Jesus' relationship with the Father becomes the pattern for his relationship with his friends, who are strengthened by the Holy Spirit to 'be where Jesus is'.

The embryonic Christian community at the Cross

In one important sense, the community of Christ's people begins at the Cross, when Jesus in his dying agony turns to his mother standing near and, indicating the Beloved Disciple, says, 'Woman, here is your son', and to the disciple, 'Here is your mother.' 'And from that hour the disciple took her into his own home' (John 19:26f.). There have many suggestions of why this little interaction was included in the Gospel, in which a new family unit is established – in the loving presence of some others, among them Mary the wife of Clopas and Mary Magdalene. This action of Jesus' compassionate suffering love stands in sharp contrast to the narrative of political dominion with its soldiers, thorns, flogging and death. Mary, whom we have not met since Cana in Galilee, is now given care of Jesus' friend – and he care of her. Perhaps Mary stands for all those who faithfully hoped in Jesus as the Messiah of the Jews, and the Beloved Disciple – who had been lying on Jesus' 'bosom' in the Upper Room – stands for those now charged with passing on what has been learned of Jesus' relationship 'close to the Father's heart' (1:18). Perhaps Mary is to be the new Eve, the mother of the followers of Jesus. Perhaps here is a new humanity, male and female, gathered at Jesus' feet. Whatever the symbolism, here is an embryonic community of the followers of Jesus, which, by way of Easter morning and the gift of the Spirit, developed into a multitude of Christian communities, of which that around the Beloved Disciple was but one.

The community of the Beloved Disciple

I am persuaded by the view that John's Gospel was written from within a group of Christians towards the end of the first century, probably led by – certainly strongly influenced by – someone whom the Gospel calls 'the disciple whom Jesus loved'. I am attracted by Richard Bauckham's proposal[211] that this 'Beloved Disciple' was an apostle, present with Jesus at the Last Supper, though not one of the Twelve. The Beloved Disciple appears at several crucial times during the Gospel. As we have said, he is the one reclining next to Jesus at the Passover meal in the Upper Room. He questioned Jesus about who was to betray him (13:23,25; cf. 21:20). He alone among the male disciples is identified at the Cross (19:26). He is the one to whom Mary Magdalene runs on Easter morning with news that the body of Jesus is no longer in the tomb (20:2), and was the first to go into the tomb – and to believe that Jesus had risen from the dead (20:8). He first recognized Jesus standing on the Galilee beach after the resurrection, and said to his fishermen colleagues in the boat, 'It is the Lord!' (21:7). And he is present at the conversation between Jesus and Peter when Jesus gives the commission 'Follow me!' (21:19).

We imagine a Christian community, gathered around this Beloved Disciple and sharing their memories, their stories and sermons, perhaps their written memos. It is a community with internal tensions, and external conflict – with Pharisees and other Judean leaders and their local synagogue. It is this community whose faith the Beloved Disciple is seeking to strengthen and whose hope to re-ignite.

If that is that case, although he would not have taken notes at the time, we can be sure that he wanted to preserve in his teaching the truth of what Jesus said to his disciples at that important last meal together. But as leader of the community out of which this Gospel originated he would emphasize those parts that particularly encouraged struggling Christians in their faith. He is writing of the events which happened *before* the Cross and resurrection *from the perspective* of knowing the risen Jesus, and having received from him the gift of the Holy Spirit. This is why some of the things which Jesus says in these chapters seem to suggest that the victory of the Cross and resurrection has already

---

211 Richard Bauckham, *The Testimony of the Beloved Disciple*, Baker, 2007.

happened. For example: 'I have conquered the world' (16:33), 'I glorified you on earth by finishing the work that you gave me to do' (17:4); 'they ... know in truth that I came from you; and they have believed that you sent me' (17:8); 'the world has hated them' (17:14); 'As you have sent me into the world, so I have sent them into the world' (17:18).

So we need to read John chapters 13–17 at different levels: first, to recall the teaching of Jesus at his 'farewell' meal before the crucifixion; and second to encourage and deepen the faith of a struggling Christian community who feel themselves to be oppressed. This 'community of Christ's people' gives us one example from the early centuries of what living in God's world, doing shalom, bearing witness to the light of truth, and 'being where Jesus is' meant in a context of struggle and uncertainty. These chapters have been drawn on by Christians of all later generations, for help in understanding what it means for Christian people, individually and together, to 'believe and go on believing that Jesus is God's Messiah' and so enjoy, learn and live hopefully to the full 'life in his name'.

Jesus' friends

In the Upper Room Jesus speaks of friendship: 'This is my commandment, that you love one another as I have loved you. No one has greater love than this, to lay down one's life for one's friends. You are my friends if you do what I command you. I do not call you servants any longer, because the servant does not know what the master is doing; but I have called you friends, because I have made known to you everything that I have heard from my Father' (John 15:12–15).

The listening disciples would remember that both Abraham and Moses were called 'friends of God' (Isaiah 41:8; Exodus 33:11), a description in each case of intimacy and mutual knowledge. It seems clear that in some sense the 'friend' is still also a servant, called to respond obediently to the Master's call and example, but now more than simply a servant, but someone who knows the Master's will and ways. Friendship with Jesus is an expression of his love – a love even to death. What holds the community of Jesus' friends together is his merciful self-giving love. Some relationships in which we find ourselves are given to us: we have no choice about them – our birth family, for example. On the other hand, friendships usually come from the freedom of choice, and depend on grace: a self-giving of one to the other. Jesus' friends are those whom Jesus loves.

It is perhaps no surprise that in our highly individualized culture, we too easily get caught up into technological ways of thinking in which we see one another as technicians, interveners in the system, problem-solvers; in which everything, even other people, become subject to our will, our control, our technique. Everything becomes a commodity. The splits in our culture that divide spirit from matter and facts from values also divide person from person. We lose the meaning of communion, fellowship, community, friends. The Way of Jesus, on the other hand, is built on other-regarding love and self-giving service.

John's Gospel introduces us to a number of individual people who, in different ways, are drawn into friendship with Jesus. Some of these are rich, some poor, some male, some female, some Jews, some Gentiles, some like Mary of Bethany with deep devotional faith, some doubtful and sceptical like Thomas, some, it seems, only 'half-believers', like Nicodemus. In the way the Gospel is written, some are included not only for what it says about their own faith; they are chosen also as representative figures (such as Nicodemus; such as the blind beggar) to illustrate some of the range of needs and responses within the community of the Beloved Disciple. We read also of John the Baptist, Andrew, Simon Peter, Nathaniel, Jesus' mother, Nicodemus, a woman of Samaria, a royal official, a paralyzed man, Philip, Jesus' brothers, Martha and Lazarus, Judas, Mary Magdalene – the first missionary – and other unnamed apostles, among them the Beloved Disciple himself.

A community of the Holy Spirit

The fullness of life seen in Jesus can be lived within the community of Christ's people as they follow Jesus' Way of suffering love, abide in him and let his words abide in them. That is, as the Holy Spirit unites them with the risen Christ. The Christian community is a 'community of the Holy Spirit'.

The Holy Spirit is rightly called 'the Lord, the giver of life'. We have commented on the life-giving work of God's Spirit in creation: 'When you send forth your spirit, [all] are created' (Psalm 104:24,27,30). We said that the Spirit's work is to bring the whole of God's 'creation project' to its fulfilment and perfection. As Abraham Kuyper put it: 'To lead the creature to its destiny, to cause it to develop according to its nature, to make it perfect, is the proper work of the Holy Spirit.'[212] That life-giving power is evident also in the incarnation of God's Word and Wisdom, in Jesus, born of Mary, to whom God's angel said, 'The Holy Spirit will come upon you, and the power of the Most High will over-

212 Abraham Kuyper, *The Work of the Holy Spirit* (1900), Eerdmans, 1975, p.21.

shadow you.'[213]

When the Spirit like a dove descended on Jesus at his baptism, and remained on him, those around knew that he was the Son of God (John 1:32–34).

The Holy Spirit, who *gives life* to every creature, who *animates* the rational minds of all human beings, *indwells* the hearts of all believers within the community of Christ's people.[214]

John's Gospel speaks about the Spirit, who 'gives life' (John 6:63), in terms of 'rivers of living water flowing' from Jesus to the believers (John 7:38).[215] The Holy Spirit, overflowing with life, will teach the Christian community, and remind them of Jesus' words (14:26); will be their helper, testifying to the truth, when the community are facing hatred and opposition (15:20–26); will guide the community 'into all truth' (16:13). The Spirit is also at work in the wider world. When the Spirit comes, inspiring the mission of the Christian community, this will prove 'the World' wrong about various things.

The Spirit will prove the world wrong about 'sin', because 'the World' has disbelieved that Jesus is the Christ – or, as the Gospel writer put it in an earlier chapter, 'This is the judgement, that the light has come into the world, and people loved darkness rather than light' (3:19). When the Spirit comes, 'the World' will also be proved wrong about 'righteousness'. Throughout his ministry, Jesus was believed – particularly by some religious leaders – to be in the wrong. His vindication as being in the right before God is his welcome at his heavenly Father's side: 'I am going to the Father' (16:10). And the Spirit will show 'the World' that it has got it wrong about 'judgement': 'Now is the judgement of this world' said Jesus (12:31), 'now the ruler of this world will be driven out' (cf. 16.11).

The community of Christ's people live now in the knowledge of Jesus' victory over the forces of darkness through the Cross and resurrection. He has 'overcome the World'. In their mission, they continue to bear witness to the truth as it is in Jesus, in a 'World' ordered without reference to God, a world of unbelief, a world under judgement. They are bound together by the life-giving Spirit of the risen Jesus. He commissioned them: 'As the Father has sent me, so I send you'; then he breathed on them, with a commission to continue his own ministry

---

213 Luke 1:35.

214 cf. Kuyper, op. cit., p.26.

215 This text may also be read as 'rivers of living water flowing from the believer', which would suggest that Christ's living water, which quenches the thirst of Christian people, can then flow out from them for the blessing of others. This was an allusion to the water used at the Festival of Tabernacles, which signified 'drawing water with joy from the wells of salvation' (as the prophet Isaiah put it, Isaiah 12:3), and is possibly an allusion to the living water flowing from God's Temple, as referred to in the Book of Revelation.

of liberation, and said to them, 'Receive the Holy Spirit' (20:21f.). This recalls God's breathing into Adam 'the breath of life' in the gift of creation, and also God's wind breathing life into the flesh on the dry bones in Ezekiel's vision (Ezekiel 37:9–10). Just as Ezekiel saw the ending of exile, and the coming into being of a new creation, here Jesus is breathing new life into the Christian community, uniting them with the new creation of his resurrection, and so sending them out to continue his mission.

A community of self-giving service and good works, 13:1–20

One of the marks of the ministry of Jesus, and therefore of the community of Christ's people inspired by God's Spirit, is self-giving service and good works.

After Jesus' symbolic action as servant, washing the dusty feet of his disciples, he tells them that their discipleship, following him as their Lord and Teacher, is also to be the way of self-giving and humble service. 'If I, your Lord and Teacher, have washed your feet, you also ought to wash one another's feet' (John 13:14).

Part of that service is to continue doing the 'good works' that have marked Jesus' own ministry. 'The Father who dwells in me does his works ... the one who believes in me will also do the works that I do and, in fact, will do greater works than these (John 14:10–12).

The reference to Jesus' 'works' is yet another favourite theme in John's Gospel. In Jesus' great prayer to the Father, he says, 'I glorified you on earth by finishing the work that you gave me to do' (17:4; cf. 4:34). 'The work' means the whole of his ministry for the redemption of the world, culminating at the Cross.

In his 'works' throughout his ministry, Jesus uses the things of earth – transforming water into wine, using clay and spittle for healing, a reshaping of the Sabbath, transforming fish and loaves into a banquet, stilling the storm – to be signs that the Messiah has come. These are the marks of God's kingdom, to which ultimately his resurrection will point: the healing of creation, that is the bringing of God's creation 'project' towards its perfection in glory.

When Jesus says, 'My Father is working still and I am working',[216] he is referring to the loving work of God in creating and continuing to sustain the world, and his own work of the new creation: healing,

---

216 John's Gospel speaks of various of Jesus' 'works' as the works also of God: 'The Father who dwells in me does his works. Believe me that I am in the Father and the Father is in me; but if you do not, then believe me because of the works themselves. Very truly, I tell you, the one who believes in me will also do the works that I do and, in fact, will do greater works than these' (14:10–12). In other words, Jesus in his ministry does the works of God the Father, works that will now be continued in the ministry of the community of Christ's people. When the disciples asked Jesus, 'What must we do to perform the works of God?' Jesus answered, 'This is the work of God, that you believe in him whom he has sent' (6:28–29). It is by 'believing into' Jesus, obeying his word and abiding in him through the Spirit, that the works of God continue.

restoring, making new. At one point the revealing of 'God's works' is linked to the healing of a blind beggar (9:3–4). Several times, Jesus says that his works bear witness that he has in fact come from the Father (5:36; 10:25,32–38), and on occasion his works provoke astonishment (e.g.7:21); indeed his brothers urge Jesus to go from Galilee up to the festival in Jerusalem 'so that your disciples also may see the works you are doing' (7:3).

Jose Miranda argues (somewhat controversially) that 'good works' and 'evil works' are very specific and technical terms in biblical and extra-biblical Jewish literature.[217] In particular, he quotes Jeremias as showing that 'good works' are most specifically defined (see Matthew 25:31–46) as such things as giving food to the hungry and drink to the thirsty, clothing the naked, and visiting the sick and those in prison. These are the issues, says Matthew, on which God's response at the Last Judgement depends. John's Gospel's comment after the conversation between Jesus and Nicodemus is similar. It matters whether a person's deeds are 'evil' (the works of 'the World' are described as 'evil', 7:7), or whether they 'do what is true' and their deeds are 'done in God'.

> This is the judgement, that the light has come into the world, and people loved darkness rather than light because their deeds were evil. For all who do evil hate the light and do not come to the light, so that their deeds may not be exposed. But those who do what is true come to the light, so that it may be clearly seen that their deeds have been done in God. (John 3:19–21)

We have already seen how in many of Jesus' works described in John's Gospel, he includes the unaccepted and marginalized, such as the woman of Samaria; he heals blind and paralyzed people; he enables people to make responsible decisions. Good work is about food for the hungry and water for the thirsty. Jesus nourishes and feeds, educates and liberates, he takes the servant's towel and bowl, he restores the fallen and commissions them for service. And in much of his work he prioritizes the poor, those without health, without food, without hope, without friends.

The fullness of life, which is following Jesus' Way, includes the service of good works, especially for the benefit of the poorest and most disadvantaged.

A community that struggles

We began in our chapter 1 with the fear of being unable to cope. There, it was about coastal erosion in Norfolk. More widely it was about the

---

217 Jose Miranda, *Being and the Messiah*, Wipf and Stock, 2006, p.97.

anxieties and uncertainties created by growing inequality, lack of sustainability, and the degradation of the natural environment. To return now to Jesus' first disciples, the dominant anxiety was about not knowing what would happen to them once it dawned on them that Jesus was to leave them. (And how would the Beloved Disciple's community cope with their uncertainties – especially in a context of opposition and persecution?) This is the point in the Gospel at which Jesus says:

> *Do not let your hearts be troubled. Believe in God, believe also in me.* (John 14:1)

We recall that this was the text on the church noticeboard in Norfolk. Just as it stands, it could read like a rather superficial panacea. We now know that the context in the Gospel is one of struggle, persecution and conflict. Although the starkness of many of John's contrasts – evil and good, darkness and light, death and life – may take us by surprise, there is nothing surprising about the fact that being a believer in Jesus creates some conflict with 'the World'. We live on God's earth, and have a responsibility to care for it on God's behalf. We live in a world of other creatures and other human beings, and are endowed with the capacity for interpersonal relationships. Yet 'the World' (in John's Gospel's sense of 'human nature organized without reference to God'), can be hostile and hateful towards Jesus and his followers, and then the community of Christ's people can find themselves – as Jesus did – the subject of murmuring, false accusation, betrayal, confrontation with corporate power, caught up in a conflict with the 'father of lies'. The word of truth in Jesus always provokes conflict and requires decision.

Towards the end of the Farewell Discourses, Jesus says: 'If the world hates you, be aware that it hated me before it hated you … If they persecuted me, they will persecute you … When the Advocate comes, whom I will send to you from the Father, the Spirit of truth who comes from the Father, he will testify on my behalf … I have said these things to you to keep you from stumbling. They will put you out of the synagogues. Indeed, an hour is coming when those who kill you will think that by doing so they are offering worship to God. And they will do this because they have not known the Father or me' (John 15:18–16:3).

It is into this context of hatred, hostility and persecution that Jesus speaks his words of strengthening encouragement. The theme continues into John chapter 15. The crucial task of the Christian community under threat is to remain together, united in common purpose. To strike out alone would be utterly counterproductive. Christ and his people need to be bound together in the Spirit, and mutually 'abide', or 'indwell' each other. 'Those who abide in me and I in them bear much fruit, because apart from me you can do nothing' (15:5).

I AM the true vine

The striking image Jesus gives at this point is of the Vine. Jesus uses the divine name: 'I AM the true vine' (15:1). The paragraph that follows describes Christian discipleship in terms of connectedness, interdependence, fruitfulness and indwelling. And it describes God as one who prunes away what does not belong, is not fruitful and so of no use. But it also goes on to speak of the Father's love, joy and friendship (John 15:8–17).

The image of the vine recalls the pictures in the Hebrew Bible that speak of the people of Israel as God's luxuriant vine (Hosea 10:1–2), which – however – is not always fruitful.[218] And just as the people of Israel stand in many ways – in the narrative of the Scriptures – for the whole of humanity under God, so an unfruitful and disappointing vine symbolizes also the failure of humanity, through its sin and selfishness, to live within God's will and God's way. Therefore, for Jesus to say, 'I AM the *true* vine' is making unmistakably clear his claim to be both Israel as she was meant to be – the *true* vine in place of unfruitful Israel – and *humanity as we were meant to be*, and as we can learn again to be, abiding in him. The harsh words about pruning out those who are not bearing fruit, probably reflect the fact – noted briefly in the Gospel (6:66), and sadly seen in the betrayal by Judas (13:30) and also made explicit in the First Epistle of John – that some of the community of the Beloved Disciple had decided to leave and go their own way. 'They went out from us, but they did not belong to us' (1 John 2:19).

The language of 'abiding in Christ' contains the sense of holding on; hanging in there when faith is tested and the going is tough. The Holy Spirit will be your Advocate. The fullness of life, which is following Jesus' Way, may be costly and painful. You may well get it wrong, hurt each other, deny your Lord, give way to cowardly betrayal. But – as Simon Peter discovered – there is a way back and a new start. Which means that the struggles can also be marked by divine love, joy and friendship.

---

218 Psalm 80:8–18 is a lament for the affliction of God's people and a prayer that God would have regard for his vine, and restore his people's fortunes. Isaiah offers a love-song concerning God's vineyard: God had expected fruitfulness – what he found was wild grapes! (Isaiah 5:1–7). Jeremiah says the same: 'I planted you as a choice vine, from the purest stock. How then did you degenerate and become a wild vine?' (Jeremiah 2:21). And there are various uses of the vine image in the prophecy of Ezekiel. The primary thrust of these Hebrew images is of the failure of Israel as a whole to live fruitfully as God's people.

A community of patient and joyful hope even through suffering, 16:12–22

There is a note of suffering throughout the whole second section of the Farewell Discourses. Abide in Christ, keep the faith during persecution, trust in the abiding presence and advocacy of the Holy Spirit, and hold on in hope to the joy that is set before you. John uses the metaphor of childbirth,[219] with the pains of labour giving way to the unshakeable joy of new life, to encourage the community of believers not to lose heart.

> When a woman is in labour, she has pain, because her hour has come. But when her child is born, she no longer remembers the anguish because of the joy of having brought a human being into the world. So you have pain now; but I will see you again, and your hearts will rejoice, and no one will take your joy from you. (John 16:21–22)

The Lord who dies will appear to them again. Resurrection will be the dawn of a new age. There will be a new understanding of who Jesus is, and of his life with the Father and the life of prayer in Christ's name will, for the believers, take on a fresh meaning (John 16:20–28).

So the import of this is: do not despair; live in hope in God's faithfulness. That can be a word also for us. Given the current environmental crisis, and as we look towards the sort of world our grandchildren and theirs will inhabit, there are many grounds for desperation and anxiety. And there can be a temptation to take refuge in what might well be a false hope.

Hope today

Authentic Christian hope is not a blind optimism that everything will work out all right, or indeed the assumption that either God or technology will provide us with a new future to resource us to keep going just as we are. As James Nash rightly puts it, '[Christian eschatology] runs counter to both pessimistic and optimistic views of the future. It cannot and does not provide any guarantee that some form of global or cosmic catastrophe will be averted.'[220] That is not to say that we should not bend every effort, draw on our technical and political skills and exercise personal restraint in our consumer lifestyles, in order as

---

219 St Paul uses a similar metaphor in his remarkable discussion of the ambiguity of the present world – a world in which we grieve, but in which also we hold out a struggling hope in God's faithfulness. In Romans 8:18–25 St Paul writes both of creation groaning in travail, subjected to futility, and yet on the basis of his gospel, he writes confidently of hope, waiting for God's new world to be born. In the centre of the complex theology of grace which he works out in the Epistle to the Romans, and of God's reconciliation with sinful humanity through Christ, Paul stands back and looks at a broader vista – the redemption of the whole of creation in God's purposes. The present world he finds ambiguous – both 'groaning' and 'eager with anticipation'. But his language is of birth – and of a new world coming into being – and that is the source of his hope.

220 James Nash, *Hope for the Earth*, Wipf and Stock, 2000, p.212.

far as possible to avert disaster. But we need a theology that is more robust than the optimistic wish that everything will work out all right. We need a theology that hears the words of judgement the eighth-century BC prophets spoke to God's people when they had abandoned God's ways, and given in to injustice. A theology that recognises that if we continue in the way of sinfulness, stupidity, over-consumption, 'extractivism' and greed, we most likely, and a future generation more certainly, are destined for some catastrophe. A theology that can address the strategies of denial among politicians and those who wield corporate power. A theology that may take us by way of Gethsemane and the Cross before we reach Easter; by way of grief and mourning and repentant change, before we can celebrate hope. Rather than blind or naive optimism, Christian hope is rather trust in God's faithfulness: that God in love holds on to us in all our uncertainties and that, in ways we do not know, God has a future for God's 'creation project'.

So the fullness of life, lived by following Jesus' Way, lives in hope rooted in God's covenanted promise and God's faithfulness. It seeks to confront the evils and injustices that cause so much suffering. But the word of Jesus is that prayerful trust in God, in all the uncertainties of the present, can ultimately be joyous.

A community marked especially by love and the quest for justice

One of the central words of John's Gospel is 'love'. To become part of the community of Christ's people is to believe into the One sent by God, to receive and respond to his love, to allow Christ's word to 'abide in you', and to bear witness by word and by deed to the truth as it is in Jesus, and to express that witness by love. In a hostile culture, opposed to the truth, antagonistic towards Christ, seeking even to divide the Christian community one from another, the commandment of Jesus is 'Love one another.'

> *I give you a new commandment, that you love one another. Just as I have loved you, you also should love one another. By this everyone will know that you are my disciples, if you have love for one another.* (John 13:34–35)

If we were to try to summaries the 'ethics' of John's Gospel in one word, it would be 'love'. It is in the discourse on the vine in John chapter 15 that Jesus first gives a 'commandment' to love. 'As the Father has loved me, so have I loved you; abide in my love. If you keep my commandments, you will abide in my love, just as I have kept my Father's commandments and abide in his love ... This is my commandment, that you love one another as I have loved you ... You are my friends if you do what I command you ... I am giving you these command s so that you may love one another' (15:9–17).

The commandment to love is addressed initially towards fellow Christian believers. They are to love one another. Maybe this points up some tensions within the circle of believers from whom John was writing his Gospel. Did they need to be reminded to love each other? Love includes willingness for suffering. Jesus loved 'to the end' (13:1). He said that 'No one has greater love than this, to lay down one's life for one's friends' (15:13). Love then becomes the standard by which all other aspects of Christian discipleship are measured. The evidence for the fact that one is keeping Jesus' words, that one is serving Christ, following him, believing in him, is the fact that believers love one another (13:34; 15:12,17).

Of course, love of God and love of neighbour were part of the faith of the Hebrew Bible (Deuteronomy 6:5; Leviticus 19:18). So what is 'new' when Jesus says 'a new commandment I give to you that you love one another'? The newness[221] is found in the next qualifying phrase: 'as I have loved you' (13:34). The account of the foot-washing in chapter 13 is a sign of this self-giving and servant-like love which Jesus has for his friends, and which they are to show to each other.

However, love is not only about loving one's friends. The great text 'God so loved the world' (3:16), means that the love of Christ's followers, modelled on God's love for us and Christ's love for his own, though beginning with the people of God, cannot end there. The other three Gospels speak more explicitly about love for neighbour, even love for enemies. John's Gospel uses rather different imagery. It speaks of the Good Shepherd, whose love is world-wide (John 10:16). The love of Christ's people, which reflects the love of Christ, must likewise be outward looking and unlimited. It is by our union with Christ 'that the world may believe' (17:21).

Love and justice

Jose Miranda's work on John's Gospel[222] reminds us that love, in John, is seen especially in love of the deprived, the poor, and the needy. He draws on the first Letter of John to identify love with social justice:

---

221 The theologian R. Schnackenburg (*The Moral Teaching of the New Testament*, Burns and Oates, 1965, p.325) refers to two things which define this 'newness': firstly, the profoundly understood idea of discipleship – following Jesus' example to the uttermost; and secondly what he calls the 'eschatological novelty', by which he means that the unselfish love which sacrifices to the uttermost has only been made possible by God's initiative, and by the mission and sacrifice of God's Son, which 'is the consequence of his incomprehensible, paradoxical love for the sinful world'.

222 Jose Miranda, *Being and the Messiah*, Orbis Books, 1977.

How does God's love abide in anyone who has the world's goods and sees a brother or sister in need and yet refuses help? Little children, let us love, not in word or speech, but in truth and action. (1 John 3:17–18)

'The defining characteristic of the God of the Bible is the fact that he cannot be known or loved directly; rather, to love God and to know him means to love one's neighbor and to do one's neighbor justice.'[223] Similarly, Nicholas Wolterstorff is right to say, 'Treating the neighbour justly is an example of loving him, a way of loving him.'[224] And further: 'Care combines seeking to enhance someone's flourishing with seeking to secure their just treatment.' Justice, in other words, is the social and political expression of neighbour-love. We are back now to shalom: peace with justice.

It is love for God and his people and his earth that will motivate transformative action for renewal.

The environmental crisis we face, and the need to move towards sustainable living, calls us to love and seek justice for our neighbours – including those overseas and those not yet born. Justice, especially for the poorest and most disadvantaged people, who have done least to cause environmental damage and are the least able to adapt. So in a world of climate change, loss of biodiversity, the need for sustainable living, we take from this that love to God and our neighbour in the doing of shalom includes bringing the environmental agenda and the developmental agenda together. As the Pope put it so powerfully in his Encyclical *Laudato Si*: we must be attentive both to 'the cry of the earth and the cry of the poor' (para.49). Christian Aid quote Nazumul Chowdhury: 'Forget about making poverty history. Climate change will make poverty permanent.' We are faced here with a radical reframing of all our values and desires. And that means costly discipleship. It means less consumption. It means restraint. It means love constrained by the requirements of justice and shalom.

That is part of our Christian mission. Justice requires an equitable and sustainable sharing of the rich resources of God's earth, and for many of us this requires the discipleship of restraint. To continue to consume earth's resources at our current rate is not only unsustainable, it is sin.

As Operation Noah's Declaration, *Climate Change and the Purposes of God*, put it, speaking of justice and love:

---

223 Miranda, p.137.
224 Nicholas Wolterstorff, *Justice in Love*, Eerdmans, 2011, pp.83,101.

> *The prophets put economic behaviour at the forefront of their call to justice ... Today, the challenge is to seek a different, sustainable economy, based on the values of human flourishing and the wellbeing of all creation, not on the assumption of unlimited economic growth, on overconsumption, exploitative interest and debt ... People in poor communities are mostly innocent of any role in causing climate change, whilst the nations that pollute the most, refuse to accept their responsibilities. Loving our neighbour requires us to reduce our consumption of energy for the sake of Christ, who suffers with those who suffer. To live simply and sustainably contributes significantly to human flourishing ... In the future, Christians may also be called to receive into their communities refugees forced to leave their lands through climate change.*[225]

The fullness of life which is following Jesus' Way is essentially a life of love, a quest for justice, the doing of shalom.

A community sent out in mission

> *From his fullness have we all received, grace upon grace.* (John 1:16)
> *As the Father has sent me, so I send you.* (John 20:21)

The Gospel of John points us to Jesus Christ, the embodied Wisdom of God. It illuminates the 'fullness of life', seen in him, that comes through union by the Spirit of God with the life of the risen Christ. That life is the corporate life of branches in the vine (John 15), what we have called the community of the Beloved Disciple. In other words, we are talking of the Christian Church, whose unity is well described by the World Council of Churches: 'The unity of the Church, the unity of the human community and the unity of the whole creation are interconnected.'[226] That corporate Church life is elaborated in rich detail in terms of discipleship, described as 'being where Jesus is' (John 17:24), and in terms of mission: 'As the Father has sent me, so I send you' (John 20:21).

The invitation – indeed command – to us is to live now, justly and healthily and sustainably, in the light of the coming of God's kingdom. The 'creation project' lives in eschatological hope.[227] It is after his great chapter about resurrection that St Paul writes: 'Therefore ... in the Lord your labour is not in vain' (1 Corinthians 15:58). In a context in which it is easy to feel that we are powerless to make any difference at all, we take encouragement from St Paul: in the Lord, your labour is not in vain. As the Operation Noah Declaration put it:

> *Hope in God motivates us to take action that can lead to transformation ... Despite the strong probability of very serious effects from global warming, for Christians despair is not an option ... We are called to live and work with hope*

---

225 http://operationnoah.org/articles/read-ash-wednesday-declaration/
226 World Council of Churches Unity Statement of the 10th Assembly, November 2013, para.13.
227 There is a whole issue of *Anvil* (Vol. 29.1, September 2013) given to 'Environment and Hope'.

in response to God's gift, and in the light of God's future: the promised coming of Christ's reign over all.

Salvation is about more than me

I think much Christian theology has become virtually overtaken by the view that salvation is essentially something to do with our individual souls, and our journey to heaven. What has got lost is the truth of the redemption of all things in Christ, the Wisdom of God in whom all things hold together, in whom all things are reconciled to God, and in whom heaven and earth are joined. We need to recover the way of Wisdom, the way of Cross and resurrection, love and service, sacrifice and restraint, and the corporate life of the Spirit. This is our human responsibility as God's image-bearers, in union with Christ and in the power of the Holy Spirit. It is also the pathway to human flourishing and the healing of all creation. To follow Colin Gunton again: people, society and all created beings can only find their true life, fulfilment and well-being, when they become part of Christ's offering of all things through the Spirit to the Father.[228]

The fullness of life, which is following Jesus' Way, is shared by a Church in mission.

A community held together by prayer and worship

It must have been extremely anxious-making for the community of the Beloved Disciple to find themselves thrown out of the synagogue. That had been their place of regular worship and corporate prayer. The first disciples had gone with Jesus to the synagogue on the Sabbath day, 'as was his custom' (Luke 4:16).

John's Gospel includes many festivals at which Jesus took part, often at the Jerusalem Temple: Passover, Booths, Tabernacles, Dedication. He speaks with the woman at the well about worship (4:24). The disciples sitting on the grass with the crowds hear him giving thanks for the five loaves and two fish. They hear him praying at the tomb of Lazarus (John 11:41). And the whole of John chapter 17 is a prayer from Jesus to the Father, partly consecrating himself for what is to come at the Cross, partly interceding for the community of his people who will continue his work when he is no longer with them. For they are to be a community of prayer, through which 'greater works' may be accomplished (John 14:12–14).

The life of the community, abiding in Christ as branches do in a vine, will be a community in which Christ's words abide. The Father will be

228 cf. Colin Gunton, *The One, the Three and the Many,* Cambridge University Press, 1993.

glorified by their fruitfulness, their life will be marked by obedience and love and joy. God responds to prayer that is inspired by the words of Jesus dwelling in the believing community.

> *If you abide in me, and my words abide in you, ask for whatever you wish, and it will be done for you. My Father is glorified by this, that you bear much fruit ... If you keep my commandments, you will abide in my love, just as I have kept my Father's commandments and abide in his love. I have said these things to you so that my joy may be in you, and that your joy may be complete.* (John 15:7–11)

The Farewell Discourse continues to speak of the persecution that the Christian community will always encounter, and it is at that point – in the pain of the present, but looking forward in joyous hope to God's future – that the writer refers to prayer. 'On that day [referring to the resurrection of Jesus from the dead] you will ask nothing of me. Very truly, I tell you, if you ask anything of the Father in my name, he will give it to you. Until now you have not asked for anything in my name. Ask and you will receive, so that your joy may be complete' (John 16:23–24).

St Paul wonderfully brings many of these themes together, rooting the Christian community in love, good works, prayer and worship:

> *So if you have been raised with Christ, seek the things that are above, where Christ is, seated at the right hand of God ... clothe yourselves with compassion ... let the peace of Christ rule in your hearts ... be thankful. Let the word of God dwell in you richly; teach and admonish one another in all wisdom; and with gratitude in your hearts sing psalms, hymns, and spiritual songs to God. And whatever you do, in word or deed, do everything in the name of the Lord Jesus, giving thanks to God the Father through him.* (Colossians 3:1,12–17)

Part IV

Hope in Today's World

This concluding section seeks first to draw together some of the many different themes we have explored in our reflections on John's Gospel, in the light of some of the questions that our contemporary crises and anxieties pose, and then to ask what this might imply for Christian discipleship today. How are we, and all God's creation, to flourish? What does it mean today to follow Wisdom's Way? Can we rediscover our hope in God's faithfulness? The chapter ends, as do many of the Psalms, with a doxology of creation's praise. It seems appropriate also to begin this chapter with a prayer:

Come my Way, my Truth, my Life:
Such as Way, as gives us breath:
Such a Truth as ends all strife:
And such a Life, as killeth death.

Come, my Light, my Feast, my Strength:
Such a Light, as shows a feast:
Such a Feast, as mends in length:
Such a Strength, as makes his guest.

Come my Joy, my Love, my Heart:
Such a Joy, as none can move:
Such a Love, as none can part:
Such a Heart, as joys in love.

George Herbert (1593–1633).

Chapter Twelve

Wisdom, Discipleship, Restraint and Worship

- • **Some of the book's main themes: the Way of Wisdom.**

- • **The meaning of Christian discipleship for today: being where Jesus is; repentance; restraint; doing shalom; living in hope.**

- • **Doxology and creation's praise.**

So who are we? What is our destiny? What are our human relationships with the rest of creation? What are our duties to the poorest people in our world? Is hope possible? What does it mean to flourish – to be fully alive? How will we deal with our fears about the future? How are we to cope?

These are the questions with which we began. Our reflections in John's Gospel have given us some perspectives from which to respond.

1. The Way of Wisdom

We have explored a spiritual wisdom that could move us away from the destructiveness of over-consumption, ecological damage and social inequality and towards justice, generosity and care for the common good.

The Wisdom literature of the Hebrew Bible opened up for us an understanding of our human place within Nature as God's creation. All we have – life and the means of life – comes to us as gift, to be received with gratitude and joy. To acknowledge that 'the earth is the Lord's' implies our dependence on God and our interdependence with all other creatures, and calls in question our persistent bias towards anthropocentrism. We need to live within limits: within the moral boundaries of God's will and God's ways, and the physical limits of the planet. We humans are part of Nature, but have a specific responsibility under God to care for all God's creation as God's priests and earth's servants and stewards.

The sad fact – and source of much of our current confusion – is that the life-giving triangle of relationships, 'God–Humanity–Earth', has been fractured. God has been 'eclipsed', and we have sinfully asserted ourselves as 'lords and possessors' of Nature.

The exciting perspective of John's Gospel is that in the incarnation of Jesus Christ – the Word/Wisdom of God made flesh – the triangle of relationships can be rebuilt: heaven and earth are brought together; coherence can be restored; creation can be healed. The incarnation of Jesus, the Man from heaven, his life, death and resurrection, changes everything. Not only does faith 'into' Jesus give us authority to become 'children of God', but in Jesus we see authentic humanity 'fully alive'.

Fullness of life – the eternal life which is knowledge of God through Jesus – is 'shalom': peace with justice. Shalom means the enjoyment and liberation, all-round health and satisfaction, of being in right relationships – with God and neighbour, with oneself, and with one's environment.

Although shalom is God's gift, it does not mean absence of all conflict. There is opposition to overcome, idols to be disposed of, healing to be worked for and freedom to be discovered. It is into this still broken and wounded world that the Light of Christ shines: a light of liberation, cleansing, healing, peace in the storm; the light of a truth that sets free. He says, 'I AM: do not be afraid.'

The resurrection of Jesus is the dawning of a new creation – and the coming into being of a new community of believers. They are commissioned by Christ, energized by the Holy Spirit, and sent into God's world to continue Christ's ministry as his followers.

This is a community committed to carrying on the 'works' of Jesus, called to be courageous and persistent under persecution and opposition, patient and hopeful in suffering. It is a community marked especially by shalom: love for God and neighbour, the quest for justice in all human affairs, and responsible care for God's creation. It is a community sent out in mission, and held together by prayer and worship.

As we put it in an earlier chapter, the story that this community of Christ's followers tells is different from the various stories being told by 'the world'. Instead of a story about over-consumption, selfishness and greed, the Way of Jesus speaks of generosity and the power of self-giving service in the interests of others. It is about equity and justice. Instead of a story about autonomous individualism, management and control, the Way of Jesus is a story of interdependence, co-operation and fellowship. It is ultimately a story of neighbour-love. Instead of a story marked by fatalism, doom and despair, the Way of Jesus is rather about compassionate love and mercy, trusting in the truth and faithfulness of God. It is about joy in creation, the promise of life in all its fullness, resurrection and as renewed and healed creation. It is a story of hope.

2. Discipleship today

So, today, who are we? What is our destiny? What does it mean to be fully alive? John, the Beloved Disciple, writing to encourage a struggling Christian community trying to cope, would reply to us: You are children of God, bearers of God's image, creation's servants and priests. Your destiny is to be where Jesus is. Your flourishing is inextricably bound up with the flourishing of others, and with the well-being of all God's creation. It is the gift and promise of the Father through Jesus Christ in the power of the Holy Spirit. It is that gift and promise to which, as a community of Christ's people, you are called to bear witness to the world. Your calling is to follow Jesus' Way, through repentance and restraint, and to 'do shalom' by loving God and your neighbours, by seeking justice in all things, and by caring responsibly for God's earth.

(i) Being where Jesus is

Rowan Williams described John's Gospel in terms of the Christian's calling is to be 'where Jesus is'.

He referred to the prayer given to us in John chapter 17: 'Father, I desire that those also, whom you have given me, may be with me where I am, to see my glory' (John 17:24).

Being where Jesus is, 'close to the Father's heart', means living – as far as we can discern it in the darkness of the world – in the light and truth of his word, seeking to be faithfully with him before the Father. It is the corporate calling of the community of Christ's people to ask ourselves before God what it means to be 'where Jesus is' in the places where we are called to be.

What does it mean, for example, to be where Jesus is in the places where there is no food and no clean drinking water? Where is he in the Maldives, as their coastline disappears under the ocean? In the Californian canyons as homes are destroyed by blazes in the hottest year on record; or in India, where the Ganges breaks previous flood records; in Brazil in the battle against the Zika virus and with pregnant women anxious for their children? Where is Jesus in the boardroom of the oil company which refuses to come clean about climate change, or with its shareholders seeking to hold the directors to account? Or in the energy departments working for clean, sustainable energy sources? Among those defining trade agreements which take no regard for environmental concerns, and the social structures which perpetuate exclusion and injustice? Among the poorest communities who have done the least to cause environmental damage, and are least able to adapt?

The community of Christ's people is called in its work and service to identify the Way of Jesus in places such as these, in love and justice, patient hope, transformative mission, prayer and worship.

Much of Jean Vanier's work with the L'Arche community of people with developmental disabilities, which he founded in 1964, has now spread worldwide. He knows what it is to wash another's feet. In his poetic book, *Drawn into the Mystery of Jesus through the Gospel of John*, he gives many illustrations of how a deeply personal and devotional spirituality, derived from a friendship with Jesus who is 'close to the Father's heart', results in a very practical, often very menial, ministry among severely disadvantaged people:

> The Gospel of John reveals that ...
> this life is not a flight from the world of pain and of matter
> but a mission into it,
> to love people as Jesus loves them.[229]

To be a follower of Jesus begins there. As we have seen in our reading of the Gospel, it can also lead into areas of social and political unrest in which love to our neighbour is expressed in the quest for justice and the fight against injustice and untruth.

This poses a huge question for today's Christian disciples. Are we in fact following Jesus in his self-giving love? Or are we as a church still too caught up in our own power struggles to be a servant to the poorest, most marginalised and oppressed? One major issue for our Christian communities is to find ways of bearing witness to God's truth as it is in Jesus, and which follow the Way of Jesus even when that – inevitably – provokes hostility from 'the World'.

We will, of course, get it wrong, make mistakes and hurt people. The community of Christ's people live in the tension and ambiguity of seeking to live in the Wisdom of God's will and God's ways in a disordered and ungodly world. We are still corrupted by sin and selfishness. We are still wedded to our idols. We are still affected by the 'lordless

---

229 Jean Vanier, Darton, Longman & Todd, 2004, p.13.

powers' of the 'father of lies'. We may get caught up in betrayal and let down our Lord. It is of enormous reassurance that John's Gospel ends not with the resurrection of Jesus, but with the gift from the risen Jesus of forgiveness and restoration for Simon Peter, and then the commission: 'Follow me.' Like Peter, we will always depend on the grace of forgiveness and the transforming energy of the Spirit to take the small fragments that we offer and multiply them into health-giving and liberating truth and blessing for the world.

(ii) Repentance

Discipleship today needs to heed a call to repentance. We have referred several times to the sin, selfishness and stupidity that have contributed significantly to our current crises. John's Gospel described life lived outside the ways of Christ as under God's judgement. We might recall how, centuries before, the prophet Jeremiah lamented the exile and the destruction of the Temple, which he described in terms of the whole of creation falling under divine judgement:

> *I looked on the earth, and lo, it was waste and void; and to the heavens, and they had no light. I looked on the mountains, and lo, they were quaking, and all the hills moved to and fro. I looked, and lo, there was no one at all, and all the birds of the air had fled. I looked, and lo, the fruitful land was a desert, and all its cities were laid in ruins before the LORD, before his fierce anger. For thus says the LORD: The whole land shall be a desolation; yet I will not make a full end.*
> (Jeremiah 4:23–27)

Perhaps one theme that we need to echo today is this sense of lament. We recall St Paul's words about the 'groaning of creation', and we share in some of that pain with sorrow and tears. We also need to hear the call for repentance, for a change of heart and mind, and change of direction. Jeremiah put it this way:

> *The word of the Lord: 'Run to and fro through the streets of Jerusalem, look around and take note! Search its squares and see if you can find one person who acts justly and seeks truth – so that I may pardon Jerusalem'.* (Jeremiah 5:1)
> *Thus says the LORD: Stand at the crossroads, and look, and ask for the ancient paths, where the good way lies; and walk in it, and find rest for your souls.* (Jeremiah 6:16).

The word that came to Jeremiah from the Lord:

> *... if you truly amend your ways and your doings, if you truly act justly one with another, if you do not oppress the alien, the orphan, and the widow, or shed innocent blood in this place, and if you do not go after other gods to your own hurt, then I will dwell with you in this place.* (Jeremiah 7:1,5ff.)

God's desire and promise, the prophets say, is to 'dwell with us'.

(iii) Restraint

A significant part of discipleship today requires restraint. The way of incarnation, we said earlier, is the way of God's self-emptying to make space for creation – and this sets a pattern for our spirituality of restraint, sharing, interrelationship, making space for others, self-giving service.

In his address at Santa Barbara in 1997, His All Holiness the Ecumenical Patriarch Bartholomew spoke of the Orthodox concept of 'encratia', or 'self-control'. He said that is an 'ascetic element' in our responsibility towards God's creation, which requires from us a voluntary restraint. 'We are called to work in humble harmony with creation and not in arrogant supremacy against it.' He speaks of the sort of asceticism which can be a form of repentance for excessive consumption, which 'may be understood to issue from a world-view of estrangement from self, from land, from life and from God. Consuming the fruits of the earth unrestrained, we become consumed by ourselves, by avarice and greed. Excessive consumption leaves us emptied, out of touch with our deepest self. Asceticism is a corrective practice, a vision of repentance – to return to a world in which we give as well as take from creation.'[230] To live well is to rediscover 'encratia, self-control, a care for the interests of others'.

(iv) Restraining our desires

Following Jesus' Way will therefore mean *restraining our desires*. Very often we are wholly ruled by our human desires – aided by intrusive advertising, the aim of which is to keep us discontented and continually wanting more. All other values get crowded out. We need to restrain, and retrain, our desires in the light of the Gospel story. Sallie McFague put it well: 'Increasingly the issue of how to live well has become one of *how to change from how we are living now to a different way.*'

Following Jesus' Way for today's disciples may well involve some very pertinent questions, such as: where do we invest our money, if we have any? What shall we eat? What transport should we use? Where will we buy our energy supplies? How often shall we choose to fly?

One of the myths by which too many of us rich Christians in the Western world have got used to living goes something like this: I realize that climate change is an important issue, but there is nothing I can do which will make much material difference. It is up to the politicians

---

230 Patriarch Bartholomew's speech to Greek Orthodox Church Environmental Symposium, Santa Barbara, November 1997.

to agree, or to the technologists to come up with a solution. It would be a huge wrench to change the lifestyle to which I am accustomed, the food habits, the air travel, other transport choices, the benefits of global trade and so on, and to change these would not only affect me, but other people dependent on me. So let us pray for those for whom the environment is a pressing concern; let us hope for good news from those with power to make a difference. But for now, for me, I would prefer not to have to think about it at all.

In the face of the questions posed for us by climate change, by loss of biodiversity, by our failure to live within planetary boundaries and the consequent environmental degradation, by growing gross inequality, by the desperate needs of the poor, by the importance of sustainable development – in the face of such questions our Christian bearing witness to truth needs to be a different way of living.

(v) Doing my little bit
We can often feel, as the lady at the Norfolk conference did, that it is all too much, and we cannot cope. In the Pope's Encyclical he gave a word of reassurance to people who feel like that in relation to the environmental crisis. Even small changes made by individual people, he said, are not negligible. It is worth quoting here: 'There is a nobility in the duty to care for creation through little daily actions... avoiding the use of plastic and paper, reducing water consumption, separating refuse, cooking only what can reasonably be consumed, showing care for other living beings, using public transport or car-pooling, planting trees, turning off unnecessary lights ... all of these reflect a generous and worthy creativity which brings out the best in human beings ... such actions can restore our sense of self-esteem; they can enable us to live more fully and to feel that life on earth is worthwhile'(211, 212).

(vi) Doing shalom
The fullness of life, seen in Jesus, displays the glory of God by showing God's abundant generosity and gracious gift; God's concern especially for those on the margins; God's compassionate tenderness and love to those suffering; God's hostility to the destructive forces of evil; God's sacrificial, loving, self-giving service, even to Jesus' death on the Cross, and so the birth of a new creation on Easter morning. The fulfilled life recognizes in Jesus the light of the true and liberating way, and finds a sense of being provided for, protected, looked out for, known and loved, within an inclusive and united community of those who follow his Way. It is concerned for education, a willingness to be taught, and

a responsive obedience to God's Word. It is expressed in loving, and sometimes menial and sacrificial service for others, within a community of love that bears fruit for the Father's glory. The Christian community is called to follow the Way of Jesus and his Way of divine Wisdom, and to be caught up into the new life of resurrection by which the whole of creation will ultimately be healed. We have called this 'doing shalom'.

Shalom tries to think through together:

- equity and the quest for social justice:
- restraint in social inequality; a commitment to cooperation instead of competition; the building of healthy communities;
- the economy, geared to human values and the common good, not merely financial gain:
- restraint in individualism; a policy for renewable energy and energy efficiency;
- ecology, and the healing of all God's creation:
- restraint in our tendency to anthropocentrism; restraint in over-consumption; restraint in our use of earth's resources; restraint in population growth; taking responsibility for sustainable development; working for the well-being and flourishing of all God's creation.

(vii) Living in joyous hope

By following Jesus' Way we will find that God holds on to us in *hope*. Richard Bauckham[231] helpfully distinguishes between on the one hand an unconditional 'ultimate hope' in the final achievement of all God's purposes for creation in 'the new heaven and the new earth' in which all creation is renewed, and on the other hand the 'proximate hopes' for what we can desire and envisage within this world, which in some way reflect the *ultimate* hope of a new creation. Our 'proximate' hopes can be disappointed. In this world, God's love can still be rejected and sin and selfishness still have power. So we need to be modest and realistic about what we hope for in this world.

In the closing chapters of the Book of Isaiah, there is a vision of a new heaven and a new earth with human and other animal life together: the Creator makes all things new:

> For I am about to create new heavens and a new earth ... no more shall the sound of weeping be heard in it ... They shall build houses and inhabit them;

---

231 Richard Bauckham, 'Ecological Hope in Crisis?', *Anvil*, Vol. 29.1, September 2013.

they shall plant vineyards and eat their fruit ... The wolf and the lamb shall feed together, the lion shall eat straw like the ox; but the serpent – its food shall be dust! They shall not hurt or destroy on all my holy mountain, says the LORD. (Isaiah 65:17–25)

Here the Creator covenant God is depicted as ruling over a peaceable kingdom from his holy mountain. The imagery is picked up in the Second Letter of Peter, where the coming Day of God is described as a 'new heavens and new earth in which justice dwells'. This recalls the vision of the psalmists and others of the time when 'justice and peace shall embrace' and God's glory will 'dwell in our land' (Psalm 85:9). The glory of God's presence, which once filled the temple, will one day 'fill the whole earth' (Psalm 72:19). The flourishing of shalom includes fulfilment for all and deliverance for the oppressed, and the flourishing of all creation.

A focus on individual salvation, important though that is, too often crowds out the bigger picture: the redemption of *all things* in Christ.[232] It is in Christ, the Wisdom of God, that all things hold together. In him all things are reconciled to God. In him heaven and earth are joined. We need to recover the Way of Wisdom, the Way of Cross and resurrection, love and service, sacrifice and restraint, and the corporate life of the Spirit. Our human responsibility as God's image-bearers, in union with Christ and in the power of the Holy Spirit, is to keep open the pathway to all human flourishing and to the healing of all creation.

3. Thanksgiving: doxology and creation's praise

I have suggested that in the context of the social and environmental crises with which we are faced, the Church's discipleship and mission must include a renewal of our worship – our joy in God and in God's creation; a transformation of our habits of thinking about our human relationship to the rest of God's earth; a reframing of our values and desires; an ethic of neighbour love and justice based on restraint; holding together ecology and economy within God's 'household', our common home; and bearing witness to the light of God's truth in a culture which is living in God's world without acknowledging God.

One of the exciting features of the Wisdom literature is the link forged between God the Creator and all God's creatures, and the invitation to all to share all creation's joy of communion with God. Prayer, Eucharist, justice, personal discipleship and social change all belong together. Heaven and earth become united in what some have called a 'sacramental universe'. George Herbert meant something like this

232 Colossians 1:15f.

when he wrote 'Teach me, my God and King, in all things Thee to see.'

One of the Psalms gives voice to the whole of creation's praise, in which we are invited to share: sun and moon, shining stars, monsters of the deep, fire and hail, snow and frost, mountains and hills, fruit trees and all cedars, wild animals and all cattle, creeping things and flying birds, kings of the earth and all people, men and women alike! (Psalm 148). 'Let everything that breathes praise the LORD!' (Psalm 150:6).

A prayer from Percy Dearmer sums up the Church's mission:

> *O God, who set before us the great hope that your Kingdom shall come on earth and taught us to pray for its coming: give us grace to discern the signs of its dawning and to work for the perfect day when the whole world shall reflect your glory; through Jesus Christ our Lord.*[233]

Joy to the world, the Lord is come!
Let earth receive her King;
Let every heart prepare Him room
And heaven and nature sing.

Joy to the earth, the Savior reigns!
Let men their songs employ,
While fields and floods, rocks, hills, and plains
Repeat the sounding joy.

No more let sins and sorrows grow
Nor thorns infest the ground;
He comes to make His blessings flow
Far as the curse is found.

He rules the world with truth and grace
And makes the nations prove
The glories of His righteousness
And wonders of His love.

Isaac Watts, 1674–1748

---

233 Used by Operation Noah in *Climate Change and the Purposes of God*, http://operationnoah.org/articles/read-ash-wednesday-declaration/

Bibliography

Ashton, J., *Understanding the Fourth Gospel*, OUP, 1991.

Atkinson, David, *The Message of Job*, IVP, 1991; *The Message of Proverbs*, IVP, 1996; *Renewing the Face of the Earth*, Canterbury Press, 2008.

Bacon, Francis, *The Great Instauration and New Atlantis* (1620), Harlan Davidson, 1980 edition.

Barker, Margaret, *Temple Theology*, SPCK, 2004; *Creation*, T & T Clark, 2012.

Barrett, C. K., *The Gospel according to St John*, SPCK, 1958.

Barth, K., 'The Doctrine of Creation' *Church Dogmatics* III/1, T & T Clark, 1958; 'The Christian Life', *Church Dogmatics* IV/4, T & T Clark, 1981.

Bauckham, Richard, *The Testimony of the Beloved Disciple*, Baker, 2007; *Living with Other Creatures*, Paternoster 2012; *Bible and Ecology*, DLT, 2012.

Berkoff, Hendrik, *Christ and the Powers*, 1953; translated from Dutch for Herald Press, 1962.

Berry, R.J., *God's Book of Works*, T & T Clark, 2003.

Bookless, Dave, *Let Everything that has Breath Praise the Lord: the Bible and biodiversity*, Cambridge Papers vol. 23. No3, Sept. 2014.

Brown, William T., *The Seven Pillars of Creation*, OUP, 2012.

Browning, George, *Sabbath and the Common Good*, Echo Books, 2016.

Brueggemann, Walter, *Theology of the Old Testament*, Fortress Press, 1997; *The Land: Place as Gift, Promise and Challenge in Biblical Faith*, 2nd ed., Fortress Press, 2002.

Brunner, Emil, *Truth as Encounter*, 1938; 2nd ed. 1945, ET SCM, 1963.

Conradie, Ernst M., *Hope for the Earth*, Wipf and Stock, 2005.

Daly, Herman E. and Cobb, Jr., John B, *For the Common Good: Redirecting the economy toward community, the environment and a sustainable future*, Beacon Press, 1989.

Dawkins, Richard, *The Selfish Gene*, OUP, 1976, 1989; *River Out of Eden*, Orion, 1996; *Unweaving the Rainbow*, Penguin, 2006; *The God Delusion*, Black Swan, 2006.

Deane-Drummond, Celia, *Creation Through Wisdom*, T & T Clark, 2000; *The Ethics of Nature*, Blackwell, 2004.

Dodd, C. H., *The Interpretation of the Fourth Gospel*, 1953.

Dorling, Danny, *Population: 10 Billion*, Constable, 2013.

Edwards, Denis, *Jesus the Wisdom of God: an ecological theology*, Wipf and Stock, 1995.

Edwards, Ruth, *Discovering John*, SPCK, 2003.

Eisenstein, Charles, *Sacred Economics: Money, gift and society in the age of transition*, Evolver, 2011.

Emmott, Stephen, *10 Billion*, Penguin, 2013.

Fiddes, Paul, *Seeing the World and Knowing God*, OUP, 2013.

Pope Francis, *Laudato Si*.

Fretheim, Terence E., *God and World in the Old Testament* Abingdon Press 2005; *Creation Untamed: the Bible, God and Natural Disasters*, Baker, 2010.

Galloway, Alan, *The Cosmic Christ*, Harper, 1951.

Goodwin, Brian, *How the Leopard Changed its Spots: The evolution of complexity*, Scribners, 1994

Gorringe, Timothy and Backham, Rosie, *Transition Movement for Churches: a prophetic imperative for today*, Canterbury Press, 2013.

Gunton, Colin, *Christ and Creation*, Paternoster, 1992; *The One, the Three and the Many*, Cambridge University Press, 1993; *The Triune Creator*, Eerdmans, 1998.

Hayek, F. A., *The Road to Serfdom*, Routledge, 1944.

Helm, Dieter, *Natural Capital: Valuing the Planet*, Yale 2015

Houghton, John, *Global Warming: the complete briefing*, Cambridge 1994; 5th edn. 2015.

Howard-Brook, Wes, *Becoming Children of God*, Orbis Books, 1994.

Hunter, James Davison, *To Change the World, Oxford*, 2010.

Jackson, Tim, *Prosperity without Growth* (2nd Edn.) Routledge, 2016.

Jacques, Peter, *Sustainability*, Routledge, 2015.

Johnson, Elizabeth A., *Ask The Beasts: Darwin and the God of Love*, Bloomsbury, 2014.

Jones, James, *Jesus and the Earth*, SPCK, 2003.

Klein, Naomi, *This Changes Everything: Capitalism vs. The Climate*, Allen Lane, 2014.

Kuyper, Abraham, *The Work of the Holy Spirit*, Eerdmans, 1900.

Lambin, Eric, *An Ecology of Happiness*, University of Chicago Press, 2012.

Lawson, Nigel *An Appeal to Reason: a cool look at global warming*, Duckworth, 2009.

Layard, Richard, *Happiness: lessons from a new science*, Penguin, 2011.

Lovelock, James, *The Revenge of Gaia*, Allen Lane, 2006.

John Macmurray, *Persons in Relation*, Faber, 1961.

Macquarrie, John, *In Search of Humanity*, SCM, 1982.

Marquand, David, *Mammon's Kingdom*, Allen Lane, 2014.

Marshall, George, *Don't Even Think About It: Why our brains are wired to ignore climate change*, Bloomsbury, 2013.

Mason, Paul, *Postcapitalism: A guide to our future*, Allen Lane, 2015.

McFague, Sallie, *Blessed are the Consumers: Climate Change and the Practice of Restraint*, Fortress Press, 2013.

McGrath, Alister, *A Scientific Theology, Vol. 1: Nature*, Bloomsbury, 2001; *The Re-enchantment of Nature*, Hodder, 2002.

McKibben, Bill, *The End of Nature*, Bloomsbury, 1989/2003; *Eaarth*, St Martin's Griffin, 2011.

Meacher, Michael, *Destination of the Species: The riddle of human existence*, O Books, 2010.

Merchant, Carolyn, *The Death of Nature*, Harper and Row, 1980.

Middleton, J.Richard, *A New Heaven and a New Earth*, Baker, 2014.

Midgley, Mary *Beast and Man*, Harvester Press, 1979; *Wickedness*, Routledge, 1984; *The Solitary Self*, Acumen, 2010.

Miranda, Jose, *Being and the Messiah*, Wipf and Stock, 2006.

Moltmann, Jürgen *The Living God and the Fullness of Life*, WCC Publications, 2016; *God and Creation* SCM 1985; The *Future of Creation* SCM, 1979.

Monbiot, George,'No fracking, drilling or digging: it's the only way to save life on Earth', *The Guardian*, 28 September 2016.

Moo, Jonathan and White, Robert *Hope in an Age of Despair*, IVP, 2013

Motyer, Stephen, *Your Father the Devil, a new approach to John and the Jews*, Paternoster, 1997

Murray, Robert, *The Cosmic Covenant*, Sheed & Ward, 1992.

Nash, James, *Hope for the Earth*, Wipf and Stock, 2000.

Newbigin, Lesslie,*The Light has Come*, Eerdmans, 1982; *Truth to Tell: The gospel as public truth*, SPCK, 1991.

Nordhaus, William, *The Climate Casino: Risk, uncertainty and economics for a warming world*, Yale, 2013.

Northcott, Michael, *A Political Theology of Climate Change*, SPCK, 2014.

Nowak, Martin and Coakley, Sarah (eds), *Evolution, Games and God: The principle of cooperation*, Harvard, 2013.

O'Donovan, O. M. T., *Resurrection and Moral Order*, IVP, 1986.

Operation Noah, Ash Wednesday Declaration 2012, *Climate Change and the Purposes of God*; available at www.operationnoah.org.

Oreskes, Naomi and Conway, Erik M., *Merchants of Doubt: How a handful of scientists obscured the truth on issues from tobacco smoke to global warming*, Bloomsbury, 2011.

Peacocke, Arthur, *Science and the Christian Experiment*, Oxford, 1971

Polanyi, Karl, *The Great Transformation: The political and economic origins of our time*, Boston, Beacon Press, 1944.

Polanyi, Michael, *Science, Faith and Society*, Chicago 1946; *The Logic of Liberty* (Chicago 1951) Liberty Fund 1998; *Personal Knowledge*, Routledge, 1958; *Knowing and Being*, Routledge, 1969.

Polkinghorne, J. and Welker, M.,eds., *The End of the World and the Ends of God,* Trinity Press, 2000.

Poole, Eve, *Capitalism's Toxic Assumptions*, Bloomsbury, 2015.

Porritt, Jonathon, *Capitalism as if the World Matters*, Earthscan, 2005.

Primavesi, Anne, *Exploring Earthiness*, Cascade, 2013.

von Rad, G., *Wisdom in Israel*, SCM, 1972.

Kate Raworth, *Doughnut Economics,* Random House, 2017.

Rensberger, David, *Overcoming the World*, SPCK, 1998.

Reynolds, Fiona, *The Fight for Beauty*, One World, 2016.

Ringe, Sharon, *Wisdom's Friends*, Westminster, 1999.

Sachs, Jeffrey D., *The Age of Sustainable Development*, Columbia University Press, 2015.

Sandel, Michael, *What Money Can't Buy*, Penguin Books, 2012.

Santmire, H. Paul, *The Travail of Nature,* Fortress Press, 1985; *Nature Reborn*, Fortress Press, 2000.

Schnackenburg, R., *The Moral Teaching of the New Testament*, Burns and Oates, 1965

Schumacher, E. F., *Small is Beautiful*, Penguin, 1973.

Scruton, Roger, *Green Philosophy: How to think seriously about the planet*, Atlantic Books, 2012.

Sen, Amartya, *Development as Freedom*, OUP, 1999; *The Idea of Justice*, Allen Lane, 2009.

Sherrard, Philip, *The Rape of Man and Nature*, Golgonooza, 1987.

Siedentop, Larry, *Inventing the Individual: The origins of western liberalism*, Allen Lane, 2014.

Skidelsky, Robert and Edward, *How Much is Enough: The love of money and the case for the good life.* Allen Lane, 2012.

Southgate, Christopher, *The Groaning of Creation: God, Evolution and the Problem of Evil*, Westminster , 2008.

Spencer, Nick and White, Robert, *Christianity, Climate Change and Sustainable Living*, SPCK, 2007.

Stern, Nicholas, *Why are we Waiting?: The logic, urgency and promise of tackling climate change*, MIT Press, 2015.

Stiglitz, Joseph, *The Price of Inequality,* Allen Lane, 2012.

Storkey, Elaine, *Scars Across Humanity: Understanding and overcoming violence against women*, SPCK, 2016.

Tawney, R. W., *The Acquisitive Society*, Harcourt Brace, 1920.

Taylor Charles, *A Secular Age*, Harvard: Bleknap Press, 2007.

Taylor, J. V., *Enough is Enough*, SCM, 1975.

Temple, William, *Nature, Man and God*, Macmillan, 1934; *Readings in John's Gospel*, Macmillan 1939–40.

Thomas, Keith, *Man and the Natural World*, Allen Lane, 1983; Penguin 1984.

Torrance, T. F., *Space, Time and Incarnation*, OUP, 1969; *God and Rationality*, OUP, 1971; *The Mediation of Christ*, Paternoster Press, 1983.

Traherrne, Thomas (1637–74), *Centuries of Meditation* (1960 edition, Clarendon Press); *The Way to Blessedness* (1675), Faith Press edition 1962.

Vanier, Jean, *Drawn into the Mystery of Jesus through the Gospel of John*, Darton, Longman & Todd, 2004

Wadhams, Peter, *A Farewell to Ice*, Allen Lane, 2016.

Webster, Charles, *The Great Instauration*, Duckworth, 1975.

Wilkinson, Richard and Pickett, Kate, *The Spirit Level: why equality is better for everyone* (Allen Lane, 2009), Penguin, 2010.

Williams, Rowan, *Faith in the Public Square*, Bloomsbury, 2012.

Wilson, E. O., *Creation*, Norton and Co. 2006.

Wink, Walter, *The Powers that Be*, Doubleday, 1998.

Wolterstorff, Nicholas, *Until Justice and Peace Embrace*, Eerdmans, 1983; *Justice: rights and wrongs*; Eerdmans, 2008; *Justice in Love*, Eerdmans, 2011.

Wright, Tom, *John for Everyone*, SPCK, 2004; *Surprised by Hope*, SPCK, 2007.

Wright N. T., *The New Testament and the People of God*, SPCK, 1992; *The Resurrection of the Son of God*, SPCK 2003.

Name Index

A

Ashton, J. 52, 123, 203
Atkinson, D. 26, 28, 203
Augustine 40, 121, 161, 165

B

Bacon, Francis 40, 41, 42, 55, 61, 118, 140, 166, 203
Barrett, C.K. 155, 203
Barth, K. 29, 71, 129, 130, 203
Bartholomew, His Holiness Ecumenical Patriarch 14, 30, 196
Bauckham, R. 6, 32, 35, 36, 43, 172, 198, 203
Berkoff, H. 129, 203
Bookless, D. iii, 36, 203
Browning, G. 71, 203
Brueggemann, W. 16, 29, 37, 38, 203
Brunner, E. 68, 160, 161, 203
Bultmann, R. 122

C

Calvin, J. 32, 90, 121
Coakley, S. 138, 205

D

Daly, H.E. and Cobb, J.B. 112, 137, 138, 203
Dawkins, R. 13, 27, 45, 138, 161, 203
Deane-Drummond, C. 60, 95, 203
Dodd, C.H. 151, 203
Dorling, D. 115, 203

E

Edwards, D. 61, 64, 69, 203
Edwards, R. 6, 123, 204
Eisenstein, C. 136, 204
Emmott, S. 146, 204

F

Pope Francis 10, 15, 25, 38, 41, 112, 113, 134, 139, 204

V

Vanier, J. 194, 207
von Rad, W. 39, 206

W

Wilkinson, R. and Pickett, K. 106, 207
Williams, R. ix, 79, 113, 141, 193, 207
Wilson, E.O. 107, 207
Wink, W. 129, 130, 207
Wolterstorff, N. 111, 112, 183, 207
Wright, N.T. 45, 96, 97, 207

Subject Index

B

beauty 24, 27, 29, 46, 59, 103, 107, 108, 118, 159, 165, 166
'being where Jesus is' 69, 76, 98, 173, 184, 191
'believing into' 51, 62, 75, 150, 158, 176
Bethany 77, 85, 87, 88, 89, 90, 91, 93, 95, 97, 162, 174
biodiversity 7, 12, 23, 30, 34, 36, 83, 115, 118, 142, 183, 197, 203
blind beggar 149, 156, 157, 174, 177
boundaries, God-given 23

C

Cana 73, 85, 87, 88, 93, 95, 97, 127, 171
Church 121, 137, 147, 169, 170, 184
Community 97, 113, 169
consumer culture 8, 11, 133, 134, 141, 142, 143, 149
courage 7, 40, 122, 123, 131, 192
creation 7, 17, 18, 24, 25, 26, 28, 29, 32, 43, 44, 56, 70, 71
Creation 21, 23, 31, 53, 113
creation in jeopardy 28, 29, 43, 111
Cross, the vii, 72, 77, 78, 79, 85, 87, 89, 93, 95, 97, 129, 149, 152, 154, 155, 157, 162, 171, 172, 175, 176, 181, 185, 197, 199

D

Disciple, The Beloved 6, 7, 8, 9, 17, 53, 62, 63, 67, 77, 85, 88, 95, 96, 104, 105, 121, 122, 123, 124, 133, 149, 156, 157, 158, 169, 171, 172, 174, 178, 179, 184, 185, 193, 203
Domination System 121, 127, 129, 130
dominion, 'having dominion' 37, 42, 43

E

Easter 85, 87, 94, 95, 96, 97, 149, 154, 155, 157, 172, 181, 197
economic growth 7, 9, 10, 82, 103, 107, 117, 136, 141, 144, 184
education 10, 34, 76, 77, 79, 81, 82, 117, 197
environmental degradation 2, 5, 7, 11, 30, 40, 107, 197

F

false gods 65, 133, 134
Father of Lies 74, 128, 130, 143, 159, 162, 178, 195

About Ekklesia

Based in Edinburgh and London, Ekklesia is an independent, citizen-based think tank concerned with the changing role of beliefs and values in public life. We have a particular interest in fresh models of Christian engagement and presence in plural, mixed-belief societies.

Ekklesia advocates transformative ideas and solutions to local and global challenges based on a strong commitment to social justice, inclusion, nonviolence, environmental action, civic participation and a creative exchange among those of different convictions (religious and otherwise).

We are committed to promoting – alongside others – new models of mutual economy, conflict transformation, social power, restorative justice, community engagement, spiritual activism and political renewal.

Ekklesia is also working to encourage alternative perspectives on humanitarian challenges in a fractured world – not least a positive, affirming approach to migration.

Overall, we are concerned with the policy, practice and philosophy of moving beyond 'top-down' politics, economics and religion.

This means that, while we are a political think-tank rooted especially in Peace Church traditions, we are keen to work with people of many backgrounds, both 'religious' and 'non-religious', who share common values and approaches.

Ekklesia's reports, analysis and commentary can be accessed via our website here: www.ekklesia.co.uk

Iona Community

The Iona Community is a dispersed Christian ecumenical community working for peace and social justice, the rebuilding of community and the renewal of worship. Its members also have a strong commitment to environmental action and care of Creation.

The Community was founded in 1938 by George MacLeod, then a Church of Scotland parish minister in Govan, Glasgow. George brought together young ministers in training and unemployed craft workers to rebuild the ancient monastic buildings of the Benedictine Abbey on Iona, which had lain in ruins since the Reformation. Through this common task they also discovered a common life together.

The Community was therefore born as a practical response to the needs of people struggling with the challenges of poverty, poor housing and unemployment in 1930s Glasgow. And out of the perception that the Church no longer spoke to the reality of their lives. Ever since, the commitment to economic justice, environmental concern, biblical witness and the inclusion of the poorest and most vulnerable in society have been central to the Iona Community's life and work.

More about the Iona Community: http://iona.org.uk and https://www.ionabooks.com

Lightning Source UK Ltd.
Milton Keynes UK
UKHW040831071118
331918UK00001B/216/P